Essays and Explorations

Essays and Explorations

Studies in Ideas, Language, and Literature

Morton W. Bloomfield

Harvard University Press
Cambridge, Massachusetts
1970

© Copyright 1970 by the President and Fellows of Harvard College

Publication of this book has been aided by a grant from
the Hyder Edward Rollins Fund

Distributed in Great Britain by Oxford University Press, London

Library of Congress Catalog Card Number 70–106956

SBN 674–26425–8

Printed in the United States of America

To Micah, Hanna, and Sam

Preface

My main motive in collecting these essays and reviews, which have
appeared in various places over the past thirty years, is to shore up a
few intellectual fragments against the scattering and centrifugal
forces which gather power and momentum with the passing of time.
The book represents an attempt to bring together some of the ideas
and explorations which have formed the substance of my thought
and which I feel indicate some of my permanent interests. My hope
is that they will stimulate other students to carry further what I
have done and perhaps to steer them clear of what I regard as mis-
taken paths.

I have included for the most part essays and reviews which are
more general in approach and less technical and detailed in manner
than the close investigations I have undertaken on scholarly topics.
One essay which I regard of considerable importance, "Episodic
Motivation and Marvels in Epic and Romance," has not as yet appeared, but since it fits well into my scheme and reflects a growing
interest of mine in problems of narrative technique I have decided
to introduce it here.

I do not claim any real unity to these pieces but, on the other
hand, they do seem to show some recurrent themes and emphases:
an interest in ideas, in method, and in historical truth. As I look
them over, it occurs to me that regrouping them here may help me
to "reculer pour mieux sauter"—at least I like to think so. Whether
they will also help others to leap forward I do not know. I hope so.

What these essays and explorations reveal as to my approach, others can say better than I. They do, however, show, it seems to me, a concern with philology in its most exact significance as well as a feeling or perhaps a groping for the underlying structure of literary, linguistic, and historical experience. I have always believed that the inner meaning of an idea or successful literary work corresponds to its outer meaning, but that the inner can only be reached through the outer. The spirit is of course more important than the body, but it is the body which makes the spirit material and accessible. The body determines the soul almost as much as the soul "doth the body make." To disregard the body in the supposed interests of the soul is to sin against creation and its wonders. I hope these essays and explorations reveal at least that conviction.

Except for minor revisions and corrections, the essays are reprinted here without any changes from their original appearance. My book *Piers Plowman as a Fourteenth-Century Apocalypse* (New Brunswick, N.J., 1962) develops at greater length and in greater depth the substance of my essay of the same title included in this book. I felt that a succinct statement of my interpretation of *Piers Plowman* might be of some interest to my readers, especially since it contains some differences of emphasis as compared with the book. I wish to thank Mrs. Laura Adams for her help in getting out this volume.

Cambridge, Massachusetts
October 1969

Contents

Contents

IV. *Language and Linguistics*

V. *Essay-Reviews*

I. History of Ideas

1. The Origin of the Concept of the Seven Cardinal Sins

Since the work of Zielinski [1] and Gothein [2] in the early years of this century,[3] it has been clear that the medieval and modern Catholic teaching of the seven cardinal sins, sometimes called the deadly sins, had a Hellenistic astrological origin. The details of that provenance, however, are still vague, and it is my purpose to add some further information tending to clarify the complex problems of origins. The material here presented will strengthen what must be a nebulous, though very probable, hypothesis. The problem, however, is not so much to show the exact origin of the concept, as it is to refute certain misleading orthodox theories of origin.

The hypothesis states that certain Egyptian Christian ascetics of the fourth century or earlier took over from heretical and pagan religions a list of seven or eight sins which were considered the chief sins and purged· them of their unorthodox associations. These sins had been linked with the seven planets and the aerial demons inhabiting them. Many Hellenistic sects believed that the soul, after death, had to journey through the seven zones of heaven,[4] while the aerial spirits, sometimes seven, sometimes not, and variously called ἄρχοντες, κοσμοκράτορες or τελώνια attempted to hinder its passage.[5] This belief appears in many forms in the mysteries, Hermetic reli-

Reprinted with permission from the *Harvard Theological Review*, XXXIV (1941), 121–128.

[1] See "Hermes und die Hermetik," *Archiv für Religionswissenschaft*, VIII (1905), 321 ff.; "Marginalien," II, *Philologus*, LXIV (1905), 21 and "Die sieben Todsünden," *Süddeutsche Monatshefte*, Zweiter Jahrgang, Zweiter Band (1905), pp. 437–442 (a popular exposition).

[2] AR, X (1907), 416–484.

[3] Both had taken up a suggestion of R. Reitzenstein made in his *Poimandres* (Leipzig, 1904), p. 232, note 2, that a form of the Soul Journey was the root of the Catholic seven cardinal sins. See below, reference no. 3. A. Bouché-Leclerq, *L'Astrologie Grecque* (Paris, 1899), p. 324, note 1, had earlier mentioned a possible astrological origin for the concept, without giving any details. He made the remark while discussing the Hellenistic division of the body into seven internal members and seven external organs. See also, F. Boll, "Die Lebensalter," *Neue Jahrbücher für das klassische Altertum, Geschichte und deutsche Literatur*, XXXI (1913), 89–154, esp. 118 ff.

[4] See G. Murray, *Five Stages of Greek Religion* (Oxford, 1925), pp. 179–180, and W. R. Halliday, *The Pagan Background of Early Christianity* (London, 1925), p. 226.

[5] For a complete study of this belief see W. Bousset, "Die Himmelreise der Seele," AR, IV (1901), 136–169; 229–273. See also, F. Cumont, *After Life in Roman Paganism* (New Haven, 1922), pp. 148 ff., C. H. Kraeling, *Anthropos and Son of Man*, Columbia University Oriental Studies XXI (New York, 1927), 189, 129 ff. *et*

3

gion and Christian Gnostic [6] sects, and has survived in modern Levantine superstitions,[7] but only in some of them can we find antecedents for our concept. The *post-mortem* journey, called by Bousset the Soul Journey, may have been represented symbolically in the rites of some of these religions, sometimes with the discarding of clothing as in the Ishtar story.[8] The journey was based on the cosmology of the time; it was scientific.

Although the question of origin is irrelevant to our purpose, Persia may have been the ultimate home of the Soul Journey. Reitzenstein suggests that a representation of the Soul Journey (which he calls the Soul Drama) is the basic concept of the Persian folk-religion which passed to the west through Babylon into various religions,[9] picking up certain Chaldean beliefs on the way. On the other hand, its origin may be less elaborate.

Perhaps it will be well to list again the most relevant passages as noted by earlier scholars in connection with the seven cardinal sins. The references which follow are arranged chronologically as far as it is possible to determine dates.

1. The Old Testament pseudepigraph, Testament of the Twelve Patriarchs, Testament of Reuben, II lists seven spirits of deceit, πορνεία (fornication), γαστριμαργία (gluttony), μάχη (fighting), κενοδοξία (vain-glory) ὑπερηφανία (pride), ψεῦδος (lying),

---

passim, and E. Schürer, "Die siebentägige Woche im Gebrauche der christlichen Kirche der ersten Jahrhunderte," ZNW, VI (1905), 63 ff. and esp. 65 n. 1.

[6] I use the word "gnostic" for convenience rather than with any precise meaning. See, e.g., Hippolytus, *The Refutation of All Heresies*, trans. J. H. MacMahon, Ante-Nicene Christian Library VI (Edinburgh, 1911), I, p. 134 (Book V, §§ 1 ff.), and Albrecht Dieterich, *Abraxas* (Leipzig, 1891), pp. 45 ff.

[7] For modern Greek survivals of τελώνια and a brief history of the word, see K. Dieterich, "Hellenistische Volksreligion und byzantinisch-neugriechischer Volksglaube," ΑΓΓΕΛΟΣ, I (1925), 17 ff. See also W. W. Hyde, *Greek Religion and Its Survivals* (Boston, 1923), p. 162, K. Krumbacher, *Mittelgriechische Sprichwörter* (Munich, 1893), pp. 170–171, and C. M. Doughty, *Travels in Arabia Deserta* (Cambridge, 1888), I, 259 (for a modern Arabic survival).

The ancient Mandaeans also used the Soul Journey in religious rites, a usage which has survived into modern times; see E. S. Drower, *The Mandaeans of Iraq and Iran* (Oxford, 1937), pp. 197 ff. The Mandaean version is very close to the ancestor of our concept. See, also, *ibid.*, pp. 365–366, 256, and 307–308.

[8] See, e.g., K. Dieterich, *op. cit.*, p. 17. For the Ishtar story, see Bruno Meissner, *Babylonien und Assyrien* (Heidelberg, 1925), II, 183 ff.

[9] *Das iranische Erlösungsmysterium* (Bonn, 1921). Bousset also believes in a Persian origin.

and ἀδικία (injustice).[10] There is a remarkable coincidence in this list with that which appears in the works of Evagrius of Pontus (†c. 400), the first orthodox Christian writer to use the scheme. There are no pronounced astrological elements in this reference. Date, 109–106 B.C. (This part may be later.)

2. Fervet *avaritia* miseroque *cupidine* pectus?
Sunt verba et voces, quibus hunc lenire dolorem
Possis, et magnam morbi deponere partem.
Laudis amore tumes: sunt certa piacula, quae te
Ter, pure lecto poterunt recreare libello.
Invidus, iracundus, iners, vinosus, amator,
Nemo adeo ferus est ut non mitescere possit
Si modo culturae patientem commodet aurem.
(Horace, Epist. I, 1, 33–40; my italics.) [11] Date, c. 20 B.C.

3. And thereupon the man mounts upward through the structure of the heavens. And to the first zone of heaven (Moon) he gives up the force which works increase and that which works decrease; to the second zone (Mercury), the machinations of evil cunning; to the third zone (Venus), the lust whereby men are deceived; to the fourth zone (Sun), domineering arrogance; to the fifth zone (Mars), unholy daring and rash audacity; to the sixth zone (Jupiter), evil strivings after wealth; and to the seventh zone (Saturn), the falsehood which lies in wait to work harm.

And thereupon, having been stripped of all that was wrought upon him by the structure of the heavens, he ascends to the substance of the eighth sphere, being now possessed of his own proper power; and he sings, together with those who dwell there, hymning the father. . . . (Corpus Hermeticum, I (Poimandres), 25–26, ed. and tr. W. Scott, I, 128 ff.) Date, 1st Century A.D. (?) [12]

---

[10] See R. H. Charles, *The Apocrypha and Pseudepigrapha of the Old Testament in English* (Oxford, 1913), II, 282 ff.

[11] There is here almost a complete correspondence with the Church doctrine, especially with that of Gregory the Great who reduced the number of sins to seven from the original eight. If we place *laudis amore* first, we even get his order. The actual terms, however, are not always the same.

[12] On the question of the date of the Hermetic writings, see Scott, *op. cit.* (Oxford, 1924–36), I, 9.

4. Corpus Hermeticum, Lib. XIII, 7b ff., lists twelve torments, some of which are similar to the Christian scheme. These are driven out by ten powers. The text is very corrupt and confusing at this spot; both seven and ten are referred to. Date, same.[13]

5. Mathematici fingunt quod singulorum numinum potestatibus corpus et anima conexa sunt ea ratione, quia cum descendunt animae, trahunt secum torporem Saturni, Martis iracundiam, Veneris libidinem, Mercurii lucri cupiditatem, Iovis regni desiderium. (Servius on Virgil, Aeneid, VI, 714.) [14] Date, end of fourth century, A.D.

It will be noted that none of the above references are Christian. Zöckler [15] and Gothein give many early Christian discussions of sin and sin-listing, but none of them offer any connection with astrology. In the course of a not too exhaustive examination of early Christian (pre-Evagrian) literature, I have uncovered several allusions,[16] corroborating by the use of terms and the aerial nature of the sins, the astrological theory of origin and providing the link between unorthodox and orthodox religion. Unfortunately, none of the following show any planetary associations.[17] The case must rest

[13] The number twelve is based upon a supposed connection with the signs of the Zodiac. Competing with the conception of seven evil planetary spirits was a similar zodiacal arrangement. Twelve, however, did not prevail. It was Egyptian in origin, as opposed to the Persian or Babylonian seven. See W. Scott, *op. cit.*, II, 384 ff., R. Reitzenstein, *op. cit.*, pp. 157 ff. and K. Dieterich, *op. cit.*, pp. 5, 6, and 16.

[14] Ed. Thilo and Hagen II (1884), 98. Servius' list, as far as it goes, corresponds closely to the Christian one.

[15] *Das Lehrstück von den sieben Hauptsünden*, Biblische und Kirchenhistorische Studien (Munich, 1893), is the best general treatment of the history of our concept, although the author is unaware of the astrological theory of origin. Zöckler has also treated the subject more briefly in both *Die Tugendlehre des Christentums* (Gütersloh, 1904), and *Handbuch der theologischen Wissenchaften in encyklopädischer Darstellung* (Nördlingen, 1885–1886), II, 114 ff. *et passim*.

[16] Some of the allusions were suggested to me by a reading of Louise Dudley's *The Egyptian Elements in the Legend of the Body and Soul* (Baltimore, 1911). The author uses the references for a different purpose.

[17] Professor A. D. Nock, in a letter to me, suggests that there is little in the following selections to suggest a Soul Journey of any kind, and that the demons can be explained by the "really well attested Iranian concept that the soul after death is met by a supernatural being impersonating its good or evil deeds and respectively appearing as a fair young maiden or an old hag." Without denying the possibility of this influence, it seems to me that, taken in conjunction with quotations 3 and 5 above

largely on the use of the word τελώνια which then, as now in modern folk-lore, probably had planetary implications.

Origen writes in a homily:

> Venit enim ad unamquamque animam de hoc mundo exeuntem princeps huius mundi; et aereae potestates, et requirunt si inveniant in ea aliquid suum; si *avaritiam* invenerint, suae partis est; si *iram*, si *luxuriam*, si *invidiam*, et singula quaeque eorum similia si invenerint, suae partis est, et sibi eam defendunt, et ad se eam trahunt, et ad partem eam peccatorum declinant. (My italics.) [18]

It is too bad that Origen is so cryptic, but enough is given to show us that he knew of the *aereae potestates* who would claim as their own the sinner of a particular sin; [19] and the four that are named are all cardinal sins. Three of the seven vices are, of course, lacking, but the basic concept is linked here closely with the sins and gives an interesting parallel to the Horace and Servius quotations given above.

Cyril of Alexandria, in a homily, conceives the sins as clustered at five *telonia* which the soul on its ascent to heaven must traverse.[20] There are gates for each of the five senses, and at each gate appropriate sins gather. Some of them are similar to the later lists of cardinal sins, but the selection, as well as the one below, is of value chiefly in showing the world view of the time and the common belief in sins as aerial demons and in guardians of the heavenly gates as reflected in a Christian writer.

St. Macarius, the Egyptian, who was one of Evagrius's masters, says in Homily XLIII:

---

and Bousset's parallels, some kind of Soul Journey is at the basis of the concept. We could hardly expect Christian writers to use pagan concepts without some cutting, and the planetary associations were especially frowned on. The use of words like τελώνια and ἄρχοντες also seem to support my position. There is no doubt that the evidence is not as strong as one would wish. On the church's attitude to astrology, see T. O. Wedel, *The Mediaeval Attitude Toward Astrology*, Yale Studies in English LX (New Haven, 1920), and L. C. F. J. de Vreese, *Augustinus en de Astrologie*, (Maastricht, 1933).

[18] Homily V in Psalmum XXXVI (Migne, PG., 12, 1366).

[19] Cf. Exod. Homil. VIII, 46 where Origen uses Luke XI as the basis of his contention that the sins are devils.

[20] Migne, PG., 77, 1074–75.

Like tax-collectors (τελῶναι) sitting in the narrow ways, and lay-
ing hold upon the passers-by, and extorting from them, so do the
devils spy upon souls, and lay hold of them; and when they pass
out of the body, if they are not perfectly cleansed, they do not
suffer them to mount up to the mansions of heaven and to meet
their Lord, and they are driven down by the devils of the air.[21]

There is another reference to the *telonia,* each of which is connected with a sin, in a vision of the same Abbot Macarius, where
unfortunately only one sin is named (*fornicatio*).[22] In the Vita
Sancti Joannis Eleemosynarii, of the Vitae Patrum, a revelation to
Saint Simeon "qui in columnis stetit" is recorded.

Quia (ut ait) exeunte anima e corpore, obviant ei cum ascen-
derit a terra in coelum, chori daemonum, singuli in proprio or-
dine. Obviat ei chorus daemoniorum superbiae, investigat eam, si
habeat opera eorum. Obviat chorus spiritum detractionis: aspi-
ciunt si quando oblocuta sit, et poenitentiam non egerit. Obviat
iterum superius daemones fornicationis: scrutantur si recognos-
cant in ea voluptates. . . .

A little further on, other sins are added. Altogether, three sins,
fornicatio, superbia and *avaritia* correspond to the later cardinal list.
Then St. Hilary's address to his soul is quoted to the effect that God
will guard our souls, to encourage the living who yet must face this
experience.[23]

In Abba Isaias' work, there is mention of *inanis gloria, superbia,
invidia, cupiditas* and *ira* in connection with seven demons.[24] The
Coptic Gnostic and Christian remains available to me afford no direct reference to the seven chief sins, but it is clear that the concept
of the aerial demons hindering the soul and of the seven guardians
was well-known.[25]

[21] A. J. Mason, *Fifty Spiritual Homilies of St. Macarius the Egyptian,* Translations of Christian Literature, Series I, Greek Texts (London, 1921), p. 274. For the
original, see Migne, PG.,34, 777.

[22] Migne, PG., 34, 223–226.

[23] Migne, PL., 73, 374–375.

[24] Or. XVI, PG., 40, 1143. Cf. C. H. G. von Zezschwitz, *System der Christlich-
kirchlichen Katechetik* (Leipzig, 1863), II, 209 ff.

[25] See E. A. Wallis Budge, *Coptic Homilies* (London, 1910), p. 214, *Miscel-
laneous Coptic Texts* (London, 1915), pp. 726–727 and 733, *Coptic Apocrypha*

8

The cardinal sins may, therefore, be conceived as a heterodox or even pagan list taken over by Christianity and purged of its unsatisfactory elements.[26] The general view of evil aerial powers was supported by the cosmology of the age and accepted by St. Paul [27] and early Christian writers. The origins of the cardinal sins are not to be sought, as some have tried, either in Greek philosophy and speculation [28] or in the Judaism of the time or earlier.[29] Also, the sins were originally independent of such concepts as penance, and it is only later in the seventh and eighth centuries, at first in the Celtic penitentials, that they were used for penitential classification. Even later they were used in questioning at the confessional. Penance provided the meeting-place for the cardinal sins and the genuinely Judeo-Christian concept of the deadly sin,[30] which had not been standardized in a list of vices. As a result, the chief sins were generally, in the later Middle Ages, considered mortal. Some theologians maintained a distinction, and Dante in the Divine Comedy uses the cardinal sins only in the Purgatorio, not in the Inferno, where one unacquainted with the distinction might expect to find them.

(London, 1913), pp. 185–186, and *Coptic Martyrdoms* (London, 1914), pp. 340 and 421. Also see the *Apocryphal Life of Joseph the Carpenter*, ed. F. Robinson, *Coptic Apocryphal Gospels*, Texts and Studies IV, 2 (Cambridge, 1896), pp. 130 ff., esp. pp. 139 ff.

[26] The Church was not completely successful in purging the seven cardinal sins of their astrological origin, for surprisingly enough, beginning in the fourteenth century, the planets are linked to the sins more distinctly than ever before in Christian literature. In fact, the best examples come from this time. Where the association existed in the interval, unless it be an accidental rewelding or in Arabic astrological lore, I cannot guess. M. Gothein suggests it existed in the interval among the folk along with black magic and unreported in literature. See, e.g., the *Miracle-Morality Mary Magdalen* (EETS. e.s. 70 and 71, pp. 53–136), the Elizabethan Lyly's *The Woman in the Moon*, and "Templum Domini," ll. 569 ff., printed in R. D. Cornelius, *The Figurative Castle* (Bryn Mawr, 1930), pp. 106–107.

[27] See 2 Corinthians XII, 2 ff., Ephesians VI, 11–17, IV, 8, etc.

[28] As Zöckler, *op. cit.*, and S. Schiwietz, *Das morgenländische Mönchtum* (Mainz, II, 1913), 72 ff. do.

[29] As in the *Dictionnaire de Théologie Catholique*, ed. Vacant, Mangenot, and Amann, Tome II, Deuxième Partie, 168a.

[30] The deadly sins were those sins which the rabbis and early Church Fathers felt led to damnation. They are usually based on the ten commandments. There are numerous references to them in Jewish and Christian writings of the age, but they must not be confused with the cardinal or chief sins at this early date. See e.g., Acts XV, 20, 2 Timothy III, 2 ff., Matthew XV, 19, and 1 John V, 16 (the theoretical point of departure for the Fathers on the subject). Zöckler gives numerous references

The Egyptian Christian ascetics chose such a list in order to deal conveniently with their chief desert enemies, the demons Satan sent against them. It was not divorced from its monastic origins until the time of Gregory the Great and even later. The sins [31] first appear, however, in the work of Evagrius of Pontus (†c. 400) as a single concept, with an ancient and complex background.

---

to the deadly sins in the Fathers, although he does not make the distinction as I do. For Jewish references, see the Midrash Rabbah on Ecclesiastes, *Midrash Rabbah*, trans. Freedman and Simon (London, 1939), VIII, 40 and 84 and 85, *The Book of Jubilees*, VII, 20–21, ed. Charles in *The Apocrypha and Pseudepigrapha of the Old Testament* (Oxford, 1913), II, 24 and A. Büchler, *Studies in Sin and Atonement*, Jews' College Publications No. 11 (London, 1928), and G. F. Moore, *Judaism in the First Centuries of the Christian Era* (Cambridge, Mass., 1932), II, 248.

[31] For convenience in comparing, I here add Evagrius' list which was somewhat modified by later theologians. As found in his Περὶ τῶν ὀκτὼ λογισμῶν πρὸς 'Ανατόλιον, (Migne, PG., 40, 1271 ff.), it runs: γαστριμαργία (*gula*), πορνεία (*luxuria*), φιλαργυρία (*avaritia*), λύπη (*tristitia*), ὀργή (*ira*), ἀκηδία (*acedia*), κενοδοξία (*vana gloria*) and ὑπερηφανία (*superbia*).

2. Chaucer's Sense of History

"Die Geschichte der verschiedenen Arten des Sehens ist die Geschichte der Welt."—Egon Friedell, Kulturgeschichte der Neuzeit.

The growth of a sense of history from the twelfth century until our own time which has culminated in the various forms of historicism, empiricism, and cultural anthropology was nourished by the importance given to history by Christianity. And Christianity emphasizes the significance of history because it is based on revelation, wherein the timeless meets time and dignifies it. It believes that profound qualitative changes essential to human salvation have occurred and will occur in history.

It is a commonplace of the history of ideas that Israel gave the Western world a philosophy of history, just as Greece gave it a philosophy of nature. The Israelite philosophy of history was based on the idea that history has a transcendental meaning and is not just a repetitive cycle, that it reveals the will of God, that God may interfere and has interfered with the process of history, and that history is partially redemptive and moves towards a final end. Unlike the gods of Greece, the God of Israel Himself has no history; but again unlike the Greek concept of its own history, Israel and the other nations have a supremely significant history.

The ancient Hebrews saw, for instance, three main stages in which man's obligations and concepts differ—a time before the Law,[1] the time after the Law, and a time to come under the Messiah before the final days and the end of all history. There is a movement forward, a *development* in history. Even the fact that the supreme revelation to the Israelites was in the Law [2] gives a historic and social character to God's activity. These ideas are not, however, explicitly stated in the Bible and ancient Jewish tradition, but they are implicit in most of the strongly existentialistic writings of the Hebrew people.

Christianity took over these basic historic postulates and beliefs from Judaism and introduced another historic stage initiated by the Incarnation in which the Law is superseded by Grace. The Pauline

Reprinted with permission of the University of Illinois Press from *JEGP*, LI (1952), 301–313.

[1] This view becomes explicit in medieval Jewish philosophy. For example, Maimonides justifies Judah's actions with Tamar on the ground that before the giving of the Law cohabitation with a harlot was not wrong; see *The Guide for the Perplexed*, trans. M. Friedländer, 2nd ed., 1936 impression, p. 374 (III, 49).

[2] The act of Creation was of course God's supreme revelation to all men; but to the Jews as such, the Law is God's highest revelation.

13

conception of eras *ante legum, sub lege,* and *sub gratia* sums up this reinterpretation of history. But Christianity also looks forward to a Coming (a second one) of the Messiah in history. No one in the Judeo-Christian tradition can ignore history, and the claims of Christianity and Judaism as religions rest upon the historicity of certain happenings in the past. They stand or fall on the truth of these events. If no revelation in time on Mount Sinai, if no Christ, Son of God, who actually lived in Galilee and Judea some two thousand years ago, then no religions of Judaism and Christianity.[3]

The Greek emphasis was, however, essentialistic, natural and metaphysical, not existentialistic, supra-natural and historic. And in its impact on the Christian and Jewish religions, it tended to develop a philosophy of religion, an essentialistic and metaphysical approach.[4] But even in St. Thomas, who more than any other Christian thinker applied the Greek categories to Christianity, the sense of the historic is not absent.

The Middle Ages generally, however, tended to ignore the implications of a historic sense on matters outside of religion. This was due in part to a lack of knowledge of other times and other cultures, and in part to an overwhelming emphasis on a few historic events of the highest religious significance. These events were often assimilated to an extra-historical reality. Christ is sacrificed every minute of the day, and man continually falls, as he did once in the long long ago. Every enactment of the Mass goes through the redemptive process all over again. By this hypostasizing of the extremely important events in the Christian story, the Middle Ages developed, in effect, an a-historic (not un-historic) approach which could—and did to some extent—blur the historic approach.

With the renaissance of the twelfth century, we find, as a result of the Crusades, new translations and other factors, the emergence of a new knowledge and a new methodology which made possible a new historic sense (or better a *Diesseitsstimmung* [5]). This may be

---

[3] It is possible, of course, as many people today do, to follow Judaism and Christianity as cultural codes even without believing in the historic truth of their claims.

[4] See Martin Foss, *The Idea of Perfection in the Western World* (1946), pp. 26 ff.

[5] There is unfortunately no good English equivalent for this German term. It is more accurate than the phrase "sense of history" which I have used in this paper. For several articles on the *Diesseitsstimmung* in the Middle Ages, see Hennig Brinkmann,

seen in Biblical exegesis,[6] in Gothic art, in the popularity and number of histories and chronicles,[7] in new historical theorizing and millenarianism, observable for instance in the works associated with Joachim of Flora and some of his Franciscan followers,[8] in the re-

---

"Diesseitsstimmung im Mittelalter," *Deutsche Vierteljahrsschrift für Literaturwissenschaft und Geistesgeschichte*, II (1924), 721–752 and the summary of W. Goetz's paper "Die Entwicklung des Wirklichkeitssinnes vom 12. bis zum 14. Jahrhundert" in *Sitzungsberichte der philosophisch-historischen Abteilung der Bayerischen Akademie der Wissenschaften zu München*, Jahrgang 1936, 11 Januar, 1936 (Munich, 1936), p. 5, and apparently printed in full in the *Archiv für Kulturgeschichte*, XXVII (1937), 33–73.

[6] The twelfth and thirteenth centuries, in part due to the influence of the Jewish exegete Rashi, insisted more strongly on the literal (which was also known as the historical) level of interpretation than on the other allegorical (and more figurative) levels, a practice different from that of earlier exegetes who tended to skip over the literal meaning. The importance of this urge to emphasize the historical level was considerable. This movement also manifested itself in current attitudes towards literature; see Charles S. Singleton's article, "Dante's Allegory," *Speculum*, XXV (1950), 78–86.

[7] The twelfth century saw an efflorescence of historical writing, especially in England and Germany. See C. H. Haskins, *The Renaissance of the Twelfth Century* (1927), pp. 224 ff. Brinkmann, *op. cit.*, p. 733, n. 1, attributes much to the Normans in the creation of the *Diesseitsstimmung*.

[8] For some works on medieval theories of history and the writing of history and related ideas, see F. Hipler, *Die christliche Geschichts-Auffassung* (1884); Marie Schulz, *Die Lehre von der historischen Methode bei den Geschichtschreibern des Mittelalters (VI–XIII-Jahrhundert)*, Abhandlungen zur mittleren und neueren Geschichte 13 (1909); Ernst Bernheim, *Mittelalterliche Zeitanschauungen in ihrem Einfluss auf Politik und Geschichtsschreibung*, Teil. I (only part published; 1918); Alois Dempf, *Sacrum Imperium, Geschichts- und Staatsphilosophie des Mittelalters und der politischen Renaissance* (1929); W. A. Schneider, *Geschichte und Geschichtsphilosophie bei Hugo von St. Victor, Ein Beitrag zur Geistesgeschichte des 12. Jahrhunderts*, Münstersche Beiträge zur Geschichtsforschung, III Folge, II Heft (1933); Ernst Benz, *Ecclesia Spiritualis, Kirchenidee und Geschichtstheologie der Franziskanischen Reformation* (1934); Johannes Spörl, *Grundformen hochmittelalterlicher Geschichtsanschauung* (1935); Paolo Brezzi, "La Concezione Agostiniana della Città di Dio e le sue Interpretazioni Medioevali," *Rivista Storica Italiana*, Serie V, III (1938), 62–94; Paolo Brezzi, "Ottone di Frisinga," *Bullettino dell'Istituto Storico Italiano per il Medio Evo e Archivio Muratoriano*, LIV (1939), 129–328; E. Gilson, *L'Esprit de la Philosophie Médiévale*, Etudes de Philosophie Médiévale, XXXIII, 2nd ed. (1944), pp. 365 ff., George Boas, *Essays on Primitivism and Related Ideas in the Middle Ages* (1948) and very generally in Chapter 1 of Ernest Lee Tuveson, *Millenium and Utopia, A Study in the Background of the Idea of Progress* (1949). Erich Auerbach (in *Mimesis, Dargestellte Wirklichkeit in der abendländischen Literatur* [1946], pp. 165, 495, 158 ff., *et passim*) associates the rise of late medieval "realism" in subject matter and style with the Franciscans and their emphasis on the life and sufferings of Jesus.

vival of interest in the Classics, and in the variety and types of vernacular literature. In some ways Aristotelianism was a retarding force from this point of view, and it was not until Aristotle began to lose his hold on men's minds in the fourteenth and fifteenth centuries that the growth of the historic sense could have full play. Yet Christian Aristotelianism with its emphasis on natural reason left a strong imprint on some of the pre-suppositions and justifications of this sense of history.[9]

What is meant by a historic sense in this new development? It is clearly not the basic historic postulates of Christianity, for they are the matrix of the new sense and were of course never superseded. It is rather basically a new heightened attention toward past, present and future. It may manifest itself in an emphasis on the pastness of the past or on the reality of the present or on a concrete hope or despair for the future. Only occasionally in its early phases, do we find in one person a three-fold emphasis, as in Chaucer, but usually it is manifested only in an awareness of one or two of the traditional divisions of time. In the Joachimite movement, the accent is on the future; in the new naturalism in art and literature it is implicitly on the present; and more rarely, in historians, a new awareness of the past is found. In sum, it is a *Diesseitsstimmung*—a this-world orientation which, however, did not deny the other world.

Approaching the question from another angle, we may also say that the new historic sense is demonstrated in (1) a more accurate sense of chronology and (2) a sense of cultural diversity. Neither is new; both may be found in the early Fathers [10] and in some of the

---

[9] Neo-Platonism as modified by Augustine provided a better basis for an historical sense than Aristotelianism. However, as will be seen, Aquinas with his clear separation of the natural from the supranatural cleared the way for an historical approach to events; and Augustine in his interpretation of the Book of Revelation (see next note) stood in its way. Augustine's views are of course indispensable for any understanding of the medieval concepts of history.

[10] The Christian concept of the seven ages of the world presupposes a strong sense of chronology. Much of the problem of history in early Christian times was centered around the question of the interpretation of Revelation—historic (urged by Victorinus) or moral (urged by Tychonius and Augustine). On this last point, see Wilhelm Kamlah, *Apokalypse und Geschichtstheologie, Die mittelalterliche Auslegung der Apokalypse vor Joachim von Fiore*, Historische Studien 285 (1935), and the two excellent commentaries on Revelations, one by W. Bousset (in H. A. W. Meyer's *Kritisch-exegetischer Kommentar über das Neue Testament*) and the other by E. B. Allo (3rd ed., 1933).

Classical writers. But they waited upon knowledge and favorable circumstances to be fully applied to the processes of history. They also in some measure demand both a sceptical or at least open spirit and a conviction that the things of this world matter (or a partially secular point of view), for a pure interest in history would be considered merely another vanity by a Saint Bernard or by a Richard Rolle. They require the existence of intellectuals who will be concerned with the problems of this world and who will be willing to forgo at least temporarily, the proper end of man from the religious point of view—the union with, or vision of, God. Or more subtly, intellectuals who believe they are doing God's work by being concerned with the things of this world. Philosophically they also need the concept of an autonomous realm of reason and a concept of natural law, which the scholastics provided or at least presented in acceptable form.

How does Chaucer stand in relation to this idea of the idea of history? Or, what is his sense of history? How does a knowledge of Chaucer's sense of history help us to interpret his work? To these questions the remainder of this article will be devoted.

In his early work there is little evidence of a sense of history, but in *The Legend of Good Women, Troilus,* and the *Canterbury Tales,* we find an increasing preoccupation with both accurate chronology and cultural diversity and a strong feeling for the past, the present and the future. I shall take for granted an increasing naturalism in Chaucer's work, a movement away from allegory toward representationalism, which in itself is a manifestation of the sense of the historic as present. We also find in Chaucer's later works, an increasing tendency to date and to localize his narratives. As a source for his changed point of view, it is possible to look to the early Italian Renaissance of which Chaucer had first hand experience. But although rare, there are also, as we shall see, signs of an incipient sense of the historic in contemporary England.

Although in Chaucer we often find flagrant anachronisms, they usually arise out of ignorance, thoughtlessness, or the superior claims of artistic fitness. We may, if we wish, make up an impressive list of Chaucer's historical errors and falsifications, probably larger than the list which illustrates his sense of history. But that is not the point. What is remarkable is that Chaucer is historically minded as compared with his English contemporaries and that on the whole, in his later works, he has a considerable sense of historic succession and cultural relativity.

At least two of his characters apologize for violating chronology. In the *Knight's Tale*, describing the "Temple of myghty Mars the rede" the Knight tells us of the murals within the building, some of which dealt with future events (after the time of Theseus)—the murders of Julius Caesar, of Nero and of Caracalla (listed in proper chronological order). He goes on to say that although they were not born yet, their deaths were, nevertheless, depicted there (ll. 2031 ff.).[11] The mere prediction is standard astrology, but significant is Chaucer's qualifying phrase "al be that thilke tyme they were unborn. . . ." The Monk also apologizes before he tells his tragedies:

> But first I yow biseeke in this mateere,
> Though I by ordre telle nat those thynges,
> Be it of popes, emperours, of kynges,
> After hir ages, as men writen fynde,
> But tellen hem som bifore and som bihynde,
> As it now comth unto my remembraunce,
> Have me excused of my ignoraunce.[12]

In the "Legend of Lucrece" (ll. 1812 ff.), Chaucer uses his sense of the past to give an ironical twist to his comments pointing toward later times.

> These Romeyn wyves lovede so here name
> *At thilke tyme*, and dredde so the shame,

[11] Chaucer was very much interested and may have believed in some form of judicial astrology as did many of the learned men of his time. The idea that the future was written in the stars is clearly enunciated in the *Man of Law's Tale*, ll. 190 ff. See however below note 14. I have avoided the subject in this article as only tangential to my purpose. It involves such large questions as predestination and science in the fourteenth century.

[12] VII, 1984 ff. All my quotations from and references to Chaucer are taken from the edition of F. N. Robinson, 1933.

That, what for fer of sclaunder and drede of death,
She[Lucrece] loste bothe at ones wit and breth. . . .[13]

This passage is a particularly happy example of the marriage of Chaucer's sense of the past with his own sense of humor and satire, the first serving the second.

Some further passages in Chaucer provide evidence both of his sense of chronology and of his awareness of cultural differences. In the *Man of Law's Tale*, Constance, daughter of the Emperor of Rome, lands on the coast of Northumberland and properly speaks a Vulgar Latin to the inhabitants. As Robinson says, "Indeed the whole account of Roman Britain in the tale conforms to historic fact to a degree unusual in mediaeval stories." [14] Chaucer may well have been aware of the fact that in the time of a Roman Emperor the inhabitants of Britain would be speaking or would at least understand a "manner Latyn corrupt" (l. 518), even though his source had the inhabitants speaking Saxon. Or at least this passage shows that he was deliberately making the ancient Britons speak Latin instead of Saxon. At the same time, however, he seems blind to the fact that a Mohammedan Sultan could not have been ruling coevally in Syria, unless he is deliberately mixing up eras here for an artistic effect of make-believe. I suspect not, however, and think rather that we have in the *Man of Law's Tale* an unconscious blend of the medieval and modern senses of chronology.

Professor Tatlock has pointed out that Chaucer is deliberately archaizing the setting of the *Franklin's Tale*. The *Tale* is made to unfold as in Roman times, and there is no suggestion for this in any imaginable source. We may see this archaism in the use of the term Armorica for Brittany, in allusions to heathens (l. 1293) and heathen gods (ll. 1030 ff.), in a reference to the worthlessness of certain aspects of natural magic "as in oure dayes is not worth a flye" (l. 1132), and possibly in the use of an ancient town of Kayrrud (l. 808). And yet we find in heathen days, a University at Orléans. Professor Tatlock suggests that "Chaucer put the whole tale back in pagan times that the Franklin might with the more propriety rail at such arts [astrological magic] as heathenish and might disavow seri-

---

[13] My italics.
[14] *Ibid.*, p. 798.

ous approval of them, or faith in their efficacy, especially for an evil purpose." [15]

It is possible that this is the explanation, but I am inclined rather to think Chaucer's method here an attempt to throw an aura of the past over the fantastic happenings reported. One reason does not necessarily exclude the other, and in any case Chaucer shows here in his accumulation of details an intense awareness of the pastness of the past and the difference between those days and his own. He turned to the past in order to make his *Tale* palatable, and in so doing reveals an awareness of the problem of time and credibility.

So too for a humorous effect does the Wyf of Bath lament the passing of incubi and elves who used to infest the land and waylay women (ll. 857 ff.). She contrasts the unhappy present when there are only friars about to carry out this pleasant function, with the happy past. *Autres temps, autres moeurs,* alas! She also points out here how the Welshmen and Britons idealize their Arthurian history.

In the famous passage in *Troilus and Criseyde* II, 22–28, we read

> Ye knowe ek that in forme of speche is chaunge
> Withinne a thousand yeer, and wordes tho
> That hadden pris, now wonder nyce and straunge
> Us thinketh hem, and yet thei spake hem so,
> And spedde as wel in love as men now do;
> Ek for to wynnen love in sondry ages,
> In sondry londes, sondry ben usages.[16]

In this melancholy stanza on the passage of time, Chaucer reveals not only a sense of chronology but also an acute sense of cultural

---

[15] See John S. P. Tatlock, *The Scene of the Franklin's Tale Visited,* Chaucer Society, Second Series 51 (1914, for the issue of 1911), p. 21. (The whole discussion is to be found in Chapter III, pp. 17–37). Some support for Professor Tatlock's position may be seen in *A Treatise on the Astrolabe,* II.c. 4, ll. 63 ff., where there is an allusion to "rytes of payens, in which my spirit hath no feith," a phrase applied to the casting of horoscopes.

[16] Cf. William of Malmesbury's comment on different literary styles when discussing Aldhelm in his *De Gestis Pontificum Anglorum,* v, 196 (ed. Hamilton, Rolls Series [1870], p. 344). He writes ". . . gentium varientur mod dictaminum. Denique Graeci involute, Romani splendide, Angli pompatice dictare solent." This is a relatively early example of medieval awareness of cultural relativity.

change in regard to the past and present. It is not merely a conventional comment on human transience, but a statement of the accumulative effect of time on human customs and manners. Here also is the medieval and Greek sense of a permanence underlying all change—the one behind the many.

A sense of historical development applying this time to the future is to be found at the end of *Troilus* (v, 1793 ff.) where Chaucer argues from the contemporary diversity of the English language and from the sound changes going on in his time to the conclusion that English may change so drastically in the future that some may miswrite, mismeter or misunderstand him. From both of these *Troilus* passages, we get a poignant sense of the inexorable quality of time. Chaucer tells us by implication that he himself will pass away along with all these other ephemera.

Shortly after (ll. 1835 ff.), he goes on to contrast the world before Christ with that after His death when He introduced a new kind of love to mankind, very different from that revealed in the story of Troilus and Criseyde which he has just been narrating. The world *sub gratia* is a very different world; a new quality or dimension has been created by God's love, dividing forever pagan history ("while men loved the lawe of kinde") from Christian history.[17]

Even more common in Chaucer is a sense of cultural diversity between the past and the present. At least three times in the *Knight's Tale*, he explains, following Boccaccio from whom he possibly derived his historic sense, the actions of his characters with the modifying clause, "as was tho the gyse" or a similar clause. The funeral customs of Thebes (l. 993), the sacrificial rites of Athens (l. 2279), and the Athenian cremation ceremonies (l. 2911) are so qualified. Similarly in "The Legend of Cleopatra" in *The Legend*

---

[17] The quotation is from the *Book of the Duchess*, l. 56. In keeping with this contrast between the pagan world under natural law and the Christian world under grace, Chaucer except in rare instances, always writes of the Trojans and Greeks in *Troilus* as if they were reasonable pagans believing in God and the basic moral law. Even though they may discuss medieval scholastic problems, they carry out pagan rites and are not Christians. A notable exception to this attitude may be found in Book III, l. 1165 (if the Robinson reading is correct which I am inclined to doubt) where Criseyde swears by the "God that bought us bothe two." In the comments of the "I" (the construct Chaucer), however, we often find, as is proper, Christian allusions and phraseology. His characters and the setting are. on the other hand, as consciously pagan as he could make them.

of Good Women (ll. 583 ff.), we find Chaucer's comment "as was usance," on Anthony's being sent "for to conqueren regnes and honour / Unto the toun of Rome."

Chaucer's awareness of the difference in human custom also extends to those two coeval peoples, the Greeks and the Trojans. Diomede's light chatter to Criseyde in his campaign to win her, includes a solicitous inquiry "if that hire straunge thoughte / The Grekis gise, and werkes that they wroughte" (v, 860–61). A pleasant enough topic of conversation, but revealing in Chaucer a knowledge that not only are customs past and present different, but also that contemporary customs in the past may vary. And again Chaucer, for purposes of his humor, makes a mock and yet true distinction between ancient mythological figures and ancient Biblical figures of names similar enough to be frequently confused. In the *Knight's Tale* (ll. 2062 ff.) we are told that Dane (i.e. Daphne), not Diane, was turned into a tree. The Pardoner is also careful to tell us he is referring to Lamuel (Lemuel) not Samuel on the evil effects of intoxication (*Tale*, ll. 583 ff.). Chaucer was no doubt aware of the medieval fondness for confusing historic figures.

Naturally then in his own time, Chaucer is aware of the variability of human habits and customs. He presents the Sultana's arguments in the *Man of Law's Tale* from the Mohammedan point of view. She tells her Council of State (ll. 330 ff.) that they will suffer Hell if they deny the Koran and God's messenger, Mohammed. The scheme of her son to become a Christian will destroy them all. Here again Chaucer goes beyond his source, which by no means sees the issue from the Saracen point of view or attempts to give credibility to the deliberations of the Council. In the earlier Council meeting held by the Sultan before Constance came to Syria, his wise men saw "swich diversitee bitwene hir bothe lawes" [18] that they could not see how he could be allowed by a Christian prince to marry his daughter (ll. 218 ff.). They were under the "lawe sweete" of Mohammed, they report. For Chaucer these Mohammedan enemies of Christianity are no silly, ignorant fools. Yet in spite of his ability to see, although not approve of, the Mohammedan point of

[18] On the canon law problem involved here, see Paul E. Beichner, "Chaucer's Man of Lawe and *Disparitas Cultus*," *Speculum*, XXIII (1948), 70–75, esp. 72–73. Beichner is only concerned with the legal issues.

view, Chaucer falls down on his knowledge (which was perhaps inevitable owing to the widespread ignorance concerning Islam) by assuming that Mohammedans sacrificed to God (1. 325). This is however a point of fact, not an attitude. But as we have already seen, the *Man of Law's Tale* is partially laid in the late Roman Empire and, as here, partially in the present.

In the *Squire's Tale*, we find an even broader attitude. For the Great Khan, who, we are told, subscribed to a non-Christian religion, was "*thereto* [my italics] . . . hardy, wys, and riche, / And pitous and just, alwey yliche; / Sooth of his word, benigne and honurable, / Of his corage as any centre stable" (ll. 19–22). May we not see in these lines a strong criticism of contemporary "Christian" rulers? Even the pagan can be just and kind. Chaucer's tolerance extends, later in the *Tale*, to the Khan's strange eating habits (ll. 67 ff.) and strange language (ll. 99 ff.). Yet in this tale, Chaucer substitutes space for time by presenting the distant Khan's Court in an almost Arthurian aura.

Purely from the point of view of the history of ideas, Chaucer's sense of chronology and of cultural diversity shows an affinity with certain emphases of the Renaissance.[19] In this, he draws close to Montaigne and Rabelais. And in his own time a comparison with Langland and other national contemporaries who manifest an almost total absence of such a sense brings out even more sharply the rarity of his point of view. In his century in England, I think he is paralleled in his sense of the historic only by the *Travels of Sir John Mandeville*, where that sense is largely implicit rather than explicit, and by Wyclif, who uses his sense of the historic for polemical purposes.

In Mandeville, we see more openly than in Chaucer, however, the workings of the scholastic concept [20] of natural reason, which is

[19] I am here using the term Renaissance in the Burckhardtian sense. A. L. Rowse entitles the second chapter of his *The England of Elizabeth, The Structure of Society* (1951), pp. 31–65, "The Elizabethan Discovery of England." Chaucer can be considered a pioneer in this characteristic of the English Renaissance.

[20] The idea of natural reason and natural law goes back to ultimately Stoic speculation. But the scholastics of the thirteenth century clearly established the distinction between the knowledge gained by natural reason and that gained by faith. Gerard Paré (in *Les Idées et les Lettres au XIII*ᵉ *Siècle, Le Roman de la Rose* [Université de Montréal, Bibliothèque de Philosophie 1], 1947, p. 301) in his excellent study of the second part of the *Romance of the Rose* writes: "Notre auteur [Jean

one of the roots of the modern sense of history. The great scholastics sought to demonstrate the existence of God by the light of natural reason, implanted, as they believed, in all men. The far-reaching implications of this attempt led to the belief that all men could arrive at some concept of the truth. This in turn involves the belief that to some extent at least even non-Christians have a grasp of the truth and hence other cultures are worth some consideration. If Professor R. W. Chambers was right,[21] this view lies behind More's *Utopia*.

Mandeville puts it thus:

> And ye shall understand that all these men folks that have reason y[t] I have spoken of, have some articles of our faith, all if they be of divers lawes and divers beleves, yet they have some good poynts of our fayth & they beleve in God of kinde. . . .[22]

What does all this mean in terms of Chaucer's art? That is not an easy question to answer. The possession of a sense of history does not guarantee its possessor artistic power. Yet I think we may say some things about Chaucer's art and point of view in terms of his sense of history. Like all problems dealing with the relationship between a man's views and his art, we cannot establish a strict causality.

It seems to me that through the Chaucerian sense of history, although it is only one element in the poetry of Chaucer, we may get a flavor of the essence of Chaucer's art. We see revealed in it the sense of poignancy, of the *lacrimae rerum* which often strikes any serious reader of the poet. Over much of Chaucer's work is a piercing sense of man's transience, of his foolish pretensions, of his comic-tragic dignity. The sense of the historic serves Chaucer in his satire and in his humor. It is one view which enables him to place the world in its right perspective for him—and for us. It is basic to the particular type of tragic objectivity which he often manifests. As

---

de Meun] se trouve ainsi à établir une distinction claire entre ce que les théologiens du 13e siècle appellent la connaissance naturelle que nous avons de Dieu, et la connaissance surnaturelle, celle que l'homme ne peut atteindre que par la foi et que procède d'une révélation divine."

21 *Thomas More* (1935), pp. 125 ff.
22 Chap. cvii, Everyman's Library, p. 226.

a comic-tragic artist, he makes use of a relatively new element in Western Civilization when he need not have done so. He grasped at it and made it part of his view of the world because it seemed to him, perhaps subconsciously, a way of expressing some of his most basic thoughts. It serves his artistic power of restraint. A sense of history is one of the ways Chaucer follows to enable attitudes to say themselves, to be objectified.

At the same time, as all choices must, it limits him. A comparison with Dante here will be profitable.[23] Dante has a more profoundly tragic view than Chaucer because, in his art, he sets eternity against time. Chaucer, who in terms of religion certainly held views similar to those of Dante, rarely transferred these religious views to his art and even occasionally exhibited the scepticism of one type of believer. Much of Chaucer's art unrolls in time aware of itself through the author, the commentator on his work. It has duration, and it conveys an awareness of this duration even as events come and go. All this will pass, Chaucer seems to say. With Dante all this has passed and is eternally judged and fixed. The actual historical events which the manifold inhabitants of hell, purgatory, and heaven participated in are laid before us compassionately, but as past and as finally arbitrated. The eternal is the merciful but stern judge of history. To this stage Chaucer rarely, if ever, comes in his art.[24] Yet his acceptance of human transitoriness and human clash of opinion and custom provides him with another spectacle from which he extracts his particular type of art. Time condemns itself and all human endeavor and hopes; and yet we cannot despair: in fact, it is only through a sense of the comic that we may fully understand dialectically our tragic dilemma. Above as within time there is need for laughter.

I do not wish to overemphasize the "modern" historical ap-

[23] Cf. T. Spencer, "The Story of Ugolino in Dante and Chaucer," *Speculum*, IX (1934), 295–301.

[24] The gates of hell proclaim:

Giustizia mosse il mio alto fattore;
Fecemi la divina potestate,
La somma sapienza e 'l primo amore
(*Inferno*, III, 4–6)

Possibly at the end of *Troilus and Criseyde*, Chaucer reaches, at one point, this Dantesque view.

proach in Chaucer at the expense of the "medieval." In history things happen slowly. In an artistic sense, Chaucer is always modern; but he is also partially a creature of history and in him are to be seen the various conflicting ideas of the fourteenth century, some destined to wax and others to wane, perhaps only temporarily if we take a point of view long range enough. For today we may see, I think, a turning away from the historic again. But the sense of history which we find in Chaucer, however undeveloped, is one element which was destined to play a very important part in the succeeding centuries; perhaps even more important, however, it is an element which gives us some clue to the heart of the mystery of Chaucer's art. Chaucer may be studied as a figure in the history of ideas as well as an artist, and in isolating at least his sense of the historic, we must eventually turn back to his art with a new awareness and a new understanding of his aims and methods.

3. Some Reflections on the Medieval Idea of Perfection

T. E. Hulme's term "critique of satisfaction" provides us with a very useful tool in approaching the history of ideas, for not only do ideas and concepts change with the passing of time but the very canons of satisfactory proof change. I do not deny a continuity in both, but as an historian of ideas I am more interested in their variability. What is it that gives a unique flavor to each historic epoch or indeed to each century or decade? The persistence of ideas and canons cannot be doubted by one who believes in reason, in certain absolute standards, and in some kind of continuity in human nature; but at the same time it must not be forgotten that there is change, growth and development, at least in the sublunar world. As historian, one must, while not forgetting the persistence, concentrate on the change without necessarily committing oneself to the metaphysical proposition that there is ever true novelty in the universe.

By the phrase "critique of satisfaction," Hulme points up the fact that what seems a satisfactory answer to one age may not content another. In the realm of natural science, no one can seriously question such a proposition. A modern would not be satisfied, in asking the question of why an apple is red, to be told that it is red because it possesses the accident of redness or that all apples, potentially red, become red in act by maturation. We would be satisfied, however, if we were told that the skin of the apple possesses, along with other qualities, the power of absorbing all the colors in the spectrum except red which is hence reflected. Whether this reply really answers the question or not depends on how deeply one may wish to probe, and I do not wish to eliminate the philosophic as opposed to the scientific question here; but at least most moderns would not feel it worthwhile to pursue the matter further. This response satisfies their critique of satisfaction, as far as the question of color goes.

One of the ways of approaching the reality of the thought of the past is through awareness of the differences in critiques of satisfaction. As soon as we delve into medieval philosophy we have the sensation that we are meeting, in at least some matters, with critiques of satisfaction different from our own. To enter sympathetically,

Reprinted with permission of the Franciscan Institute, St. Bonaventura University, from *Franciscan Studies*, XVII (1957), 213–237.

This article was delivered in substantially this form as a speech before a meeting of the East-Central Conference of the ACPA held at the Pontifical Josephinum College, Worthington, Ohio on March 24, 1957.

then, into medieval thought, whether for the purpose of discovering truth or for establishing what was then believed to be truth, we must be conscious of this difference in answering questions at different times.

On many matters there is no problem at all. We silently make the adjustment and do not let it interfere, if the point under discussion can otherwise be substantiated to us, with our belief or with our awareness. In the matter, for instance, of the etymological mode of argument, we have no difficulty. Until fairly recent times it was believed that the history of words provided us with a clue to their present meaning. When we find in St. Thomas, for instance, a passage in a brilliantly argued "questio" which deals with the etymology or even worse an assumed etymology of the word or words involved in the proof being used as an additional argument in its favor, we silently excise the passage; and if the rationality of the rest of the argument is strong, we can accept the truth of his answer, provided of course that in general we accept his intellectual premises.[1] We do the same when St. Thomas makes use of antiquated science to support an argument. There is, however, more difficulty with certain other canons of verificability and response, and it is with one of them, the notion of perfection, that I wish to deal today.

I have deliberately entitled this address some reflections on the medieval idea of perfection, for I am very conscious of the enormous extent of the subject and of my own limitations. It was, however, the paucity of both discussions and studies of the concept which led to the research which lies behind this paper today. If I may intrude some autobiography, I became convinced of the importance of the subject, especially in its moral aspect, when trying to understand a Middle English poem, *Piers Plowman*, in which I am very much interested. Naturally, I sought scholarly aids and interpreters, but I

---

[1] I do not wish to deny that the etymological mode may still have some rhetorical value but am only questioning its use for verification and proof. See "Etymology as a Category of Thought" in Ernst R. Curtius, *European Literature and the Latin Middle Ages*, trans. Willard R. Trask (London, 1953), pp. 495–500, and E. Gilson, "De quelques raisonnements scripturaires usités au Moyen Age," *Les idées et les lettres* (Paris, 1932), pp. 155 ff., esp. pp. 164 ff. St. Thomas does, however, point out in *ST* I, q. 29, a. 3 ad 2; II, II, q. 92, a. 1 ad 2 that words have deeper meanings than their etymologies indicate.

found so few guides that I was forced to do the job myself with the result that a nonphilosopher had to do work for which he was not well equipped. I hope, in view of the circumstances, you will forgive the rash attempts of an amateur in a field where one must tread softly.

Perfection is an extremely common concept in the writings of classical and medieval philosophers and, indeed, of modern philosophers, at least down to Kant; and some important changes have taken place in our attitude towards it which have not, I think, always been taken into consideration by those of us who study the thought of the past. In fact, except in its application to the moral and religious life, in for instance the idea of Christian perfection on which there is an extensive bibliography, the metaphysical idea of perfection has been, as far as I am able to determine, little studied. One comes upon the word in its nominal, verbal, adjectival and adverbial forms very frequently in the writings of philosophers of the past, and yet there is hardly any book or article to which one may turn for enlightenment on its significance.

My purpose here is to try to analyze the various meanings of the term and to show how some of them are contradictory, or at least demand careful precision in their use; how this idea provides us with a clue to understanding medieval thought; and finally how we stand today in regard to this term if we wish to preserve the insights and truths of scholasticism, for it does pose, I think, a difficulty.

The notion of perfection is not only a philosophical concept in many philosophical systems of the past but also an important canon of decision, or in other words it is both a philosophical idea and part of the critique of satisfaction for certain kinds of philosophical questions raised in the past. The appeal to perfection in settling an issue is a final court in much historical philosophical reasoning, and it is this aspect of the word in which I am most interested. I am in general going to limit my reflections to the ontological and metaphysical aspects of the subject, although I shall touch upon the moral and religious sides of the concept at times, especially as one of my major points is that the idea of perfection is a common bridge between the various orders of thinking—or being—theological, ontological, social, psychological and ethical. Although often the term itself is not used, it is only in the latter realms that the idea is very much alive today. In ordinary parlance it has come to mean the *summum bonum* in any particular order of experience and discipline. It is often romantically thought of as the object of deliberate striving with the stress thrown on the striving. It is equated with the ideal. In all these modern popular senses of the term there is some trace of the word's former high dignity, but much has happened to it since it fell out of philosophical and scientific favor.

Many of the philosophical terms of the past need justification and redefinition today. "Perfection" is by no means in a class by itself in this regard. With it, as opposed to some of the other metaphysical concepts of the past, I think we have special difficulties, and it is to these that I hope to direct your attention. For some Platonic and Aristotelian concepts, although modern science has repudiated them, concepts like act, form, idea, final cause, and so forth, one can make a very good defense as to their relevance in philosophical argument whether Thomistic or not, but for perfection it is not so easy and except in the idea of Christian perfection, it is my impression that modern traditional and scholastic philosophers do not use the term very much. They have in fact bowed here to modern science. And indeed it is perhaps well that they do so. But the abandonment of the concept of perfection has certain significant implications of which it is well to be aware.

The sources of the idea, like those of many other ideas in Western Civilization, are Greek and Hebrew, and many offspring have been huddled together under its capacious wings. The meanings of the term are numerous and interlocking, yet in order to grasp its complexity one must distinguish as far as possible these various elements. I am taking as my norm in this essay at definition the employment of the term in medieval philosophy, and my approach is systematic rather than historical and chronological.

It may be said that the very notion of a rational universe, a universe capable of being understood by the human mind, implies to some extent the notion of perfection. The rise of Ionian philosophy in Thales, Anaximander, and their successors elsewhere meant that to some minds at least there was a possible fitting of the multiplicity of the changing universe to certain patterns or principles which implied that a perfection in at least the sense of rationality is possible. There was a δίκη in things, in the physical world. Later in the fifth century we get a widespread recognition of an antinomy between φύσις and νόμος, between eternal laws of nature and artificial human conventions, which also contains within it an idea of perfection. But actually it was Plato who first developed the notion of perfection latent, and if we possessed the texts, perhaps open in earlier speculation.

The classical idea of nature which intersects the concept of perfection at many points, may be subdivided into three major definitions—nature as norm and reason associated with Plato, Platonism and Stoicism; nature as completion and act associated with Aristotle; nature as generation and blind striving associated with Democritus and the Epicureans. These three definitions have persisted into modern times, and from the twelfth century on, the last definition has been ever more dominant. The first two definitions, although they certainly allow for chance and contingency conceive of nature as rational and in a sense as supranatural [2] as compared to the last definition. In a rational nature, whether Platonic or Aristotelian, nature is perfect or at least perfectible. And in the Hebraic tradition this view although not with the metaphysical categorization of the Greeks is also dominant. The third definition emphasizes the irrational and contingent aspects of nature. Its blind striving, its endless cycles, are the dominant mode of its appearance. Perfection is not a natural concept, but if it exists at all it is beyond nature. The Aristotelian definition is a bridge between the rational and irrational views of nature, but in Aristotle himself the concepts of a final cause and of act brings his view of nature within the realm of the rational.[3] To follow the story of perfection further, however, we need to make some more distinctions and definitions.

I think we may overall distinguish between two types of definition—the relative and the absolute. In the first, the idea of perfection implies an opposition of two middle excluding alternatives, or a universal dichotomy one of which is more desirable than the

---

[2] "Natura est ratio cujusdam artis, scilicet divinae, indita rebus, qua ipsae res moventur ad finem determinatum," Thomas Aquinas, *In Physic*. II, 14., one of the various definitions of nature found in his works.

[3] See, for the Aristotelian and Thomistic view of nature, Joseph M. Marling, *The Order of Nature in the Philosophy of St. Aquinas*, A Dissertation . . . of the Catholic University of America (Washington, 1934).

other and hence in certain senses can be thought of as perfect. The opposite concept is however always implied. In the second, the term means something in itself and possesses a positive definition. I am also assuming here that the idea of perfection is closely associated with the idea of good although not by any means equivalent to it. "Good" itself is defined in a variety of ways, but in general, I am using it in the sense of utility in all its senses and relating it to the will as its principle of movement.[4]

First, let us take up some of the relative meanings of perfection. Rest is perfect as opposed to motion. In many ways this is one of the basic components of the *perfectio* complex and goes back both to Aristotle and Plato on the one hand and to the Old Testament on the other. One of the characteristics of most of Greek thought and science is its suspicion of motion and change as opposed to rest and stability. The essential problem in Greek physics was to explain change; in modern physics change and movement are taken for granted. The chief charge of Plato against the world of experience and the senses is its mutability, and it is the unchangingness of the world of ideas which provides one of its greatest appeals to the intellect. Change cannot be apprehended per se; in order to explain it we must assume a changeless world of which it is the reflection. Although Aristotle has no world of ideas, he too is motivated by similar reasons. How can we explain movement? What are the changeless principles behind change? And ultimately Aristotle is led to his unmoved mover as the source of all change, generation and corruption. The general concept of a final cause and a teleological universe is an essential presupposition of all this.

This conception, although given a social and ethical twist, is also part of the thinking of the ancient Hebrews. Although they are never argued as such, I do not think that metaphysical assumptions are absent from their views. The prototype of all rest is the Sabbath, which commemorates the resting of the Lord after creation. The full exegesis and meaning of this idea which is profound and demanding I am not equipped to undertake. The idea of rest as be-

---

[4] See, e.g., the good is "that which all things aim at," Aristotle, *Nic. Ethics* I, 1094a; John Damascene, *De fide orthodoxa* I, 1 (PG. 94, 791); Boethius, *De consolatione* III, pr. 11; Dionysius, *De div. nom* IV, 1 ("bonum est, quod est sui diffusivum vel communicativum") and *De caelest. hier.* 4, 1; Alain de Lille, *De articulis cath. fidei* II (PL 210, 603) ("bonum est quod utiliter habet esse").

ing part of creation and of its perfection is a deep theological mystery, as deep as the creation itself. But from the human point of view this idea with its concomitant weekly commemoration which impressed its significance on the Jewish people and through them other peoples did make the idea of perfection accessible to mankind in a way Greek philosophy could not. And yet the conception of perfecting and perfection is remarkably similar in both traditions. The sabbath is the symbol of heaven, of paradise, of the world to come, of the kingdom of God. The Hebrew word for peace, *sholom*, the chief characteristic of rest, is a variant of *shalem*, a word meaning perfect.

The history of this definition of perfection could be made the subject of a monograph, but for our purposes we may say that the sense of rest as perfection was widely distributed in the Middle Ages and rested upon Greek and Hebrew antecedents. *Quies*, one of the chief characteristics of heaven, was a moral and religious goal, and rest as the exemplar of all change was a fundamental way of thinking about the nature of the universe. We might, for the Middle Ages, make a whole series of parallels which are based upon this one opposition of rest versus motion—heaven versus the earth, intellect versus reason, eternity versus time, the center versus the circumference and so forth.

The next relative meaning of the term *perfectio* is in form as opposed to matter, which may also be conceived as act versus potentiality or intelligibility versus unintelligibility. The actual is always more perfect than the potential, and God as pure act is metaphysically the most perfect of all. Insofar as a thing is in act, it is perfect.[5] Probably it was an examination of the concept of growth and maturation which gave Aristotle the clue to this idea. Implied in this is the belief that the material cause "est infima et minime perfecta"[6] than the other causes and of course the formal cause. The contrast between form and matter, between pure form at the one extreme and prime matter at the other, is closely bound up with the hierarchy of being on which we shall say more later. Here we are deal-

---

[5] Things are perfect "secundum quod est in actu," *ST* 1, q. 4. a. 1 (cf. *SCG* I, 43 [7]).

[6] John Wyclif, *Summa de ente*, ed. S. Harrison Thomson (Oxford, 1930), tr. 1, c. 1 (p. 13).

ing with formal perfection as opposed to material potentiality and final perfection.

St. Thomas defines perfection in many ways and according to many subdivisions. He sometimes considers *formaliter* and *operatio* both of which are based on the concept of form and act equivalent to perfecting and perfect.[7] This point, however, is clear, I think to all who have any understanding of Aristotelian philosophy.

Closely related to this idea is a further definition—substance is more perfect than accident, because it is, although dependent on the Creator in general, self-subsistent and independent of change. The more independent a thing is the more perfect it is. Accidents cannot exist of themselves; they must be manifest in a substance, and hence they are imperfect as compared to the latter. This whole definition may be reworded as the dependent is less perfect than the independent, or the relatively dependent is less perfect than the relatively independent. Perfection depends upon the degree of freedom or self-sufficiency a being attains.

The next dichotomy is a more complicated and ambiguous one— that of finite versus infinite, or limited versus unlimited. A characteristic of much Greek philosophy is a suspicion of the infinite and the unlimited because of its unintelligibility. The limited and finite is perfect as opposed to its opposite. As Lovejoy puts it in speaking of Plotinus, "Nothing that is perfect or fully in possession of its own potential being, can lack determinate limits." [8] I have found it difficult to find a plain statement of this principle in Plotinus [9] or Aristotle, yet there is discernible at least a suspicion of the infinite and indeterminate.

Christian speculation on this subject took its departure from the famous verse in *Wisdom* 11:21 which is one of the most frequently

[7] See Philip H. Wicksteed, *The Reactions between Dogma and Philosophy Illustrated from the Works of St. Thomas Aquinas* . . . The Hibbert Lectures, Second Series (London, 1926, reprint of 1920), p. 616 n. (cf. p. 614).

[8] *The Great Chain of Being, A Study of the History of an Idea* (Cambridge, 1936), p. 66.

[9] In the *Enneads*, VI, 6, Plotinus recognizes an intelligible and an unintelligible infinity.

Plato in *Philebus* 16cff has a difficult section on the infinite and finite. He seems to argue in 27e–28a that only the infinite can be perfectly good. In 66b, however, he appears to equate the symmetrical, beautiful, perfect and sufficient.

quoted Biblical verses in medieval philosophy and susceptible to many uses: "but Thou hast ordered all things in measure and number and weight." The context indicates that the author was referring to a specific situation, the limit of the punishments with which God afflicted the erring children of Israel; but it is enunciated as a general principle. Of this principle which the author of *Wisdom* probably got from Stoic and Middle Platonic circles, medieval philosophers and even earlier the Fathers made much. To medieval philosophy this principle posed the difficulty of keeping the perfection of God intact. If perfection implied a limit, it must also in the case of God imply a limitlessness. Another line, that of the negative theology, was to put God above perfection.[10] It was simple to keep the Creator above and different from the created in whatever way, but actually if the nature of God was a subject for human rational speculation, even analogically, as most medieval philosophers believed, it was necessary to introduce a number of distinctions into these principles to preserve the rationality of the concept of God. I am not sure that this end was always achieved in practice, although St. Thomas devotes some of his most brilliant reasoning to it.[11] At least, one may say that there is a paradox here, and it is one which dogged the footsteps of philosophy for a long time.

St. Thomas uses this principle to prove the philosophical necessity of a last judgment or at least an end of the world,[12] that Christ's grace is not finite (for it too is created),[13] that concupiscence is limited,[14] that the precepts of the decalogue are suitably formulated,[15] and so forth.

St. Albertus Magnus is concerned with showing that the goodness or perfection of created things lies in their number, measure and weight and based his arguments on St. Augustine's long treatment of the subject.[16] He attempts to see vestiges of the Trinity in

[10] In Dionysius, *The Divine Names* XIII, God is called both perfect and beyond perfection.

[11] See e.g., *ST* III, q. 10, a. 3.

[12] *ST.*, I, II, q. 1, a. 4.

[13] *ST.*, III, q. 7, a. 11 and 12, and *De Veritate* XXIX, a. 3.

[14] *ST.*, I, II, q. 30, a. 4.

[15] *ST.*, I, II, q. 100, a. 1.

[16] *De bono* I, q. 2, a. 1 (ed. H. Kühle, C. Feckes, B. Geyer, and W. Kuber in *Opera Omnia* XXVIII [Münster i. W., 1951], p. 23).

this trinity but admits the difficulties.[17] W. J. Roche [18] has given us an excellent study of "measure, number and weight" in St. Augustine and shows us how central it is to his conviction of the goodness of the world. St. Augustine relates these three qualities to modus, species, and order, which are his most general metaphysical principles of being. They form in creatures the principles of their perfection.[19] Significantly enough, St. Augustine often uses *pax* and finality as synonymous for *pondus*.[20] But *pondus* is also the drive towards good in all creatures in its two moments of *usus* and *fructus*.

Cassiodorus developing the Augustinian notion went further and argued that God created all things according to number, measure, and weight so that we may understand the world. It is an evidence of his goodness. As he says, "For this reason God's extraordinary and magnificent works are necessarily confined to definite limits, so that just as we know that He has created all things we may in some measure learn to know the manner of their creation. And hence it is to be understood that the evil works of the devil are not ordered by weight or measure or number, since whatever iniquity does, it is always opposed to justice . . ." [21] On this last point I don't think Cassiodorus would have had the approval of St. Augustine as loath as he was to concede these intelligible principles to the prince of darkness. On the other hand, however, St. Augustine had to maintain the devil's creatureliness or fall back into Manicheeism.

Another relative definition of perfection is the simple as opposed to the diverse, or completeness as opposed to incompleteness. In its application to God, this definition also caused difficulties in connection with the principle of plenitude. It creates, as Lovejoy pointed out,[22] the problem of why a complete perfect and simple Being—

[17] *Ibid.*, I, q. 2, a. 3. Cf. Robert Kilwardby's similar attempt in his *De imagine et vestigio Trinitatis*, ed. Stegmüller in *Archives d'histoire doctrinale et littéraire du moyen âge*, X and XI (1935–36), 324–407.

[18] In *New Scholasticism* XV (1941), 350–76.

[19] Cf. Cicero's discussion of perfection from the Stoic point of view in *De natura deorum*, II, 13, and 14, wherein it is proved that the world is perfect and moves toward perfection.

[20] Cf. "Bonum enim in numero est diminutum et in mensura perfectius, sed completum in pondere." Albertus Magnus, *De bono.* I, q. 2.

[21] *Institutiones* II, 2 trans. L. W. Jones *An Introduction to Divine and Human Readings* (New York, 1946), pp. 142–43.

[22] *Op. cit.*, pp. 39 ff.

God—should desire to create an incomplete, imperfect and diverse world. The usual answer is that God could not begrudge existence to anything that could conceivably possess it, for He delights in diversity [23]—and imperfection then is led out of perfection. Some even defend divine punishment and damnation on an extension of this theory. Duns Scotus argues against this view strongly. ". . . nullus defectus culpae sive ponae est de perfectione per se universi; igitur nec per se requiritur ad manifestationem divinae bonitatis. Et per hoc patet, quod non est simile de differentiis rerum in esse naturali et morali . . ." [24] but as one can see he accepts it in the physical world.

The philosophical root of perfection as simplicity is in Aristotle's *Metaphysics* V, 16 where two of the four definitions of perfection make essentially this point. The perfect is "that outside which it is impossible to find even a single one of its parts" and "goodness is a kind of perfection, for each thing and every substance is perfect when and only when, in respect of the form of its peculiar excellence, it lacks no particle of its natural magnitude." [25]

Two of the three definitions Deferrari in his lexicon to St. Thomas [26] gives for this word fit our concept of perfection—simple, uncomposed, without parts, synonym of *indivisibilis*, the opposite of *compositus*, and simple, absolute, not connected with anything, synonym of *incomplexus*, the opposite of *complexus*. These definitions in Aristotle and St. Thomas run over into other concepts in the *perfectio* complex—the good and the absolute, of which we shall say more later.

The common Hebraic word for perfect—*tam* or *tamim*—has I believe this idea translated into ethical terms at its base—the idea of singleheartedness and integrity. The term is applied to the oneness or wholeness of a thing or person and is found in the Old Testament, *inter alia* in connection with both the Law and Noah. Both

[23] ST I, q. 23, a. 5, n. 3. See Wicksteed, *op. cit.*, p. 396, quoting from St. Thomas ". . . ad perfectionem universi pertinent diversi gradus rerum"; and ". . . Perfectio universi requirit inaequalitatem esse in rebus, ut omnes bonitatis gradus impleantur," *ST* I, q. 48, a. 2 .

[24] *Oxon.* I, d 14, q. unica, n. 6 (Vivès X, p. 693).

[25] Ed. H. Tredennick (Loeb Classical Library), I, p. 267. Cf. "Perfectio simpliciter sit absolute melius quorumque incompossibili," Duns Scotus, *De primo principio*, IV, 69 (ed. Garcia, [Quaracchi, 1910], p. 670).

[26] Washington, 1949, p. 1029.

are whole and unified, one commanding an integrity of spirit and full obedience, the other manifesting these qualities.[27] The use of the term perfect in the New Testament ($\tau\acute{\epsilon}\lambda\epsilon\iota os$ and its relatives) is probably very close to the meaning of this Hebrew word. The word is very frequently used in the Epistles and has given rise to much comment. I shall get back to this point a little later. At the moment I merely wish to show that the idea of simplicity as perfection is present in both Greek and Hebrew writings, although in the former it has more of an ontological and essential meaning and in the latter, more of a moral and existentialist significance.

Related to the above definition of the term is a number of similar oppositions—complete versus incomplete, the whole versus the part, the one versus the many, order versus disorder, necessity versus contingency—which we may consider as further definitions of this much defined concept we are attempting to analyze.[28] In all cases the first is considered perfect as opposed to the second, and criteria such as intelligibility and rest are presupposed. We need not spend more time on these, other than to note them. They only add to our sense of the complexity of the concept and help us to account for particular uses of the term in the writings of the scholastic philosophers. They are similar to the idea of the perfection of the purely simple and are related to it.

We may now turn to what I have called above the absolute meanings of the term. The major concepts here are final causes, the Greek, originally Platonic, idea of $\mathring{\alpha}\rho\epsilon\tau\acute{\eta}$ or virtue, the hierarchial view of the world, the idea of the diffusion of the good and the idea of intensity.

One of the central meanings of the term perfection may be defined as correspondence to a final cause or as the end as opposed to the other principles of movement or change. Just as the formal cause is more perfect than the material cause, so the final cause is more perfect than the efficient cause and even further the final

[27] The Talmud sometimes links the idea *tam* with the pure as clean or opposed to the unclean and impure (Zebahim 116a) which is an important rabbinic concept and related to the Jewish idea of separateness.

[28] Some of these definitions account for the statement in *ST*, II, II, q. 35a, 3c that a mortal sin is perfect—i.e., a complete manifestation of the sinful will in regard to its end.

40

cause is the most perfect of all causes.[29] As implied above this idea is related to the concept of the superiority of rest to movement and of act to potentiality. Both the universe's and man's perfection may be defined in terms of their final causes—God and the vision of God or deification. These ideas are both Greek and Christian and have been very influential in medieval and modern thinking. Final causes and ultimately the Final Cause of all final causes may even be said to provide the definitions for all created beings. We may qualitatively and religiously define every being by its immediate and ultimate final causes. They give a rationale to the world and are a guarantee of its meaning. This, I may add, is not the only way of defining things and living beings, but it is a most important method, and from the religious point of view perhaps the ultimate method of thought. As St. Thomas puts it in one of his many definitions of perfection, "perfectio consistit in hoc quod pertingat ad finem" [30] or again "unumquodque dicitur esse perfectum, in quantum attingit proprium finem, qui est ultima rei perfectio." [31] In these two definitions we see the double aspect of this definition of perfection —an approximation to the end or final cause and the attainment of it, combining both the notions of movement and striving and of rest and peace. The original source is no doubt the Aristotelian emphasis on the final cause and his whole conception of entelechy. This definition is so widely known that I need hardly spend any more time on it; it is perhaps the commonest definition of perfection and has still not lost, in general philosophical and nonphilosophical circles, its power. It seems to be an incurable way of human thinking possibly because it is so closely related to man's own purposive activity. Scientists in their struggle against theology and Aristotelianism were quite right from their point of view to center their attack on teleological thinking; and although it is a misuse of the concept to use it thus, to some extent it did in fact hamper scientific investigation.

[29] ". . . in rebus naturalibus primo quidem est perfectio dispositionis, puta cum materia est perfecte ad formam disposita; secundo autem est perfectio formae, quae est potior, nam et ipse calor est perfectior, qui provenit ex forma ignis, quam ille, qui ad formam ignis disponebat; tertio autem est perfectio finis, sicut ignis perfectissime habet proprias qualitates, cum ad locum suum provenerit," *ST* III, q. 27, a. 5 ad 2.

[30] *ST* I, q. 6, a. 3 and q. 73, a. 1.

[31] *ST* II, II, q. 184, 1c.

Related to the above definition of perfection is the concept of a virtue or excellence inhering in all things. Both Plato and Aristotle believed that everything has its proper perfection or ἀρετή. The ἀρετή of the cobbler is to make good shoes and the ἀρετή of the house is to give shelter. This concept is best seen in Plato's *Republic*,[32] where it is discussed in its narrow sense, and further the whole subject of that great dialogue may be said to be concerned with defining the ἀρετή of man and of society, which is justice. It does not occupy the same importance in Aristotle's thinking unless it be assimilated to his teleological mode, but it is assumed by him. He discusses some of the implications of this concept in the *Nicomachean Ethics* I, vii, and raises the most crucial question there. "Are we then to suppose, that while carpenter and cobbler have certain works and courses of action, Man as Man has none, but is left by Nature without a work? Or would not one rather hold, that as eye, hand, and foot, and generally each of his members, has manifestly some special work; so too the whole Man, as distinct from all these, has some work on his own?" [33]

This concept is of course closely tied in with the idea of a final cause, but it is not identical with it. It does emphasize that all things have a proper use and exist for a proper employment, principles which imply final causes. The accent here is however on employment and a correct use of faculties, rather than on an explanation of generation and corruption or of change. As the quotation from Aristotle above shows, the real interest of this definition arises when we turn to man. What is the ἀρετή of man? What is the proper activity or activities for man? It was to this question that the Cynics, Stoics, and Epicureans turned following the death of Aristotle. Every being must live according to its essence if it is to attain happiness. If we discover the true philosophical anthropology, we can answer the question of how to live. The concept of a proper activity, however, is not limited to neutral or useful creatures but even includes evil ones.

When Christianity came upon the scene, it was possible to say that the final end of man was the vision of God or assimilation to

[32] 335 B–E and 353 D ff. See A. J. Festugière, *Contemplation et vie contemplative selon Platon*, 2nd ed. (Paris, 1950).
[33] Trans. D. P. Chase in Everyman's Library.

God, but the issue of the way to attain that final end, the proper employment of his faculties, his ἀρετή, still remained to be much debated in the light of the Bible and the Apostolic tradition.

From one point of view, the Law, the Torah, might be said to have provided the Jews with their ἀρετή and the wisdom and authority of the Church established by Jesus to have provided Christians with theirs. It can be seen how this aspect of perfection soon looms large in the whole problem of the Christian meaning of life. I do not here wish to enlarge upon this, but one can surely see its scope. The notion of a right use of things and other living beings and self is a common-sensical idea which has somehow or other been neglected in modern times. It is not perhaps that anyone if asked would deny its truth, but that moderns simply do not think consciously in this way. It is taken for granted that the purpose of a knife is to cut and that tools and instruments must perform their proper functions, but it is not extended to the universe as a whole or to man in particular. Uncommitted man may still ask for the meaning of life, but he will not pose this question in terms of man's proper excellence or function. Plato's crucial definition of justice, based on the notion of "each man must perform one social service in the state for which his nature was best adapted" (IV, 10),[34] reflects a mode of thinking very strange to the man trained in modern science and the modern *Weltanschauung* which insists on, at least for methodological purposes, a universe devoid of ends or excellences.

Another important constituent of the *perfectio* complex is the notion of the ontological hierarchy in the universe or the great chain of being. The qualitative distinction between each level is its degree of perfection. The whole universe may be looked upon as a machine or organism for the production of increasing degrees of perfection. The chain took its origin in perfection and is characterized by a straining back towards its source and original perfection. Creation is a great flowing out from God and a movement back to Him in a series of ontic steps. This flow and ebb may be termed a vertical rather than a horizontal movement such as may be applied to the Aristotelian entelechy. In the *De Primo Rerum*, Chap. 1,

[34] Trans. P. Shorey in Loeb edition, p 367.

Duns Scotus divides the order of essences into an *ordo eminentiae* and an *ordo dependentiae*. The chain of being is the *ordo eminentiae* in which the degree of nobility and perfection is the decisive criterion. The *ordo eminentiae* is indivisible, whereas the *ordo dependentiae* may be divided as to causes. Although "perfection" may be applied to both orders, in the order of eminence the quantity of perfection is the basic criterion, whereas in the order of dependence the prior and the degree of approximation are the tests.[35]

There is in this definition of perfection a conception of relativity, but the relativity is not based on a dichotomy and hence it is not included among my relative definitions. All creatures, insofar as they are creatures in a hierarchial universe, are perfect, but the degrees of perfection vary. The relativity here involved is that of position leading up to God, although analogy relates all of the levels. The root of this idea is to be found in Neoplatonism and was developed for Christianity by Philo and the pseudo-Dionysius. It is closely related to my next definition of the term, and it was the Aereopagite who is chiefly responsible for popularizing both ideas.

This next definition equates the good with the perfect [36] and is a parallel to the chain of being concept. The great law of the universe, the medieval second law of thermodynamics, one may say, is the principle of the diffusion of the good. It is natural for the good to extend itself as far as possible. St. Thomas in *De Veritate*, XXVII a. 1 in discussing the question "Do all things tend to good," says in part, answering it affirmatively: "Since all things are destined and directed by God to good, and this is done in such a way that in each one is a principle by which it tends of itself to good as if seeking good itself, it is necessary to say that all things naturally tend to good." In *Quaestiones disputatae de potentia Dei*, q. 2, art. 4, obj. 11, St. Thomas also says echoing the ps.-Dionysius, "Goodness is

---

[35] Duns Scotus also uses the term perfections to classify a subgroup of transcendentals as well as to be a synonym for all the transcendentals (the most general predicates, those which cannot be included under any genus). They are irreducibly simple and in some sense at least all equal. See Allan B. Wolter, *The Transcendentals and Their Function in the Metaphysics of Duns Scotus*, Franciscan Institute Publications, Philosophy Series No. 3, St. Bonaventure, N. Y., 1946, esp. pp. 162 ff.

[36] "Nam per hoc tendunt in suam perfectionem quod tendunt ad bonum, quum unumquodque in tantum bonum sit in quantum est perfectum" (Aquinas, SCG III, 24).

44

the principle of diffusion." [37] Ulrich of Strasbourg, following his master Albertus Magnus, puts it in another way, "Et quod desiderant omnia, verum est vel in se, ut Sancti Deum desiderant, vel in sua similitudine, sicut omnis res desiderando suam perfectionem quae est similitudo perfectionis divinae, desiderat ipsum summum bonum per se, et per accidens desiderant illam perfectionem secundum id quod est." [38] Or in other words, the whole universe attempts to imitate God its source of being and its end because all creatures are somewhat similar to Him. "The very effort of natural entities to reach their end or perfection is an endeavor to be like God." [39] Not only does man but also the whole universe, animate and inanimate, naturally imitate God.

The basic conception of the goodness of the created world is Hebraic rather than Greek. Greek philosophy, except perhaps for Stoicism, tended to despise the phenomenal world, and its characteristic dualism in this matter is well-known. The essential goodness of the world of experience is clear from the very first pages of the Old Testament. "And God saw that it was good." Even though sin was later introduced into creation, the Hebraic faith in the goodness of the world was never lost, and in Philo, the first philosopher, properly speaking, of the Hebrews, this basic principle is enunciated. In Philo we find that combination of Platonic levels with the notion of the good which is also characteristic of the pseudo-Dionysius. Although the Christian tradition has on the whole kept to the Hebraic notion of the goodness of the created and visible world as Philo envisaged it, sometimes a more purely Platonic view would dominate and the wickedness of the world would be emphasized. This latter view I regard as erratic and unusual, even though it is sometimes strongly emphasized for pastoral reasons.

In late antiquity, Boethius in praising God in his *De consolatione philosophiae* III, m. 9 emphasizes the perfection of the universe.

"Thus thou perfect the whole, perfect each part dost frame" and

[37] See J. Peghaire, "L'axiome 'Bonum est diffusivum sui' dans le néoplatonisme et le thomisme," *Revue de l'université d'Ottawa*, Section Speciale I 1932), 5*–30*.

[38] *Summa de bono* II, tr. 3, 1, ed. F. Collingwood (in *Nine Mediaeval Thinkers*, Pontifical Institute of Medieval Studies, Studies and Texts I [Toronto, 1955]).

[39] Marling, *Order*, p. 175. Cf. "Si igitur res omnes in Deum sicut in ultimum finem tendunt, sequitur quod ultimus rerum finis sit Deo assimilari" (Aquinas, *SCG* II, 20).

through him as through Dionysius this notion of a perfect universe found widespread support in medieval times.

The Dionysian picture of the universe however was the one which impressed the notion of the hierarchy of being and perfection, and by analogy that of society, the Church on earth and the progress of self, on the medieval world, especially through the Victorines. Roques calls this the "Alexandrine vision of the world" [40] which the Ps.-Dionysius systematized for Christianity. The whole universe and everything that is in it is a series of graded and analogical levels, all of which tend to perfection and in a sense to the negation of all negations beyond all perfections. This magnificent scheme combines the various orders of being and existence, including the historic, in a sweep and amplitude which can only make one truly humble. It is the crumbling of this complete and universal hierarchy in modern times, largely the work of science and of the growth of the generative view of nature which has increased the difficulty of defending rationally the existence of God and His providence in the world. The collapse of the Ptolemaic universe becomes almost insignificant beside it.

Finally at the end of this long catalogue of definitions comes the idea of intensity or excess with which the idea of perfection is also associated. In the *perfectio* complex there is a quantitative element applied even to nonquantitative concepts.[41] The idea of measurement is involved, implicitly or explicitly, with the notion of perfection in many of its aspects. The really important application of this idea lies in the measurement of qualities, for the "size" of qualities lies in their perfection. "In formis dicimus aliquid magnum ex hoc quod est perfectum" (St. Thomas, *ST* II, I, q. 52, 1). Sometimes St. Thomas even uses intensity as a synonym for perfection.[42] The scholastic definition of virtue as the "principium motus vel actionis" could lend itself well to a quantitative approach towards what we would consider inaccessible to physical measurement.

---

[40] *L'univers dionysien, Structure hiérarchique du monde selon le pseudo-Denys* (Paris, 1954), p. 29.

[41] See Joseph de Tonquédec, *Questions de cosmologie et de physique chez Aristote et St. Thomas* (Paris, 1950), pp. 103 ff.

[42] ". . . docitur magnus color propter suam intensionem et perfectionem," *ST* I, q. 42, a. 1, ad 1.

46

St. Bonaventure distinguishes between two infinities [43]—an "infinitas per defectum" and an "infinitas per excessum." The latter is indeed the "summa perfectio." Tied up in all this is the much debated late scholastic issue, going back to Peter Lombard, of whether there can be a quantitative increase in charity or love to infinity. Indirectly this speculation led to the development of some important scientific concepts related to the calculus and the notion of inertia and acceleration, but this is not the place to probe into that.[44] Perfection as growth and development and flowering implies always an increase in intensity which may possibly be raised to infinity. The more intense a quality, the more perfect it is, and in some the greatest intensity becomes a kind of excess. This notion of perfection is somewhat at variance with the notion of limit as perfection; however the contradictory definitions usually appear in different contexts of argument and there is less of a contradiction than might a priori be imagined.

Although I am not sure that I have been exhaustive in my definitions of metaphysical perfection, I am sure that I have covered a wide ground and possibly have exhausted you.[45] As yet I have not touched on the moral meanings of the term, but to allay your fears I may at once say that I am going to be very brief here, for on the subject of Christian perfection there is a large bibliography,[46] even

[43] I. Sent. d. 35, a 1, q. 5, ad 4.

[44] See, e.g., A Maier, *Die Vorläufer Galileis im 14. Jahrhundert, Studien zur Naturphilosophie der Spätscholastik* (Rome, 1949).

[45] I have not here touched upon the "ontological" argument for the existence of God or St. Thomas' Fourth Way, which make use of the conception of perfection, as these arguments properly speaking employ or assume the concept rather than provide new definitions of it. They both, to some extent, at least, presuppose the principles of plenitude and hierarchy.

[46] To list a few titles: Gerhard Ladner, "Die mittelalterliche Reform—Idee und ihr Verhältnis zur Idee der Renaissance," *Mitteilungen des Instituts für österreichische Geschichtsforschung*, LX (1952), 31–59; R. Newton Flew, *The Idea of Perfection in Christian Theology, An Historical Study of the Christian Ideal for the Present Life* (London, 1934); Frederic Platt in Hastings, *Encyclopaedia of Religion and Ethics*, IX, 728–737; Dayton Phillips, "The Way to Religious Perfection According to St. Bonaventure's *De Triplici Via*," *Essays in Medieval Life and Thought Presented in Honor of Austin Patterson Evans*, ed. J. H. Mundy et al. (New York, 1955), pp. 31–58; Arnoldo M. Lanz, "Perfezione Christiana," *Enciclopedia Cattolica* (Vatican City, 1952), IX, col. 1173–1175; A. Fonck, "Perfection Chrétienne," *Dictionnaire de Théologie Catholique*, ed. A. Vacant et al., XII, 1219–1251; Martin Grabmann, "Katholisches Priestertum und christiches Vollkommenheitsideal nach der Lehre

if not complete agreement, to which one can turn for enlightenment.

The question of Christian perfection is the basic question of the Christian life. Jesus Himself commanded his followers to be perfect in the words "Be you therefore perfect, even as your Father in heaven is perfect" (Matthew 5:48). In the parallel passage in Luke 6:36, Christ's words are different, "Be you therefore merciful, as your Father is merciful." Both of these passages are the culminations of the great injunction to love one's enemies, and I am inclined to agree with Foss [47] that Luke reports more accurately Jesus's words on the occasion. God is never called perfect in the OT, although many attributes are predicated of Him. However whatever that may be, and I cannot lay any claims whatsoever to being a Biblical exegete, the words in Matthew are full of meaning and have ever since been the concern of all good Christians, beginning with St. Paul.

This sentence of Jesus as A. Fonck in his long article on "Perfection Chrétienne" in the *Dictionnaire de Théologie Catholique* points out seems relatively simple, but it is not, and the history of the interpretation of this injunction amply bears this out. For one thing, it may run into moralism or Pelagianism, and for another it raises the question of the difference between counsels and commands. Classic western Christianity at least has tended to recognize the existence of social levels and levels of perfection and has real-

---

des hl. Thomas von Aquin," *Zeitschrift für Aszese u. Mystik*, II (1927), 189–209; Felix Vernet, *Mediaeval Spirituality*, trans. (London and St. Louis, 1930?); Otto Zimmermann, "Arten der Vollkommenheit," *Zeitschrift für Aszese und Mystik*, I (1926), 229–51; P. Laurentius, "Das aktive und das kontemplative Leben nach der Lehre des hl. Thomas von Aquin," *Divus Thomas* (*Studia Friburgensia*), III, Serie III (1925), 171–184; Ottavio Marchetti, "La perfezione della vita cristiana secondo S. Tommaso," *Gregorianum*, I (1920), 286–98; Dom Anselme Stolz, *L'Ascèse Chrétienne* (Chevetogne, 1948); Marcel Viller, *La spiritualité des premiers siècles chrétiens* (Paris, 1930); Aidan Carr, "Poverty in Perfection according to St. Bonaventure," *Franciscan Studies*, n.s. VII (1947), 313–323; 415–425; Dom Jean Leclercq, *La vie parfaite, Points de vue sur l'essence de l'état religieux* (Turnhout and Paris, 1948); R. Garrigou-Lagrange, *Christian Perfection and Contemplation According to St. Thomas Aquinas and St. John of the Cross*, trans. Sister M. Doyle (St. Louis and London, 1937).

[47] See M. Foss, *The Idea of Perfection in the Western World* (Princeton, 1946), p. 29. Foss' book is one of the very few that I have been able to find on the subject of metaphysical perfection. Because of his desire to prove a thesis, however, it must be used with caution by the historian of ideas.

ized that not all human beings are called upon to follow the most perfect life in both status and endeavor. This interpretation also raises difficulties into which I shall not go. In general since the twelfth century, the term has been interpreted as urging the *imitatio Christi*, with emphasis upon charity as the highest of all the virtues. The Eastern Church has tended to think of the injunction more in terms of the deification of man, giving a much more mystical interpretation to the term perfection. I wish to say, however, that both principles are to be found in East and West, and it is largely a matter of emphasis.

Most vital to the history of the notion of Christian perfection has been the role played by monasticism as a force making for perfection. R. Newton Flew writes "Monasticism is the boldest organized attempt to attain to Christian perfection in all the long history of the Church" and "the motive that drove all the chief founders of monasticism to forsake the world was the desire of perfection." [48] The cloister as the prototype of heaven, as the equivalent of the earthly paradise, sustained and strengthened those men who withdrew from the world in order to win a better one. It is only recently that the philosophy of the cloister, the meaning of monasticism in the development of Western thought, has begun to be fully recognized.

The monasteries as centers of learning and preservers of culture in a dark age have, of course, been long appreciated, but these functions, important as they were, are not of the essence of monasticism but rather accidents. On the other hand, it is not purely fortuitous that both St. Thomas More and François Rabelais portrayed their Utopias in terms of a monastery or that Dante speaks of Jesus as the Abbot of the cloister of heaven. An important root of much Utopian and indeed characteristic Western thought is to be sought in this philosophy of the cloister. Ideas of rebirth, reform and renewal were nurtured in the monasteries. They are, in modern times, frequently a secularization of what was a religious ideal. The Ps.-Dionysius with his picture of the monk as the most perfect type of the ecclesiastical order, which is a reflection of the angelic and divine orders, provided monkish thinkers and historians with the theoretical basis for the picture of themselves which they sincerely believed

[48] *Op. cit.*, p. 158.

to be true—the leaders of the human race in its attempt to live up to the injunction of Jesus to be perfect.

In the West, the idea of different grades of perfection resting on the concept of a Dionysian world has always been widely current, although there have been different definitions of these grades. Sometimes the grades are expressed in terms of beginner, progressor and perfect, sometimes in the terms of marriage, widowhood, and virginity, sometimes in terms of social classes, sometimes in terms of the mystic trinity of purgative, illuminative, and unitive, sometimes in psychological terms like meditation, prayer, and contemplation, sometimes in terms of virtue—civil, purifying, pure, and exemplary. Nor are all these necessarily mutually exclusive. Basic to all these, however, is the notion of analogical levels and of analogical demands on those Christians in each level. Each Christian must be as perfect as his status demands. All thinkers recognize that, although the various statuses are hierarchically arranged according to perfection, not every member of a more perfect status is necessarily more perfect than a member of a less perfect status. Indeed, he may be much worse because of his failure to live up to the higher demands he has professed. I think it may be said, however, that a conscientious member of a more perfect status is more perfect than a conscientious member of a less perfect status.

My interest, however, is in the concept of levels here. The guarantee of this idea lies in a conviction of a many-levelled universe of perfection. This underlying concept is in large measure gone today. Or at least it has to be redefined.

Science and theology are not theoretically at variance in their respective fields, but in practice they are. It is not the conclusions of science which have destroyed the essence of the medieval world view but rather the attitude involved. Science and theology are only opposed in this way, for their methods of approaching reality do not conflict with each other. Fundamentally they and the humanities as well are merely different types of knowledge of reality. The modern scientific emphasis on the efficient cause, and even more fundamental the replacement of the very notion of causality by statistical inference, force, however, a crucial reorientation of religious thinking which is only now beginning to show itself. I know that many scientists are religious personally and that the best of them recognize that their antimetaphysical thinking should be merely methodological in certain fields. Yet in effect their attitude, their opposition to teleology, to the notion of perfection as I have here outlined it, and their refusal to wonder have a weakening effect on the religious attitude. And besides in a way science works and produces immediate results. What need do we have, some say, of superfluous hypotheses. The very way of putting this question reveals the gap most glaringly.

In some ways the most crucial question here is the method of the social sciences with their adoption of the quantitative and statistical method and their refusal to philosophize. I recognize among the social scientists notable exceptions to this charge, but in America there is a strong tendency to avoid the philosophical basis which true social science needs.

Medieval thinking not only applied the notion of perfection to the realm of being, the realm of society and the realm of self, but also to some extent to the realm of history. In some ways the problem of the perfection of history is the most interesting of all. The concept of perfection is closely connected with a rationalistic view of the universe, that is, the conviction that the universe is for the most part capable of explanation by reason, or in short rational. It assumes that the multiplicity of singulars in the universe can be reduced to or subsumed under certain principles. The unknowable particular can be explained as a manifestation of a knowable general. The singular, the particular, the unique are unknowable in a philosophical sense. Even in Scotism which admits an intuitive knowledge of singulars, this knowledge is of a limited kind and not fully scientific and rational. But the realm of history is the realm of the unique, when recognized as a separate realm at all. If the concept of perfection is to be applied to history, we must consider the latter at least somewhat rational and meaningful. To put it another way, if history is meaningful, as we are taught by the Judeo-Christian tradition to regard it, it is related to some extent at least to perfection. History is not merely the arbitrary and the capricious.

Although the Classical world produced many great historians and in practice the ancient Greeks and Romans were no doubt much interested in history, in theory, however, their thinkers and philosophers tended to ignore history or to reduce it to nature by giving it a cyclic form. The concept of the eternal return made history into a more unruly, but nevertheless rational, nature. There is no true progress in history any more than one spring is basically qualitatively different from another. As Shelley puts it,

> Another Athens shall arise,
> And to remoter time
> Bequeath, like sunset to the skies,
> The splendour of its prime.

In effect, however, all this is making history meaningful by making it meaningless or denying its importance and uniqueness. To the Greek thinkers, the historic, although it could be exemplaristic, was a mere accident of things, an unessential detail in assessing the meaning of an event.

In the Christian tradition, following the Hebraic emphasis, history must be meaningful. God is a God of history and his providence extends overall. To the Israelite, in both flesh and spirit, history has a meaning because salvation has come and will come through it. It is not just a repetitive cycle, it reveals the will of God. God may interfere and has interfered with the process of history. History is partially redemptive and moves towards a final end. Unlike the gods of Greece, the God of Israel Himself has no history; but again unlike the Greek concept of its own history, Israel and the other nations have a supremely significant history. No one in the Judeo-Christian tradition can ignore history, and the claims of Christianity and Judaism as religions rest upon the historicity of certain happenings in the past.

Then, of course, there is the eschatological side. The Day of Judgement sets a termination to the world, and the end explains the beginning. The problem of the kingdom of God to which all the saved belong is also involved here. Etienne Gilson points out quite correctly,

> En annonçant la bonne nouvelle, l'Evangile n'avait pas seulement promis aux justes une sorte de béatitude individuelle, il leur avait annoncé l'entrée dans un Royaume, c'est-à-dire, dans une société de justes, unis par les liens de leur commune béatitude.[49]

The end of history is social as well as individual perfection.

49 *L'Esprit de la philosophie médiévale*, 2nd ed. (Paris, 1944), pp. 367–368.

The meaning of history could not be purchased, however, as with the Greeks, at the cost of its uniqueness. This was the Judeo-Christian historical problem—how can uniqueness be wedded to meaning. The uniqueness could be maintained easily enough if one gave up the hope of significance, and the significance if one gave up the unique, the historical. The answer generally was the concept of world ages, which, as opposed to the Greek cycles, combined the unique and the pattern. Paul speaks of or implies the ages before the law, under the law and under grace. St. Augustine adds to this division a sevenfold periodization. And one can list many more systems of dividing history. There are repetition and progress in history. In terms of itself each age is justified and unique, and in terms of later ages it is a preparation and a type of it. In the eyes of some, such as Hugo of St. Victor, within each age there is progress too. To him the history of man since the fall is a long *restauratio* to paradise in which the central but not the exclusive event is the Incarnation. Not all medieval thinkers were to take such optimistic views, but such a theory was not uncommon.

History then in spite of its intellectual intractability could be brought under the aegis of perfection. It was rational and could be understood and justified both because of the soteriological events which happened within it and because of its end in a Resurrection, Final Judgment, and a Kingdom of God to embrace all the saved. To some this historical perfectibility has been a heady brew, and, secularized, it has led to much Utopian thinking, not all of it bad. With the kingdom of God as the goal, however, history does have a rationale and is in some sense perfecting and perfectible. This seems to me a sound religious principle.

The marriage of the Judeo-Christian concept of perfection with the Greek was not always a happy one. We have already seen certain contradictions and inherent difficulties in Greek thought on the subject. These were multiplied greatly when Christian theology with its concept of a perfect God, of Christian perfection, of the final perfection of history was combined with the Greek categories. But the early interest in perfection in Christianity bespeaks an enthusiasm, a drive in those to whom the Master had appeared and their followers. Life could no longer be the same. Perfection could not merely be a pale metaphysical concept, but something which must come down into everyday life. The hopelessness of the pagan with his merely metaphysical idea of perfection was sin. Joy was one of Christ's messages, and a new man more perfect than the old must be born. In their own salvation the early disciples saw the wondrous workings of the Lord who at one stroke abrogated the shadow and brought in the sun. This was reflected in a new attitude toward the self. A new dispensation called for a new man, and newness could only be justified if it were more perfect.

Although there are probably traces of Greek thinking on perfection in the New Testament, especially in the Epistles, as there are in the later books of the Old Testament and in the noncanonical late Jewish writings, it was actually in Alexandria that the first attempts at combining the Greek, mainly Platonic, and Hebrew concepts were made. Philo himself was not unconcerned with the question and uses these ideas frequently. In him, as in the early Christian Fathers at Alexandria and elsewhere, the concept of perfection is rather assumed than argued. In a world of Greek philosophy and Greek categories of thought, perfection as an assumption of thought, as a critique of satisfaction, was almost impossible to avoid. These early theologians wished to show that the Judeo-Christian existentialistic concept of perfection could be satisfactorily combined with Greek, especially Platonic, thinking on the subject.

The completion of this union did not take place until the high Middle Ages, when the great scholastics presented their syntheses to the Christian world. Until very recently, this synthesis in one form or another has been universally accepted, even by Protestant and secular thinkers. Even more than Cartesian dualism which could still use at least the metaphysical concept of perfection, the very recent developments of science which "live no longer in the faith of reason" have made its acceptance difficult.

How can we maintain the notion of Christian perfection in a universe in which, science tells us, is no perfection in any of its senses, not even causality, which is perhaps the last of the cosmological and ontological categories to go? Must we redefine Christian perfection? The new interest in Christian moral philosophy and in Biblical theology today seems to me to point in that direction. Ethics in the last analysis must rest upon metaphysical presuppositions.

54

In what sense can we say today that the world is perfect? In what sense can we say that it is subject to rational explanation? and that it is qualitatively real? Perfection is closely tied up with the rational and qualitative approaches to the universe. I think that for one thing a thorough-going defence of the notion of final cause, not necessarily exactly as Aristotle conceived it, is necessary. The notion of the hierarchy of being can, as Maritain has shown, be reorganized and fruitfully applied to modern problems. Although I do not think that the present presuppositions of science are necessarily correct, the chief task of rehabilitation, if rehabilitation is at all possible, must be with the philosophers, even those of the "analytic" persuasion. It may be, too, that we shall have to reconsider our concept of the perfection of the world. It may be that the profound Greek categories have to be reapplied to the world in new ways. If philosophy is to be more than the history of philosophy this has to be done. A blind adherence to the past can help to destroy the true values of the past. The great scholastic systems are very much alive today in the general world, more alive than they have been for a long time. I do not think, however, that we can rest on our oars and let the boat drift into harbor. The general sympathy for scholastic philosophy should be used as a constructive force. The intellectual difficulties facing all traditional philosophy must not be by-passed or avoided by all who have the concern for truth and reason at heart. A mechanical repetition of traditional philosophical concepts will weaken respect for true philosophy. We, as teachers, must not aim at producing Platonists, Thomists, Scotists, and Kantians, but philosophers in the true sense of the word, who using the past will be prepared to reconstruct philosophy, if necessary, from the ground up discarding, if need be, what should be discarded and defending what should be defended. The abdication of the role of natural philosopher by the scientist may in fact be the greatest help to the reconstruction, and the return to metaphysics in at least some sense by modern philosophers may be taken as a healthy sign. We cannot conjure up a Plato, an Aquinas, or a Kant, but we can help create the conditions for his appearance. What is at stake is the preservation of human values, even if all philosophical systems by their very nature may contain contradictions and antinomies.

II. Approaches to Medieval Literature

4. Understanding Old English Poetry

In order to understand Old English poetry, there are a great many things one should know—its language, its literary traditions, its ideas, the culture out of which it came, and so forth. I am concerned here with only one of these desiderata—the social function of this poetry because I think it has been the most ignored of all. We have been too long under the domination of the notion well expressed by John Middleton Murry when writing of a poem by Sir John Squire, "it is not really a poem, because it did not have its origin in any compulsive emotion, but was the outcome of a desire to write poetry rather than the urgent need to express a perception." [1] This attitude, which might be called the evacuation theory of poetry, is, I am convinced, extremely misleading when applied to our oldest poetry and has led to serious distortions of understanding. To regard our older poetry chiefly in terms of the poet's need to extrude or express an emotion and to ignore the poetry's social function can only give rise to a one-sided and inadequate comprehension of that poetry.[2] I do not believe that we can ever read poetry or literature intelligently, particularly pre-Romantic literature, unless we have some idea of what role it played in the society out of which it came, a notion which involves the expectations of the audience, the practical function of literature, literary genres, rhetoric, word magic, and other social elements.

My underlying purpose is to try to rid our minds of certain romantic presuppositions which have controlled for too long our approach to Old English poetry. The German scholars who created Anglo-Saxon studies were under the domination of nineteenth-century assumptions about poetry and culture. One of their concerns was the attempt to find the original Germanic pagan spirit in Old English literature, the oldest and most extensive Germanic literature. As a result they posed the problem of understanding in terms of pagan and Christian influences and elements. This pagan-Christian dichotomy has bedeviled Anglo-Saxon scholarship to this day and only recently have we begun to put matters in a more reason-

Reprinted with permission from *Annuale mediaevale*, IX (1968), 5–25, copyright The Duquesne University Press.

Given as the Strub Lecture at Duquesne University on March 14, 1967. I have preserved in this version much of the informality of its original delivery.

[1] Quoted in *TLS*, March 9, 1967, p. 187.

[2] Cf. Kenneth Burke, *The Philosophy of Literary Form* (New York, 1957), p. 75.

able and exact perspective. This matter will not be my concern today. I am interested in another issue: the exaggerated individualism and psychologism of their attitude. These scholars thought of Anglo-Saxon poetry either as a mysterious product of the *Volkgeist* or as the product of a poet trying to express his feelings, as a romantic poet might, in verse. They did not neglect the historical; on the contrary, they overemphasized it; but their view of history was inevitably too narrow and it was vitiated by false social and psychological assumptions.

I do not wish to deny personal expression in this body of poetry, but I do not believe we can evaluate this element until we recognize the rhetorical stance of the poet and the social role of the poetry insofar as we can recreate it. "The first purpose of art, of which the medieval mind was fully self-conscious was usefulness." [3] The preserved poetry of the early Middle Ages was created as far as we know by men who had a definite role in society as either teachers or officials of a sort who were what we would call today priests, historians, archivists, or scientists. Popular poetry of this period has simply not survived. Much poetry was occasional. We live in an age and a society where, except perhaps for advertising, the literary man has no fixed social role. This is not true of the non-Western world, where the social role of artists is well recognized and his output carefully controlled. But in the Western world, the artist is essentially a free lance. His value is personal and only incidentally social. If we would understand the past social role of literature, we must look either at the advertising profession in our society or at the artists under communism or fascism or perhaps if any truly tribal societies are left in parts of the world such as Africa, at the poets and craftsmen of such societies. [4]

Anglo-Saxon society in its early centuries was a tribal society or a society beginning to emerge from its tribal state. The conquest of Britain was both part of the disintegration of the Roman Empire

[3] Frank P. Chambers, *The History of Taste, An Account of the Revolutions of Art Criticism and Theory in Europe* (New York, 1932), p. 10. See also A. Van Gennep, *La formation des légendes*, Bibliothèque de philosophie scientifique (Paris, 1910), pp. 16, 39, 306–309, *et passim.*

[4] See, e.g., H. F. Morris, *The Heroic Recitations of the Bahima of Ankole*, with a Foreword by A. T. Hatto, Oxford Library of African Literature (Oxford, 1964) and I. Schapera, *Praise-Poems of Tswana Chiefs, ibid.*, (Oxford, 1965).

and the beginning of the transformation of Germanic tribal society into the nation-state, a transformation in which Christianity played an important part. Anglo-Saxon literature as studied today is a reflex, largely accidental because contingent upon the chances of manuscript preservation, of a social breakdown and a social rehabilitation of great magnitude. Because written literature belongs largely to the later Anglo-Saxon period, our Anglo-Saxon literature reflects the recovery rather than the decline. Anglo-Saxon literature is closely related to the society of which it is a part.

The changeover from a social to an individualistic art [5] began, no doubt, in the West with the Renaissance of the twelfth century, but the process was long; it was not until the late eighteenth and early nineteenth centuries that it was widely victorious, although perhaps never completely so, for we still have occasional coronation odes and poems of that sort. The arts were primarily useful socially, and the emergence of a non-useful, purely decorative and expressive art which began in the twelfth century at first tentatively and then with the increasing luxury of society and its gradual atomization more rapidly, was a long, slow process.

For a long time the new arts which did not serve a recognized social purpose were clearly separated from the socially useful arts. In seventeenth-century France the newer role of the arts was at last recognized in the emergence of terms like *beaux arts* and *belles lettres*, both of which stressed their purely aesthetic function. It is true that *belles lettres* at least in English gradually became rather limited in application, but it originally signified all the newer kinds of literary art. *Beaux arts* was generally replaced in English by *fine arts*, a term used for the same aesthetic function in the plastic arts. Sculpture and to some extent painting never lost their social function to the same degree as the literary arts.

[5] "Our present concept of literary form is, in several respects, related to privacy. The practice of reading a book to oneself, in silence, is a specific, late history development." George Steiner, "A Note on Literature and Post-history," *Festschrift zum achtzigsten Geburtstag von George Lukács*, ed. Frank Benseler (Berlin, Neuwied, 1965), p. 503. Herman Meyer calls the change in the audience over the past centuries as the creation of a Leser-Diaspora in "Von der Freiheit des Erzählers," *Festgabe für L. L. Hammerich, Aus Anlass seines siebzigsten Geburtstags* (Copenhagen, 1962), p. 186. On the history of the word *ars*, see Tullio de Mauro, "Per la storia di *ars* 'arte," *Studii mediolatini e volgari*, Istituto di Filologia romanza dell'-Università di Pisa (Bologna, 1960), VIII, 53–68.

As recently as the late eighteenth century, the usefulness of the arts was stressed in theoretical and practical treatises. We may take as an example of this attitude Rudolph Erich Raspe's *Critical Essay on Oil Painting* written in 1781. Raspe, who is better known to the world as the author of stories about the Baron Munchausen than as the author of a work on oil-painting, speaks at the beginning of this treatise on the usefulness of the arts as compared to the uselessness of the sciences. It is very much indicative of the transformation in values which our world has undergone in the past two hundred years that today we would reverse that judgment.

The very word itself *art* or its Latin original *ars* indicates the transformation. In medieval times—to avoid the complication of the history of the word in classical times when in Roman civilization art itself could be individualistic—*ars* was applied to an organized body of knowledge. The medieval use of the term goes back ultimately to Varro, mediated through Isidore of Seville. The servile arts were the crafts: the liberal arts were the pure sciences.

The application of a word *art* to literature, painting, and so forth probably did not take place until the eighteenth century. Earlier uses relating to what we should call the arts are somewhat ambiguous and probably just mean "skill." However, with the first discourse of Sir Joshua Reynolds of 1769 there can be no doubt that he is using the word in our sense of artistic activity, especially in art and literature. In other words, the meaning of the word *art* underwent the same change as we see in the arts themselves, and *science* took over many of its old meanings. The notion of liberating skills of the "liberal arts" provided the bridge to its use for "useless," that is, pure, art.

The social role of poetry is intimately connected with the social role of the poet. In order therefore to pursue this subject further, we must turn to the Anglo-Saxon scop to see what we know of him. We do have some information about the Irish *filid* and the Welsh bards and Norse skalds, but unfortunately very little about the Anglo-Saxon poet. Some Old English poetry was written by monks, and the subject matter can often tell us when we can safely assume monkish authorship. These men were teachers and had a very definite didactic purpose in their saints' lives and biblical paraphrases. Monks may have written other kinds of literature too, but when the subject matter does not help us to decide, we must only guess. The real problem, however, is not the monk but the scop. Was he a wandering minstrel low in social standing or was he a man of importance at the king's or nobleman's court? Here the paucity of information hurts us.

Some scholars, most recently Eliason,[6] have denied any importance to him at all. Others have seen in him a kind of court poet and prophet.[7] However, whether the court scop was an important man or not, that he performed a useful social role cannot, I think, be doubted.

My belief in his importance is based on analogy with other cultures like the Icelandic and Irish [8] and even the Frisian, and on the evidence of the poems themselves. The closeness of the scops to their lords, their freedom in addressing their masters, their pride all appear in Old English poetry. Tacitus and Procopius give us a similar picture of Germanic tribal minstrels from earlier times. Most of this native evidence was collected for us in L. F. Anderson's monograph of some years ago, which is still valuable, and more recently in Egon Werlich's dissertation.[9] No doubt there were also popular and folk singers, but the pictures of Germanic scops that we have are all aristocratic. They were attached to kings.

[6] See his "Two Old English Scop Poems," *PMLA*, LXXXI (1966), 192.

[7] "The mere fact that he [the scop] was the preserver of tradition with something of the priestly about him, was sufficient, perhaps, to account for part of his high esteem. . . ." Karl Julius Holzknecht, *Literary Patronage in the Middle Ages*, A thesis . . . of the Unversity of Pennsylvania . . . (Philadelphia, 1923), p. 22.

[8] "The Celtic poet and sage was a functionary in society, and was an essential part of the aristocratic structure of that society. His prime duty was to praise and celebrate his chief and his chief's family in panegyric verse (which was traditionally what 'poetry' meant above all to the Celt), to preserve and recite his genealogy, and in all other ways to further his fame; hence the necessity for his existence as a court official," Kenneth Hurlstone Jackson; *The Oldest Irish Tradition: A Window on the Iron Age* (Cambridge, Eng., 1964), p. 26.

[9] *The Anglo-Saxon Scop*, University of Toronto Studies, Philological Series 1 (Toronto, 1903), and Egon Werlich, *Der westgermanische Skop, Der Aufbau seines Dichtung und sein Vortrag*, Inaugural Dissertation . . . der Westfälischen Wilhelms-Universität zu Münster (Münster, 1964). The latter to be used with caution; the attempt to penetrate the role of the scop by etymology has not been too successful. The word, though, has been related to Germanic words meaning *to create, to scoff, to dance*, etc.

63

They were the ancestors of the late medieval court poets and heralds who were keepers of records, coats of arms, and genealogies,[10] whereas the popular singers no doubt found their continuers in the wandering medieval minstrel. The scop as portrayed in *Beowulf* sang victory, religious and funeral songs as well as panegyrics. Saxo Grammaticus tells us of an English scribe Lukas, "historiam scientia apprime eruditus," who encouraged by song the Danes in a battle against the Estonians in 1170. The scop's chief was his employer, usually a king or high nobleman—a role later taken over by the patron.[11] Just as one of the major subjects of poets is poetry itself, so minstrelsy is a major subject of Anglo-Saxon poetry as *Widsith*, *The Wanderer*, and *Deor* testify to. Like their Irish and Welsh counterparts, scops may even have been professional cursers and satirists like Balaam in the Old Testament.[12] Unfortunately our evidence for this activity among the Anglo-Saxons is slight,[13] but it may very well have been so. Unferth, the thyle, in *Beowulf* may have had this function as one of his tasks. The Court Jester of the later Middle Ages and Renaissance no doubt is a descendant of this professional curser.[14]

Although we have not proved anything, I think it can be said that it seems most likely that the Anglo-Saxon scop performed various important functions in his society and was attuned to the needs of his audience. In order to proceed further, I think we should look at the corpus of Old English poetry to try to analyze it in terms of its societal purposes. Can we explain most of the varieties of Old

[10] On the relation between heralds and minstrels, see N. Denholm-Young, *History and Heraldry, 1254 to 1310, A Study of the Historical Value of the Rolls of Arms* (Oxford, 1965), esp. pp. 15–16 and 54 ff., although the author is rather surprised by the connection. These heralds carried on the archivist aspect of earlier medieval scops.

[11] See Karl Julius Holzknecht, *op. cit.*, pp. 4–5 *et passm*. Cf. M. Dominica Legge, "The Influence of Patronage on Form in Medieval French Literature," *Stil- und Formproblem in der Literatur*, Vorträge des VII Kongresses der Internationalen Vereinigung für moderne Sprachen und Literaturen in Heidelberg, ed. Paul Böckmann (Heidelberg, 1954), pp. 136–141.

[12] See Robert C. Elliott, *The Power of Satire: Magic, Ritual, Art* (Princeton, 1960).

[13] All of this material, together with other Germanic parallels, may be found in Anderson, *op. cit.*

[14] See Enid Welsford, *The Fool: His Social and Literary History* (London, 1935). For further comments on the scop, see below pp. 68–69.

64

English poetry in terms of satisfying the needs of its audience? If so, we shall have gone some distance in trying to prove our contention that we must not ignore the social and useful aspects of this poetry if we hope to understand it. Poetry does have social functions in most early societies and is not fundamentally the expression of personal whim and emotion. Even though few panegyrics, victory songs, or laments survive, it is reasonable to assume a parallel situation in England even when direct evidence is lacking. It also seems to me to be unlikely that Anglo-Saxon England was filled with Shelleys and Brownings expressing their personal emotions on every occasion.

The first step in our investigation of Old English poetry is to eliminate our easy problems. Much of Old English literature has a definite Christian purpose. Such writings were created to encourage and instruct the faithful. Their didactic or pastoral purpose is usually very obvious. Much of this literature, especially sermons, was written in prose and will not be our concern here. But there is still a substantial amount of Christian poetry extant in the vernacular. The poetic saints' lives fall very clearly into a pattern of Christian exemplarism. They no doubt carried over with them from the secular heroic lays and epics some of their magical sense of participation, but the Christian sense of history, the Christian desire to honor its holy men, are no doubt the main motives in their creation and preservation. Possibly on occasion less worthy motives like propaganda for a particular monastery entered into the situation. They are, however, a main mode of Christian instruction and fitted into the aims of a Christian society. To keep attention, no doubt marvels and miracles were overstressed, and borrowings from secular, folk, and learned motifs and topoi can be found. With saints' lives, the problem of authentication is acute, and much ingenuity is expended on obtaining complete assent to the truth of the legend. A term like "suspension of disbelief" is not properly applicable to these tales, for I believe their audiences, accustomed to learning their history through tales, were only too ready to believe what they were told. I suspect the question cannot be posed in these terms. Anglo-Saxon audiences would not concentrate on particular performances and acts, but consider every version a particular realization of the true story. Albert Lord in his important *The Singer of*

65

Tales [15] has pointed out that the modern Yugoslav folk singer does not think that he is telling a different poem on different occasions if the general subject is the same no matter how much he may vary it. Nor does he think his poem, if it deals with the same hero as that of another singer's, is different from that other poem. As the word *story* itself indicates by its etymology, all heroic stories are considered true history. The problem for the teller of saints' lives is not to make his audience "suspend disbelief" but to entertain them and strengthen their belief in the truth of what he is saying. They are *legenda*, narratives to be read or listened to.

These Christian narratives then, the *Andreas* or *Guthlac* for instance, are in an ancient Judeo-Christian tradition and serve a definite purpose in leading men to God. Their language and marvels do in fact reveal strong affinities with those of secular heroic tales, but as I hope to show, the attitude towards Beowulf was no doubt similar in kind if not in degree of intimacy, to that towards Christian saints.

Besides poetic saints' lives, we also have Biblical paraphrases in verse of which the *Genesis* and *Exodus* provide notable examples. The Christians, like the Jews, are people of the book; and the Bible had to be taught to men so that God's great mercy and goodness could be recognized. We also find lyrical or semi-lyrical poems close to the liturgy at times in the three Christ poems. The majestic Harrowing of Hell and the Day of Judgment which occupied such important places in early medieval and Patristic theology are also subjects of a number of Anglo-Saxon poems. We also find many short poems of Christian wisdom and riddles, about which we shall say something later.

The two Christian poems which do give us some trouble are the *Battle of Maldon* and *The Dream of the Rood*. Let us look at them somewhat closely. The *Battle of Maldon* at first glance seems to be a late secular short heroic poem celebrating the heroism of a historical figure, Byrthnoth, who goes down to defeat possibly on account of his pride, at the hands of the heathen Vikings. His exploit is referred to in the Anglo-Saxon *Chronicle* for 991 and celebrated in a monk's Vita Oswaldi about 1000 and the *Liber Eliensis* some hundred and fifty years later. The poem itself has lost its head and

[15] Cambridge, 1960, pp. 99 ff.

66

tail so that rather vital parts for its general interpretation are lacking. Byrthnoth, it has recently been argued by N. F. Blake and myself,[16] "had a religious dimension in the minds of his compatriots"; and his tale was influenced by legends of the saints. Byrthnoth, as he is about to die, prays for immediate and safe passage to heaven as a saint might pray. Death was ordinarily a horrible ordeal to the soul as it emerged from the body to find devils awaiting it. Only the good and the martyrs could expect an easy passage to heaven. Mr. Blake has also shown how the poem parallels saints' lives in many ways. I assume that the *Battle of Maldon* is an unofficial saint's life. As a purely heroic secular poem it is a little late.

The Dream of the Rood poses even more difficulties for my thesis. It would be easy of course to say that this poem is an exception and that here we find an individual interpretation of Christ's passion which seems to have no immediate didactic purpose. It could very well be an individualistic creation on the part of a subjective poet. There are no doubt some such poems in the Anglo-Saxon corpus. I think perhaps *Resignation* with its emphasis on the speaker's own sins may be one such. But as may readily be understood, I am loth to allow too many exceptions; and *The Dream of the Rood* can possibly be explained on other and—to me at least—more congenial grounds.

The poem is presented through two "I" speakers. The poet or his persona speaks at the beginning and end, and reports in the middle a speech a tree addresses to him. The persona speaks of a dream in which he sees a tree in the form of a richly decorated cross. The cross then tells him of its history—how it was cut down and shaped into a cross and how Jesus as a young hero mounted on him and went to his death as all Creation wept. It saw the burial of Jesus and then it was buried itself. The tree tells the poet to report his vision to the world and to praise the powers of the cross. The poet then worships the cross and speaks of the joy it gives him. The cross will enable him to attain eternal life. The poem closes with a reference

---

[16] N. F. Blake, "The Battle of Maldon," *Neophilologus*, XLIX (1965), 332–345, and Bloomfield, "Patristics and Old English Literature: Notes on Some Poems," *Studies in Old English Literature in Honor of Arthur G. Brodeur*, ed. S. B. Greenfield (Eugene, Ore., 1963), pp. 37–38 (the following quotation is from p. 38).

to the Lord's redeeming power as manifested in the Harrowing of Hell.

The influence of the classical figure of prosopopeia (whereby an inanimate object speaks) [17] and of the first person address of many riddles (one of which incidentally is the Cross) is apparent in this poem and firmly fixes it to the literary tradition of the age. It is also obviously connected with the veneration of the cross and may even have been inspired by Pope Sergius I's discovery of a fragment of the true Cross in 701.

I think it is clear that the poem has a didactic purpose and is related to the rhetorical modes of the age. The problem is its genre. It has been praised for its uniqueness; and until we have further information in the form of its source, I am afraid we must at least at present recognize a strong personal element in it. It cannot, however, be considered, even on the basis of what we do know about it, as the completely personal meditation of an individual on a venerated object. We need only compare it with later and more personal meditations on the cross to see this. There is no interest in the self, and the "I" is a visionary who is *seeing* the crucifixion and *hearing* the cross speak.

Turning to secular literature, I shall concentrate on epic, which in effect means *Beowulf*, and on what I call wisdom literature, a category which comprises a very large number of OE poems, many more than have been recognized under the rubric of gnomic poetry.

One of the major functions of the scop was to be the historian of early traditions, and *Beowulf* can be best approached in these terms. It exists to pass on to the generations a tale of a noble hero whose life can be a model to his tribe. J. W. Saunders tells us that "these (early) bards, like Homer, were employed to preserve in metrical form, the form best calculated to assist memorization and thus transmission from one generation to the next, the religious legends and early history, half historical, half mythical, of the community.

[17] See Margaret Schlauch, "*The Dream of the Rood* as Prosopopeia," *Essays and Studies in Honor of Carleton Brown* (New York, 1940). One must always hesitate before considering older lyrics as personal. Many personal lyrics are only apparently so. See for instance "The Feúch Féin controversy" as discussed in James Carney, *Studies in Irish Literature and History* (Dublin, 1955), pp. 243 ff. I am indebted to Mr. Patrick Ford for this reference.

The bards, then, were the authors of each new nation's holy book, the repositories of the highest truths in which men believed, and they were revered for their priesthood." [18] This is an admirable statement of the scop as historian. That Beowulf was a Geat does not lessen the value of the knowledge of his life for Anglo-Saxons. Besides the general consciousness of a Germanic unity not yet completely faded by the eighth century when Beowulf was written and proved by the links between Germania and England, we know from Sutton Hoo and elsewhere that the Scandinavians and Anglo-Saxons had close and friendly contact with each other before the Viking raids began in the ninth century.

It is also possible but less probable that some of the more primitive attitudes towards myth prevailed in the *Beowulf* audience. As Mircea Eliade has written, "an object or an art becomes real insofar as it imitates or repeats an archetype. Thus reality is acquired solely through repetition or participation; everything which lacks an exemplary model is meaningless, i.e. it lacks reality." It is possible that to an Anglo-Saxon of the eighth century, listening to the story of Beowulf was a way of attaining greater reality. Some of the power of the hero would be transferred to him as he participated vicariously through words in his deeds. Participation in epic sessions would be a considerable advance over cannibalism and had the advantage of being repeatable.

Deor and Widsith, who appear as scops in the poems bearing their names, both possess extensive historical and mythic information, not confined to Anglo-Saxon lore. Saxo Grammaticus in the Preface to his great Danish history considers his work to be the continuation of earlier poems which celebrated the deeds of his ancestors and indeed he claimed them as his sources. We have evidence from the Frisians, the closest Germanic relatives of the Anglo-Saxons geographically and linguistically, that their minstrels sang songs of their heroes. In Altfrid's life of St. Liudger, we are told about Berulef who sang of "the acts of the ancients and the rivalries of kings." [19] It is only reasonable to assume Anglo-Saxon scops did likewise. *Beowulf*, in spite of its fundamentally Christian point of view and its mixture of praise and criticism of its pagan

[18] *The Profession of English* (London and Toronto, 1964), p. 21.
[19] Pertz, MGH, Scriptores II, 412 (referred to in Anderson, pp. 10–11).

heroes, belongs to the category of historical works and in its reciting, the tradition of society was being carried on.

Although I do not think that *Beowulf* as we now have it was orally composed, there can be no question but that an oral tradition lies behind it and that if the poem as we now have it was diffused at all, it must have been largely by oral performances. These oral performances were guided by the score of our text and were not oral composition in the Parry-Lord sense. The oral background and oral diffusion of *Beowulf* have left their mark on the poem in the shape of formulas, organization of the plot, and perhaps even in the characterization. I must admit that the artistry of *Beowulf* as manifested particularly in its wealth of historical and mythological allusions would perhaps argue against its oral diffusion as it certainly argues against its oral composition. Given the rarity of literacy, however, it is hard to think of the early *Beowulf* audience as primarily readers rather than listeners. If it was diffused as seems likely, it must have served somewhat the same function in society as the saints' lives did as well as narrative generally—except that its audience was probably more restricted and perhaps more knowledgeable. The audience must have known the Beowulf legend in some way [20]—possibly through genuine oral performances and through their traditions. The fact that Beowulf himself may not have been a real man who lived at one time does not at all affect my argument, for all we have to assume is that the Anglo-Saxons believed him to have been a historical personage. The historically reliable information in the poem—for Beowulf lives in an environment which can be proved to have existed—reveals to us the assumed historicity of his own person. As de Vries has argued,[21] the anonymity of most epics would argue against the view of original creation. The poets who composed heroic lays and epics must have felt that they were links in carrying on history as it was understood through the centuries.[22]

Beowulf is not then an individual new creation which a modern

[20] See Jan de Vries, *Heroic Song and Heroic Legend*, trans. B. J. Timmer, Oxford Paperbacks 69 (London, 1963), p. 45.

[21] *Ibid.*, pp. 165–166

[22] See Lars Lönroth, *European Sources of Icelandic Saga-writing: An Essay Based on Previous Studies* (Stockholm, 1965), p. 10, on the Icelandic conception of saga in the classical period as history.

poet might make about traditional materials—about the Conquistadores or the American Civil War—but a written or oral performance of a traditional legend which gave strength and a model to the audience. The personal element is there of course, but it is kept subordinate to a wider and more impersonal purpose. The epic poet is not revealing consciously his soul but rather the soul of his people so that they may know who they are and may be.[23] The poet is partly a historian and partly a priest.

This picture fits fully only the age before our preserved poems, but enough of it applies to our earliest OE poems so that it can help us to understand them.

I have no intention of going through all of Old English literature in this fashion, but I have saved for the last a category which I do not think has been taken seriously enough in Anglo-Saxon studies—wisdom literature. I shall spend the remaining time discussing this type of literature, widening its scope and showing how it gives a social dimension to a large body of OE poetry.

Few topics in the history of culture have occupied such a large place in men's minds and have been at the same time so widely ignored as the whole subject of wisdom and wisdom literature. It almost seems as if there had been a conspiracy of silence on the part of the scholarly world about it except perhaps for some narrow categories of wisdom literature like proverbs and riddles. Even when these last have been discussed, their affinity with a broader category of writing and activity has been more or less ignored.

One cannot make up in part of a paper for such colossal neglect, but some few general comments seem called for. Whenever we turn to the literature of the past, we always find a certain part of it devoted, in one way or another, to rules for conduct or control of environment or to information about nature and man. The purpose of wisdom and its literature is to suggest a scheme of life in the broadest sense of the world, to ensure its continuance, to predict its variations and to associate humanity with the fundamental rhythms of nature. It is an attempt to control life by some kind of order, to

---

[23] The remarks of Lönroth, "It is difficult, therefore, to accept the popular image of the Icelandic saga writer as an artistic layman, inventing and creating, pen in hand, all by himself . . . ," *op. cit.* p. 14, may also be applied to the Anglo-Saxon epic writer.

reduce the area of the unexpected and the sudden.[24] It is the step beyond shamanism and prophecy. One can control life by wisdom rather than by dependency on special revelations. The early laws are its first manifestation, and in Hebrew history, it is the Sinaitic code which as a divine gift, organizes life for man. Torah is wisdom; and although it needs supplementation, it provided the basis for all Hebraic wisdom literature, not to speak of normative Judaism. It is the rational, as opposed to the irrational and inexplicable part of the law. Wisdom provides us with a store of knowledge to enable us to discover the right time ($\kappa\alpha\iota\rho\acute{o}s$) for things. It controls sacred time and classifies it. It is the discernment of the particular. It is the science of time and of the possible. It is presented to us by wise men or by folk culture[25] and is modeled for us by the ideal king or ruler who embodies wisdom (*sapientia*) and force (*fortitudo*) in his being. It originally depended on memory and continued so for a long time. Certain truths were acquired and passed on.[26]

Like most wide and basic categories, it is difficult to define wisdom literature. As far as I know there is no book treating of this general category in an international way. There are many books and

[24] "The unexpected is feared. It is too often evil, and in any case its constant potential intervention conflicts with the deep-rooted need for security." David Daube, *Suddenness and Awe in Scripture*, Robert Waley Cohen Memorial Lecture (London, 1963), p. 10.

[25] See Harvey H. Guthrie, *Israel's Sacred Songs. A Study of Dominant Themes* (New York, 1966), pp. 171 ff. See also for some recent studies of ancient Israelite, Biblical, and Eastern wisdom, Hans Heinrich Schmid, *Wesen und Geschichte der Weisheit, Eine Untersuchung zur altorientalischen und israelitischen Weisheitsliteratur*, Beihefte zur Zeitschrift für die alttestamentliche Wissenschaft 101 (Berlin, 1966); Johannes Jacobus Adrianus Van Dijk, *La sagesse suméro-accadienne, Recherches sur les genres littéraires des textes sapientiaux*, Proefschrift . . . Rijksuniversiteit te Leiden . . . (Leiden, 1953); W. G. Lambert, *Babylonian Wisdom Literature* (Oxford, 1960). On the notion of the wise man, see Lorenz Dürr, "Heilige Vaterschaft im antiken Orient, Ein Beitrag zur Geschichte der Idee de 'Abbas,'" *Heilige Überlieferung, Ausschnitte aus der Geschichte des Mönchtums . . . Ildefons Herwegen zum silbernen Abtjubiläum* ed. Odo Casel, Beiträge zur Geschichte des alten Mönchtums und des Benediktinerordens, Supplementband (Münster, 1938).

[26] See Ernst Heitsch, "Wahrheit als Erinnerung," *Hermes*, XCI (1963), 36–52 (mainly on Plato). This notion no doubt accounts for the widespread concept of remembrance in older literature; e.g., Marie de France in *Equitan*, lines 1–8 and numerous other examples. The whole Judeo-Christian tradition is closely connected with the notion of wisdom and remembrance. We remember God's mercies to us, we remember our ancestors, we remember our martyrs—all in order to recreate the basis for our own salvation.

articles on Babylonian, Sumerian, Egyptian, and above all Hebrew wisdom literature, but nothing on the category as such. This lack is partly due to the vagueness and all-encompassing quality of the concept. It is clear that much literature in the Oriental, Classical and Western traditions belong to this category, but to be precise about its limits and genres is not an easy matter. It is found all over the near-East and in the Graeco-Roman sphere. It consists of proverbs, riddles, fables, anecdotes or exempla, dialogues, list science (inventories, e.g., "there are three types of men . . . etc." sort of thing), didactic rules, gnomes, charms, and reflective poems. Its general tone is pessimistic and worldlywise. It is sometimes witty and sometimes primitivistic. It may inveigh against civilization, and in Graeco-Roman times is associated somewhat with Cynic and Stoic philosophies. Like utopianism, primitivism is almost always didactic and reformist.

The Cynic type of wisdom literature stressed the artificiality of social conventions, the importance of passivity, the value of labor. The Cynics were antiurban and cosmopolitan. The Stoics shared similar attitudes but did not stress absolute passivity nor favor labor. Little anecdotes about great men were popular forms of instruction.[27] These stories are the literary ancestors of the later medieval exempla.

Wisdom literature is ethically, not ritually, oriented. It consists of practical wisdom and reflections on earthly existence and on the nature of things. This last is especially to be noted, as the "scientific" aspect of wisdom has not always been recognized. Nature as well as human nature and society are its concerns. As Alcuin tells Charlemagne when the Emperor asks him "what is prudence," "knowledge of things and natures."[28] The nature of things is moral and rational. In a hierarchical and harmonious world, to learn about

---

[27] I am indebted to a lecture by Professor Henry A. Fischel delivered at the Conference on Jewish Philosophy, Brandeis University, April 24, 1966, for some of the above ideas. On the anecdote or Χρεία in classical literature, see Elizabeth Hazelton Haight, *The Roman Use of Anecdotes in Cicero, Livy, & the Satirists* (New York, 1940), and Wilhelm Gemoll, *Das Apophthegma, literarhistorische Studien* (Vienna, Leipzig, 1924).

[28] Ed. Wilbur Samuel Howell (Princeton, 1941), p. 146. For a recent work on prudence, see Pierre Aubenque, *La prudence chez Aristote*, Bibliothèque de philosophie contemporaine, Histoire de la philosophie et philosophie générale (Paris, 1963).

the stars is to learn about one's self. The wise man wishes to learn about the nature of existence which includes what we would call science as well as ethics. Living together in society and on this planet depended on wisdom.

The classical rhetoricians analyzed wisdom literature as diatribes, riddles, fables, and exempla. But classical wisdom literature also embraces didactic treatises and poetry, dialogues (such as those of Plato, Seneca, and Boethius), proverbs.[29] Hesiod's *Works and Days* is an early example of the type. It is threaded upon the outline of a useful farmer's life addressed to Hesiod's brother Perses, who seized Hesiod's share of his father's property. It is not, however, limited to advice to farmers. It contains proverbs, practical wisdom, and admonition, and list science of various types. It is above all a poem of καιρός—to give us the proper time for doing things, even things for which there should never be a καιρός and hence not to be done at all.[30]

Proverbs and *sententiae* tend to be passed on from people to people—or at least to be repetitious. The wisdom of the folk and of the educated people was preserved in pithy sayings as well as in other ways. Tracing sources is very difficult because wisdom tends to be universal. Proverbs are close to gnomes which present less dramatically wisdom in brief form. Some gnomes are simple statements about nature. Kenneth Jackson prefers to call these "nature" gnomes "quasi-gnomic."[31]

Riddles are closely related to proverbs and sentences although not all belong to the category of moral wisdom. Some force the bearer to speculate on the nature of things. They expect an answer. They may have had their origin in ritual. Entertainment is also one of their purposes.

All these pithy sayings are closely related to the older phenomenon of prophecy, for God speaks through prophets in riddles,

[29] See, e.g., Henry Chadwick, *The Sentences of Sextus, A Contribution to the History of Early Christian Ethics*, Texts and Studies, n.s., ed. C. H. Dodd, V (Cambridge, Eng., 1959). These sentences are a reworking of pagan proverbs circa 180–210.

[30] See P. Mazon, "Hésiode, la composition des *Travaux et des jours*," *Revue des études anciennes*, XIV (1912), 352–353.

[31] See Kenneth Jackson, ed., *Early Welsh Gnomic Poems* (Cardiff, 1935), and *Studies in Early Celtic Nature Poetry* (Cambridge, Eng., 1935).

gnomes and proverbs. The Koran tells us that God speaks in metaphors. The divine rhetoric is usually indirect and often ambiguous to mortal ears.

Another type of wisdom literature, not always recognized as such, is the charm. Charms are the practical, action side of wisdom and are aimed at producing desired-for effects. Behind them are various ancient magic notions like the power of the word [32] and homeopathic magic (i.e., like produces like). Possibly the more sententious type of wisdom as seen in proverbs and gnomes arose from charms and magic. The wise man is the man who knows how to do things properly and bring them about. Charms belong to the category of other types of action literature like prayers and hymns which rest on a *do ut des* basis. Charms escaped the spiritualization of prayers and hymns which Christianity brought about. Charms and primitive prayer attempt to gain practical results for the well-being of man. They often allude to myth or recite it—to bring about a like result.

More important than Graeco-Roman wisdom literature, and it was indeed important, was Hebrew wisdom literature, in the shaping of Old English poetry of this type. Wisdom was not merely a virtue, even the supreme virtue, but an attribute of God. In being wise, we are imitating God. The semideification of wisdom was also a characteristic of Plato and his school, but in Hebrew literature it reached its apogee and finally was applied to Jesus Himself the Λόγος. It was through wisdom that the world itself was created. Wisdom was highly honored.

Hebrew wisdom literature as it is extant consists in the main of two types—proverbs and reflective poems. To the first category belongs the Book of Proverbs and to the second Ecclesiastes, Ecclesiasticus, Wisdom, and in dialogic form Job. (Some psalms like number 49 belong to this category.) These latter works have certain interesting characteristics in common. They are usually in the first person or are dialogues. They consist of comments on the mutability of the world and on the immutability of God. They speak of worldly wisdom and recommend certain lines of prudential action. They do not neglect nature, but usually nature is used to provide evidence of the moral and divine fabric of the universe. Sometimes

---

[32] See, e.g., Toshihiko Izutsu, *Language and Magic*, Keio University, Studies in the Humanities and Social Relations I (Tokyo, 1955).

they are attributed to rulers (as in Hebrew literature often to Solomon), sometimes addressed to rulers, and sometimes they are addressed to the Lord. We have sometimes a shifting addressee. In *Ecclesiasticus* or *Sirach*, a father addresses a son. The line of organization is loose. There are sudden shifts in emphasis. The history of the Chosen People offers examples to underline points. These works are full of proverbs and gnomic sayings, and we find examples of list science.

Job has a narrative line, but is basically a dialogue. It is common to find wisdom poems cast in dialogue form. Babylonian literature offers several noteworthy examples, *The Theodicy* being especially notable.[33] There are also Babylonian fabulistic contest poems. We have already noted classical wisdom dialogues.

The existential quality of direct speech and admonition is a strong characteristic of this type of wisdom literature, in fact of many types. The traditional role of the teacher who may be a father or a wise man instructing his pupil who may be a son or a disciple was no doubt carried over into writing and literature. The vividness of direct discourse when well done makes teaching more palatable. No doubt this is why riddles, which are more concerned with the nature of things than with ethics, are also often in the first person. We are addressed when we learn. The teacher is talking to us not writing a philosophical treatise. Direct speech whether of only one or of two or more characters is characteristic of wisdom literature.

There is then a long tradition of direct address and "I" speakers in wisdom literature. Dante in the *Convivio* I.2 discusses the use of "I" in poetry. A writer should speak of himself only on needful occasions, he writes, of which there are two main cases. He should speak only to squash great infamy about himself as Boethius did to protect his good name or, and this is important for our purposes, to instruct others as Augustine did his *Confessions*. It is for this latter reason, based on the confrontation of teacher and pupil, that I think that many wisdom poems are cast in dialogue form or are addresses by the poet as teacher. Riddles expect an answer. Charms are addressed to the supernatural and hence are often apostrophes.

Wisdom literature consists of a number of genres which interact with each other and with related genres like the *consolatio*. There

---

[33] See Lambert, *op. cit.*, pp. 63 ff.

is no science of literary genres, but an awareness of the general type to which a literary work belongs, even if it is not a pure example, gives us some idea of the social function and rhetorical gambits of such a work. If we see a considerable body of Old English poetry as part of wisdom literature we look at it differently and estimate it differently. Genre study of this sort is normative; it is not concerned with particular examples of poems but rather with the ideal form (or occasionally forms) they presumably illustrate.

That a part of the extant OE poetic remains may be called wisdom literature has been, of course, recognized for a long time. Blanche Williams, some years ago, edited a group of gnomes with a lengthy introduction.[34] She also made reference to the many gnomic reflections buried in other poems. I believe, however, that wisdom literature is much more extensive in OE literature than has hitherto been recognized, that it is essentially traditional and not personal, and that the notion needs to be used in order to understand such puzzling pieces as the so-called elegies.

Proverbs, gnomes, riddles, and charms are all found among OE poetic remains and have, with the possible exception of charms, usually been recognized as wisdom literature. They also have the characteristic of being able to be used in longer works, and they are not only found by themselves in OE and Old Norse literatures but also embedded in other works such as epics, sagas and religious literature.

The elegies I believe are not really elegies at all. We may if we wish call these OE poems elegies, but we must recognize that a world of difference lies between the classical notion of elegy which was either a lament over the death of someone or of a people or over the destruction of a city or army;[35] or a love poem, and all

[34] *Gnomic Poetry in Anglo-Saxon*, Columbia University Studies in English and Comparative Literature (New York, 1914). See also Hugo Müller. *Über die angelsachsischen Versus gnomici*, Inaugural Dissertation . . . an den Universität Jena . . . (Jena, 1893), and R. MacGregor Dawson. "The Structure of the Old English Gnomic Poems," *JEGP*, LXI (1962), 14–22.

[35] There are of course Biblical parallels as in Lamentations and in David's lament over the death of Saul. For an earlier criticism of the notion of elegy, see B. J. Timmer, "The Elegiac Mood in Old English Poetry," *English Studies*, XXIV (1942), 33–34. On eighteenth and early nineteenth century concepts of elegy, see Edgar Mertner, "Thomas Gray und die Gattung der Elegie." *Poetica, Zeitschrift für Sprach- und Literaturwissenschaft*, II (1968), 326–347.

written in elegiacs. There are true elegies in OE poetry—the famous lament of the last survivor in *Beowulf* springs to mind, but most of the "elegies" in OE, as in Welsh and medieval Latin, are really moral reflective poems and not elegies in the strict sense of the word at all.

The term elegy was first applied to these poems in the nineteenth century. But by that time, the word had lost most of its original meaning and had been subjectively interpreted. Coleridge in *Table Talk* (Oct. 23, 1833) defines "elegy" as follows: it "may treat of any subject but . . . of no subject for itself . . . always and exclusively with reference to the poet." In other words, any personal poem may be called an elegy. When Anglo-Saxon literature was recovered in the nineteenth century, this word was applied probably first by Conybeare to poems like *The Wanderer, The Seafarer,* and *Deor* which seemed to be personal and for which no ready literary generic term sprang to mind. The use of this word for these poems has been mainly responsible, I believe, for the misunderstanding of their true nature.

These poems, affected no doubt by other genres such as the charm and gnome and consolation, are types of wisdom literature and are close in spirit and form to Hebraic and classical reflective poems. They were employed to teach men about the nature of the world, society and their own selves in terms of the Germanic life with which they were familiar.

The speaker, or speakers in wisdom literature, is the poet speaking as prophet and teacher. He is mediating wisdom and is not speaking primarily of himself. His experiences are to be taken as representative experiences not personal experiences. (They may of course incidentally have been personal, but only incidentally.) The poet is urging his audience to the practice of the four cardinal virtues particularly prudence from a Christian point of view. Or he may emphasize particular Christian notions though not dogma. He is giving us not ritual and dogma, although as a Christian he would presuppose these, but practical ethics based on wise knowledge. This tone is reflective and sad.

But these speeches are not monologues but dialogues even when a second speaker does not appear. Unlike romantic poetry which is a monologue expressive of self or a dialogue with a "real" person, these are addressed to everyman or to God. They are not self-expression but the communication of inherited wisdom to society at large. They teach, and although the rhetoric of persuasion is alive in them when they are successful, they do not claim originality or individual psychological acuity.

The Seafarer begins with the rather long exemplum of the sailor, trying to explain the hardships of this kind of life, which is a paradigm for the life of all men. *Ecclesiastes* begins in similar fashion. The speaker, supposedly Solomon, tells us that he tried to seek out wisdom in the world because he discovered that nature and life seem meaninglessly circular. "One generation passeth away, and another generation cometh. . . . The sun also ariseth, and the sun goeth down. . . . The wind goeth toward the south, and turneth about unto the north. . . . All the rivers run into the sea; yet the sea is not full . . . the eye is not satisfied with seeing, nor the ear filled with hearing . . . and there is no new thing under the sun."

The seafarer speaks, "I have borne bitter sorrow in my breast, made trial of many sorrowful abodes on ships. . . . Afflicted with cold my feet were fettered with frost . . . hunger within rent the mind of the sea-weary man. . . . The hail flew in showers. . . . No protector could comfort the heart in need. . . . The man knows not . . . what some of those endure who most widely pace the paths of exile." (R. K. Gordon translation.) The similarity of tone, even allowing for the original language differences, is striking.

Then both the preacher and the seafarer go on to general reflections about the earth and give us wisdom. Both give us lists. The seafarer tells us that three things lie in wait for us: illness, age or hostility. The preacher tells us that there is a season for everything: a time to be born, and a time to die and so on. Both use proverbs and gnomic sayings, and both stress the joys of heaven and God as a contrast to our earthly lot. The Hebrew poem uses the imperative more frequently than the Old English one. The preacher also speaks longer and is perhaps a little more pessimistic, but we have in both a poem organized around the same themes and with the same general structure.

The Wanderer shows a similar structure although the speaker is a scop. *Deor* uses historical examples and the poet casts his poem in the form of a charm.[36] But all stress mutability, the weariness of the flesh, the irreliability of life and its relations in comparison with God's eternal realm. They are teaching us wisdom—justice, temperance, fortitude and above all prudence—and the Christian attitude toward life.

The Wanderer and *The Seafarer* have a meditative reflective line and move from thought to thought. They represent Judeo-Christian wisdom at its best. They serve to lead us to God through the paths of wisdom rather than through the sacraments.[37]

Wisdom literature is a large and perhaps somewhat vague category of world literature, but it has many masterpieces to its credit. That it should appear in Anglo-Saxon is not surprising, but that its scope has not hitherto, as far as I know, been recognized, is. This is a contribution I hope to the understanding of this literature and to some of its Old English examples. Wisdom literature, in its usual manifestations, is practical advice told directly or through exempla or fables, and it serves an important role in teaching man to face the trials and tribulations of this world. It may on occasion be dull, but when properly animated in noble language, it strikes the hearts of men everywhere especially and enables them to rise above sorrow and grief and to live properly.

[36] See M. W. Bloomfield, "The Form of Deor," *PMLA*, LXXIX (1964), 534–541.

[37] It is currently fashionable to call these OE elegies (as well as their Celtic counterparts) penitential poetry (see e.g., P. L. Henry, *The Early English and Celtic Lyric* [London, 1966?]). The parallels offered are usually the penitential psalms which belong rather to a different genre of literature altogether. These "elegies" are not penitential at all—they do not castigate their speakers and pray for forgiveness. Using such a term obscures the relationship with their true generic siblings—meditative, reflective wisdom poems. Although they may refer to God and end with a prayer to him, they are didactic and addressed to man, not a plea for forgiveness addressed to God. I am, of course, only referring to the OE poems, not the Irish or Welsh, poems alluded to in Henry's book. Henry is right, however, to stress the importance of the exile motif in these poems. The exile is the image *par excellence* of the religious man in the Judeo-Christian tradition.

5. Symbolism in Medieval Literature

Unde in nulla scientia, humana industria inventa, proprie loquendo, potest inveniri nisi litteralis sensus; sed solum in ista Scriptura, cujus Spiritus sanctus est auctor, homo vero instrumentum.— Thomas Aquinas, Quaestiones quodlibetales *vii. a.16.*

It is exceedingly fashionable today in the general intellectual flight from history to interpret literature symbolically or, as it is often called, "allegorically." The particularity of fact and event is passed over for the general, the cyclic, and the mythical, which is presumably more universal and more meaningful. Unless the significance of a literary work can be subsumed in a system of interpretation—usually Christian, although not always—it is assumed to have no real meaning.[1] Parallel to this revolt against history is a revolt against psychology, which is another facet of the same disregard for the unique. Those works which may easily be interpreted symbolically, such as Melville's *Moby Dick*, have leaped into new favor, and the great classics of English and American literature are everywhere, as far as possible, being reinterpreted along symbolic, usually Christian, lines.

Needless to say, this movement has not left medieval literature untouched, for in the Middle Ages there is at hand a fully worked-out, even if contradictory, theoretical symbolical system, especially in the works of the early Fathers. The general awareness in medieval studies outside theology and the history of theology, at least in English-speaking countries, of the so-called four or three levels of meaning theory which goes back chiefly to Origen [2] and Philo and the Alexandrine school [3] and ultimately to the Stoics, dates from

Reprinted from *Modern Philology*, LXI (1958), 73–81.

[1] Unless the system implied by them really gives meaning to the world and man, the general, the cyclic, and the mythical are no more meaningful than the particular, the unique, and the fact. This axiom is not always kept in mind by the "symbolists." The mere cycles of nature, for instance, are as meaningless as any unique fact unless one is satisfied by a purely biological vision of the world.

I am indebted to Professor Phillip W. Damon for several suggestions which I have used in this paper.

[2] For a recent treatment and defense of Origen's exegetical method see Henri de Lubac, *Histoire et esprit: L'intelligence de l'Écriture d'après Origène.* Théologie: études publiées sous la direction de la Faculté de Théologie S.J. de Lyon-Fourvière (Paris, 1950); see, however, P. Th. Camelot, "La Théologie de l'image de Dieu," *Revue des sciences philosophiques et théologiques*, XL (1956), 453, n. and 455, where the literalness of Origen's biblical exegesis is emphasized.

[3] The Antiochene school, which emphasized the literal more than the spiritual sense (to use inexact but common terms for the sake of convenience), was, however, always opposed to Alexandrine flights of fancy. Its influence, chiefly expressed through Theodore of Mopsuestia (although Ambrosiaster, John Chrysostom, and Junilius must not be neglected), never completely died in the Middle Ages, and in the early period is to be found in Ireland and elsewhere, notably England and north-

the publication of Harry Caplan's article "The Four Senses of Scripture" in *Speculum* in 1929 and of Dr. H. Flanders Dunbar's *Symbolism in Medieval Thought and Its Consummation in the Divine Comedy* in the same year.[4] Since that time, medieval scholars and literary students have increasingly concentrated on interpreting medieval literature in terms of the exegetical method used

ern France. See M. L. W. Laistner, "Antiochene Exegesis in Western Europe during the Middle Ages," *HTR*, XL (1947), 19–31; Alberto Vaccari, "La Teoria esegetica della scuola antiochena," *Scritti de erudizione e di filologia*, I (Rome, 1952), 101–142 (reprinted from *Biblica*, 1920 and 1934); and the important article by Bernard Bischoff, "Wendepunkte in der Geschichte der lateinische Exegese im Frühmittelalter," *Sacris erudiri*, V (1954), 189–281. The latter protests against the facile setting of Alexandria against Antioch in the early Middle Ages. He points out that even Bede, who did much to push the Alexandrine method, was essentially historical in his exegesis. In fact, the whole subject seems to be hopelessly confused. One thing is certain that, except for typology (the veiled prediction of Christ in the Old Testament), at no time did any biblical exegete repudiate the importance and often the primacy of the biblical letter. There are, however, degrees of emphasis.

Even Augustine's *De doctrina Christiana*, which is supposed to have established the fourfold method for the Middle Ages, contains no reference at all to it. In fact, the whole point of that work as regards the Bible is that what is taught is clearly taught, and, if it is occasionally obscure, it is elsewhere in the Bible made very plain. Augustine does refer, it is true, to a four-fold method of interpreting the Bible in *De utilitate credendi* 3 (PL, XLII, 68 ff.) and *De genesi ad litteram* 2 (PL, XXXIV, 222), but the four meanings are history (the letter), etiology (normal explanation of difficult biblical passages to a Christian), analogy (typology or agreement of the two Testaments), and allegory (figurative meaning, usually typology). The recognition of the figurative meaning of parts of the Old Testament is either typology as found in the New Testament itself or the normal application of a criterion of meaning to a written text. In practice, however, Augustine frequently does indulge in symbolic biblical exegesis. Gregory the Great by his practice did perhaps more to make the early Middle Ages pass over the literal for the figurative (usually moral) meaning of the Bible than anyone else. He had great influence on Bede and Rabanus Maurus, the most important of the early medieval biblical commentators. For some recent discussions of Augustine's exegetical methods see Maurice Pontet, *L'Exégèse de S. Augustin prédicateur*, Théologie: études publiées sous la direction de la Faculté de Théologie S.J. de Lyon-Fourvière (Paris, 1944?), and Allen A. Gilmore, "Augustine and the Critical Method," *HTR*, XXXIX (1946), 141–163. Neither Augustine, Gregory, nor Bede thought of a consistent and continuous multileveled interpretation of Scripture but that the nature of the particular text determined the "level" desired. Bede, for example, gives as an example of tropology I John 3:18, which he says must be taken literally, and of anagogy Matt. 5:8, which also must be taken literally (see his *De tabernacula* i [PL, XCI, 410B–411B]).

[4] There are, of course, earlier treatments of the subject in English: e.g., Frederic W. Farrar, *History of Interpretation: Eight Lectures Preached before the University of Oxford* . . . (London, 1886), and H. Preserved Smith, *Essays in Biblical Interpretation* (Boston, 1921).

in medieval biblical criticism, at least in the earlier Middle Ages.[5]

It seems to me that this method, while not totally wrong, is essentially erroneous as a method of understanding most medieval literary works historically, and it is the purpose of this article to discuss briefly the implications and limits of this method in the study of medieval secular literature, especially of the later Middle Ages.

First, it must be admitted that all meaning is at least partially symbolic. A literary work of any sort and of any period always has some symbolic meaning. Beyond the fact that language itself is a system of sound and written symbols, which is of little significance to my main point, the substance and figures of literature must stand for more than themselves if they are to be fully meaningful. The unique has a meaning of a special sort. If Hamlet is only Hamlet, he is a primary datum; but if he stands for man in a dilemma, or a truth-seeker, or a ditherer, he has another dimension. Although its attention may be captured by it, the human mind comprehends the singular in a special way and not completely intellectually—a limitation, incidentally, of human creatureliness to medieval scholasticism. Meaning in literature comes through the unique but is not equivalent to it.

In this sense, all literature has a *nucleus* and a *cortex* and conveys *sententia*.[6] This is no peculiarity of medieval literature and thought. Historically, of course, medieval man tended to think in Christian categories, and most frequently the *sententia* he put into or discovered in literature was a Christian one. Indeed, no proper understanding of medieval literature is possible without a good knowledge of the Christian categories of thought and beliefs. Yet medie-

---

[5] For a good summary of early Christian exegesis and a review of recent literature on the subject see Walter J. Burchardt, "On Early Christian Exegesis," *Theological Studies*, XI (1950), 78–116. The literature on patristic and medieval exegesis is too vast to be suitably summarized here. My comments in this paper should not, of course, be interpreted to mean that I do not believe that traditional biblical exegesis is not of great value in interpreting biblical allusions and symbols when used by medieval authors.

[6] On the history of *sententia*, see G. Paré, A. Brunet, and P. Tremblay, *La Renaissance du XIIᵉ siècle, les écoles et l'enseignement*, "Publications de l'Institut d'Études Médiévales d'Ottawa," Vol. III (Paris and Ottawa, 1933), pp. 267 ff. Isidore of Seville interprets it to be an impersonal general dictum from which its general, but not only, medieval meaning of "meaning" or "truth" probably derives.

val man was also the heir of late classical antiquity and of barbarian cultures, and their categories of thought, their literary genres, their points of view, were also part of this heritage. He was well aware of a secular tradition which had not been completely transformed by Christianity.

Christianity gave meaning to existence for medieval man, was the framework of his thought generally, and was backed by the state and society with a strength and vigor no longer displayed today. The very form of the universe, with its hierarchy of being, as reflected in nature, in society, in the church, and in the next world, supported a view of a providential and ordered universe. What could be more natural—indeed, inevitable—than to see a Christian *sententia* in secular literature if that literature were to have any deep and important meaning at all. The Bible was, of course, in a class by itself, as the composition of God through various gifted and graced men to reveal his Truth to all men.

What also could be more natural than that students should be taught the letter and the *sensus* and the *sententia*[7] of a text. Although we do not use the terms, we still do so today if the instruction is more than memory work. However, then as now, I suspect, the *sensus* and *sententia* got less emphasis in practice than in theory. A glance at medieval commentaries, especially of the earlier period, on secular works and even occasionally on the Bible shows for the most part an overwhelming interest in the purely grammatical and rhetorical.

The first objection, then, to the symbolic approach is not that it finds a Christian *sententia* in medieval literature, but that it assumes that this symbolic method is unique to the period and that there is no essential difference between literary works and theological or pastoral works. It misunderstands the nature of meaning and of literature. It neglects the concrete for the universal and assumes that the concrete exists only for the universal in a work of art,[8] which is

---

[7] As at least John of Salisbury and Hugh of St. Victor put it (see Paré, Brunet, and Tremblay, p. 116).

[8] ". . . All the senses are founded on one—the literal—from which alone can any argument be drawn" (Thomas Aquinas, *ST* i, q.1, a.10). "He [Aristotle] has to do this [criticize the obvious sense of Plato's words] because Plato's method of teaching was faulty; he constantly used figures of speech, teaching by symbols and giving his words a meaning quite other than their literal sense" (Aquinas, *Com-*

not true even of the Bible. It is as if one were to love a woman because she represented eternal beauty or eternal good. Her particularity—her figure, face, skin, and personality—is submerged in her "meaning." She is what Professor Wimsatt would call a "sign," not an icon. There is no "concrete universal" in the world of the symbolists, only the universal.

The second objection is that the emphasis on the symbolic as opposed to the literal⁹ approach to the Bible is not characteristic of the later Middle Ages, except perhaps in sermons, which are very conservative and must, of necessity, stress the moral. Although there are warnings earlier against neglect of the literal or historical sense of Scripture,[10] beginning in the twelfth century the symbolic method as applied to biblical exegesis underwent strong attacks, and in the later Middle Ages, except for certain standard interpretations dealing mainly with the prediction of Jesus in the Old Testament and the normal interpretation of any tale or event, the literal sense was the one which received the major attention.[11] In

---

mentary on De anima i. 3, lectio 8, trans. K. Foster and S. Humphries [London, 1951], p. 107). Cf. Wyclif (*De benedicta incarnacione* iii, ed. Edward Harris [London: Wyclif Society, 1886], pp. 37 ff., esp. p. 40), who argues for the importance of the literal meaning of Scripture. This attitude can be found everywhere in later Middle Ages (see below, pp. 87–88).

[9] In the earlier period the word "literal" had a much narrower meaning than it has in the later Middle Ages of today. We include a sense of the "plain meaning of the text" in the term; to the Middle Ages "literal" tended to be limited to the form of the words. "Most of the Fathers considered the meaning behind a metaphor not a literal but a secondary sense" (R. E. Brown, *The "Sensus plenior" of Sacred Scripture: A Dissertation . . . of St. Mary's University, Baltimore . . .* [Baltimore, 1955], p. 6). This shift in meaning explains some of the confusions in our understanding of what the Fathers mean by their comments on and practice of biblical exegesis. Yet Thomas writes: "Quamvis spiritualia sub figuris rerum corporalium proponantur, non tamen ea quae circa spiritualia intenduntur per figuras sensibiles, ad mysticum pertinent sensum, sed litteralem; quia sensus litteralis est qui primo per verba intenditur sive proprie dicta, sive figurate" (*In Job* [Parma ed.], XVIII, 6).

[10] See Henri de Lubac, "Sur un vieux distique, La doctrine du 'quadruple sens,' " *Mélanges offerts au A. P. Ferdinand Cavallera . . . à l'occasion de la quarantième année de son professorat à l'Institut catholique* (Toulouse, 1948), p. 352 n.

[11] Our recent awareness of this trend is largely due to the important work of Miss Smalley, *The Study of the Bible in the Middle Ages*, 2nd ed. rev. and enl. (Oxford, 1952). The author has emphasized the importance of the exegesis of Andrew of St. Victor in the development of later medieval biblical study. Bonaventure writes: "Qui litteram sacrae Scripturae spernit ad spirituales eius intelligentias numquam assurget" (*Breviloquium*, Prologue 6).

other words, at the time of the rise of the great vernacular literatures, we find a corresponding decline in the emphasis put on the symbolic method in biblical interpretation. In fact, both movements may be viewed as manifestations of a change of attitude in Western man, a new interest in the world of the senses and experience, which is seen in much else and which culminated in the Renaissance and the modern period.

Third, even in the period of its greatest use the symbolic method with its three- or fourfold levels was never mechanically or completely applied to Scripture. These levels should rather be viewed as possible ways of interpreting the manifold meanings in the Bible. All meaning at any time is multiple. The cross, for instance, can stand today for Jesus' sufferings, for Christianity, for the church, for the truth, for good as opposed to evil, and so forth. To attempt to systematize various possible meanings, without understanding what is involved, can lead only to a debased and mechanical interpretation of the highest mysteries. Such attempts reveal a profound misunderstanding of all historical study and, even though the Middle Ages loved system theoretically, medieval history in particular. Besides, in effect, no one can consistently apply the fourfold criterion except to a few hackneyed terms like Jerusalem.

One has only to look at the *Distinctiones*,[12] those symbolic dictionaries chiefly of the twelfth century, to see that there was no science of symbolism. The commonest objects and animals embrace a wide variety of meanings, often contradictory.[13] The meaning could be interpreted only in context, if at all, and even then multiple interpretations would frequently be possible.[14]

---

[12] See M. D. Chenu, "Théologie symbolique et exégèse scolastique aux XIIe–XIIIe siècles," *Mélanges Joseph de Ghellinck* (Gembloux, 1951), II, 509–526; and Smalley, pp. 246 ff.

[13] Augustine (*De doctrina Christiana* iii. 25) recognizes that one and the same thing (his examples are the lion, serpent, and bread) may have different and even opposing meanings; see also G. G. Coulton, *Art and the Reformation*, 2nd ed. (Cambridge, Eng., 1953), Appendix 18, p. 554, who refers to the sixteen meanings for the peacock and D. W. Robertson, Jr., and Bernard F. Huppé, *Piers Plowman and Scriptural Tradition* (Princeton, 1951), pp. 5–6, who point to the seven meanings of *dormitio*.

[14] Dante in *De monarchia* III, iv, 6, recognizes how easy it is to misinterpret the "sensum misticum."

It was also at all times recognized that the Bible could be taken symbolically only partially. Much in the Old Testament is literally binding on Christians, and parts of the New Testament must be metaphorically interpreted.[15] Although some parts and elements of the Old Testament were usually interpreted symbolically, there is no evidence whatsoever for a consistent application of any level-of-meaning interpretation in Scripture. One of the basic arguments for the truth of Jesus' claims is that he fulfils certain Old Testament prophecies and, in general, gives a profound (christological) sense to that collection of divine books. Typology, as it is called, is found in the New Testament itself where Old Testament prophecies and figures are applied to the fulfilment in Christ.[16] Certain other parts of the Bible tend to be morally interpreted. Babylon and Egypt, for example, are always the supreme types of evil. This interpretation is obvious and does not require any special insight or method beyond a normal intelligent reading of the text.

Fourth, the polysemantic school makes no difference between the Bible which was dictated by God in the form of the Holy Ghost and literary works written purely by sinful and erring man. There

---

[15] See Jean Daniélou, *Essai sur le mystère de l'histoire* (Paris, 1953), p. 211.

"Si vero aperte fidem predicat vel bonos mores astruit, sive hoc sit ita quod vetat flagitium vel facinus, sive sit ita quod utilitatem vel beneficentiam iubet, sive sit ita quod radicem omnium malorum exstirpat . . . non est ad aliud refferendum quasi figurative dictum, quia per hoc vigor eorum eneruaretur" (Ulrich of Strassburg, *Liber de summo bono* i, tr. 2, cap. 11, ed. J. Daguillon [Paris, 1930], pp. 59–60).

"We must discover first of all, whether the [biblical] expression which we are trying to understand is literal or figurative" (Augustine, *De doctrina* iii. 24, trans. John J. Gavigan, *The Fathers of the Church: A New Translation* [New York, 1947]). Gerald of Bologna in his *Summa Q.* XI, a.1, written in 1317, makes this same point (that the Old Testament is not always to be taken allegorically) (see Paul de Vooght, *Les Sources de la doctrine chrétienne* . . . [Bruges, 1954], pp. 425–426).

[16] For a study of the use of typology by the New Testament writers and its general background, see Leonhard Goppelt, *Typos: Die typologische Deutung des Alten Testaments im Neuen* ("Beiträge zur Förderung Christlicher Theologie," ed. Schlatter and Althaus, Vol. II, No. 43 [Gütersloh, 1939]).

St. Thomas Aquinas says that the literal is what the author intends, the spiritual what God intends. In the eyes of God the whole Bible is, however, clear and literal: "Quia vero sensus litteralis est quem auctor intendit, auctor sacrae Scripturae Deus est, qui omnia simul suo intellectu comprehendit: non est inconveniens . . . si etiam secundum litteralem sensum, in una littera Scripturae, plures sint sensus" (*ST* i, q.1, a.10, in c). This statement implies that only God composes polysemously. See below, next paragraph.

is very little evidence that the latter were written to be interpreted consistently in a symbolic manner, beyond the normal demands of literary figurative expression.[17] To suppose that medieval man would presume to put himself on the level of God in the writing of literature of whatever sort is surely most astounding. To think that he would write literature, which to him was both for *sentence* and *solace,* merely to convey profound religious truths clothed in many-colored "allegory" seems to me to involve a great misunderstanding of that literature and that man. I do not deny an occasional symbolic reference based on standard biblical interpretations, but to imagine a consistent and elaborate systematic application of a multilayered web of symbolism is unthinkable.

It is also true that certain classical works especially venerated by the Middle Ages, the *Aeneid,* the *Metamorphoses,* for example, were also occasionally interpreted by the symbolic method. Even these special cases, however, did not pass without protest.[18] No medieval writer would ever think of himself on a level with these masters, and the method was chiefly used to Christianize pagan writers. And no one ever maintained that Ovid or Virgil had put the symbolism there himself.

It must be remembered that the advocates of secular literature in

[17] "Auctor sacrae Scripturae est Deus in cujus potestate est ut non solum voces ad significandum accommodet (quod etiam homo facere potest), sed etiam res ipsas" (Aquinas *ST* i, q.1, a.10). Thomas specifically denies a spiritual sense in writings other than the Bible in *Quodl.* vii, a. 16, quoting Gregory the Great, *Moralia* 22. The whole point of the creed is that it is literally true on the authority of faith as interpreted by the church, unlike art, which is only metaphorically true. In one sense the Bible is not symbolic at all but completely literal, i.e., true. Cf. "In caeteris igitur scripturis solae voces significantur, in scriptura divina non solum voces, sed etiam res significativae sunt quamvis non in omnibus" (Conrad of Hirasau, *Dialogues super auctores sive Didascalon,* ed. G. Schepss [Würzburg, 1889], p. 75) and "sciendum est etiam quod in divino eloquio non tantum verba, sed etiam res significare habent" (Hugo of St. Victor, *PL,* CLXXVI, 790).

"In liberalibus disciplinis ubi non res sed dumtaxat verba significant, quisquis primo sensu litterae contentus non est, aberrare videtur mihi" (John of Salisbury, *Polycraticus,* ed. Webb, vii. 12, p. 144). I owe this last reference to Jean Misrahi's excellent review in *Romance Philology,* IV (1951), 350.

[18] See Paré, Brunet, and Tremblay, pp. 119–121. It was Macrobius who probably first suggested for the Middle Ages that the great classical poets consciously used "allegory" (see, on the allegorizing of Virgil, Pierre Courcelle, "Les Pères de l'église devant les enfers virgiliens," *Archives d'histoire doctrinale et littéraire du moyen âge,* XXII [1955], 5–74). Much earlier, of course, the Stoics and Alexandrines had "allegorized" Homer to their taste and no doubt set a pattern.

the Middle Ages were on the defensive. The pagan worldliness of much of it clashed with Christian otherworldliness, and those who loved the ancient poets were hard put to defend their poetry. The only way out, as the accessus and glosses to many a classical and pagan work show, was to argue strongly for the *utilitas* of such literature, and *utilitas* meant finding a moral meaning.

The medieval scholastics following Aristotle gave, in general, a very low position in the soul to imagination and a very low rank to poetry in the hierarchy of the "sciences." [19] To most, poetry was a branch of logic, but the lowest and weakest branch. This created difficulties, as Thomas' remarks show:

> The science of poetry pertains to those things which because of their lack of truth cannot be grasped by reason; therefore it is necessary that reason be almost beguiled by such similitudes. Theology, however, pertains to those things which are above reason, and so the symbolic method is common to both as neither is proportioned to reason [*In sent.* i. prol. a. 5.3].

Yet, having quickly removed the problem of certain similarities between poetry and theology, Thomas gives no more thought to this useless art. Those on the defensive were the men who, like Boccaccio, felt that they must defend the claims of poetry and could do so only by arguing that it contained a "sentence." Yet this argument was obviously never taken very seriously by the real thinkers of the Middle Ages, who were content to ignore the so-called claims of poetry as beneath reason and the concern of rational men, who did not need *ficta* to see the truth. Reason, authority, and divine revelation were the ways to truth. We have little evidence that the supporters of poetry did in fact interpret their poetry as symbolic, in spite of the theories of some of them.

Then common sense must step in. In a poem like *Piers Plowman*, as in many medieval literary works, the obvious technique is personification, not symbolism. Personification is making what is abstract concrete. It cannot normally have more meanings than what it says. If Mercy kisses Peace, what else does that mean than that

[19] See Ernst Robert Curtius, *European Literature and the Latin Middle Ages*, trans. W. R. Trask (London, 1953), p. 224.

peace and mercy embrace? [20] Symbolism is used but not in any wide and consistent pattern.

St. Eucher of Lyons is apparently the only patristic author who admitted that secular works could have levels of meaning.[21] All the other Fathers or theologians I have been able to examine, when they do not tacitly assume its applicability only to Scripture, reserve the method exclusively for biblical exegesis.

If the purpose of scholarship is to determine the historical circumstances surrounding a work of art and the probable intention of the author in terms of his background and the evidence of the text itself, then the burden of proof lies with those who would claim a religious symbolic multileveled meaning for medieval literature. If this is not the aim of scholarship, then, of course, there is no objection to finding any meaning or meanings one wants in the literary relics of the past. The really serious reason for opposing this procedure is the historical exactitude which is claimed or implied. One can, if one chooses, interpret a work of literature in any way whatsoever, provided that one does not claim to be thereby revealing the conscious intention of the author.

In view of the fact that the historical trend was moving away from the heavy symbolic interpretation of Scripture and that a secular tradition of entertainment and literature was very much alive in the Middle Ages, it seems to me that to believe that the medieval author would presume to write as God wrote through his chosen servants in Holy Scripture is the height of folly. This, of course, is not to deny that in certain literary works—possibly the *Divine Comedy*, in the case of which there is some evidence for the assumption, although not totally above question—the multiple method may have been used. It is, however, the task of the historical scholar who makes such a claim to substantiate it in each case. The *Divine Comedy*, if it is an exception, is almost the exception which proves the rule. It is significant, as Auerbach points out,[22] that Dante arrogates

[20] See Robert Worth Frank, Jr., "The Art of Reading Medieval Personification Allegory," *ELH*, XX (1953), 237–250, for an excellent discussion of this point as well as other related ones.

[21] See André Pézard, *Dante sous la pluie de feu* (*Enfer, Chant XV*), "Études de philosophie médiévale," Vol. XL (Paris, 1950), pp. 382–384.

[22] See his "Figurative Texts Illustrating Certain Passages of Dante's Commedia," *Speculum*, XXI (1946), 475, n. 5. Cf. "To claim to use the allegory of the theo-

to himself, against all precedence, polysemy—a special mission in keeping with his high view of himself as poet and prophet. Even in the *Divine Comedy*, however, it is impossible to work out a consistent fourfold scheme of meaning.[23] The basic and important meaning of the *Divine Comedy* except in the case of a few obvious symbols is its literal meaning. Individual symbols are often used therein in multiple senses, but this fact is not equivalent to discovering a consistent four- or threefold level of meaning. And, as we have already admitted, all meaning is, at least to some extent, symbolic. In every sin there is something of the sin of Adam; in every goal there is something of the Promised Land.

Nor do I mean to deny that in many medieval works a Christian meaning is aimed at or assumed, but this need not imply the acceptance of a multileveled system of symbolism, which in any case for the most part did not exist. The Christian meaning of medieval literature is usually very clearly underlined by the normal meaning of the words, as in Chaucer's *Troilus and Criseyde* or the *Divine Comedy*, where we are expressly told by the authors what the poems mean in Christian moral, dogmatic, or mystical terms.

The multileveled interpretation cannot be consistently applied to any work, including the Bible, without involving contradictions, omissions, and denials. The long history of biblical exegesis proves this to the hilt. To assume that a medieval author would be so proud and unperceptive as to take a system which is largely the creation of modern systematizing scholars and the mere repetition of

---

logians (as Dante did in his letter to Can Grande) is to remove *The Divine Comedy* from the category of poetry as his contemporaries understood it" (Joseph A. Mazzeo, "Dante's Conception of Poetic Expression," *Romanic Review*, XLVII [1956], 241; see also his "Dante and the Pauline Modes of Vision," *HTR*, L [1957], 275–306). Dante thought of himself as prophet rather than poet, and perhaps on a level with Paul and Moses (see also Curtius, pp. 221 ff. and 377: ". . . Dante believed that he had an apocalyptic mission").

[23] A recent attempt is by Dorothy L. Sayers in *Introductory Papers on Dante* (London, 1954) who presumes at last to tell the simple truth. She finds most astoundingly that the allegorical (in its narrow meaning of a level) sense has to mean the historical or political level of meaning (pp. 104–105) and gives us only a few generalized clues to this quadruple meaning that she claims to have found in the poem. A number of great Dante scholars have denied that there are systematic levels of meaning in the poem at all. I have never seen this fourfold meaning completely worked out in the case of any literary work, including Dante's.

patristic formulas and apply it to the composition of secular literature is most unwise.[24]

Literature has ends of its own, and even if in a Christian society
these are fundamentally Christian, they are not exclusively so. If
the work is felt as literature, it would belong to one or more genres
which had traditions of their own generally going back to classical antiquity. A work of literature cannot have been written fundamentally to expound in Bible-wise the truths of Christianity.
These would be assumed by the writers, or if Christian themes
were to be the main point of a work, as in, say, *Piers Plowman*,
these are openly discussed or at least in a normal rhetorical manner.[25]

Fifth, above all, the multileveled system of symbolism provides
no criterion of corrigibility except, as in the case of biblical exegesis,
tradition. There is no way, seeing the wide variety of symbolic interpretations of the same thing, to correct any particular interpretation. At the most, one might say a certain interpretation is not right,
but of many alternative explanations there is no way of deciding
which one is correct, for supporting texts from the wide variety of
medieval and patristic theology can be found for each one. Con-
sistency to some extent could, it is true, be used as a criterion of
truth; but, as the history of Dante scholarship abundantly shows, it
is easy enough to work out a variety of consistent interpretations of
at least cantos of a poem, and, in most cases, there is no way of deciding between them. It was this strong subjective element in medieval symbolism, which was so patently misused for various selfish
interests in the later Middle Ages, that, along with other factors,
led to the strong attacks on and even repudiation of the method
from the thirteenth century on, and by the Reformers. In the four-

---

[24] An easily available fourteenth-century discussion of the problem of multiple
meanings (of Scripture) may be found in the second article (pp. 43 ff., esp. pp. 46 ff.)
of *Quaestio de Sacra Scriptura et de veritatibus catholicis* of Henry Totting of Oyta
(d. 1397), edited by Albert Lang ("Opuscula et textus, series scholastica," ed. J. Koch
and Fr. Pelster [Münster i.W., 1953, editio altera]). Totting was much influenced
by English thought of the period—in particular by Scotus, Woodham, and Fitzralph.
His discussion of the question is surprisingly modern; he is well aware of the difficulties. He struggles to preserve the validity of the symbolic approach to the Bible. This
whole *Quaestio* reveals interestingly some of the doubts raised in Totting's time about
scriptural accuracy.

[25] See above, p. 90.

teenth and fifteenth centuries, the gloss on a biblical text was frequently treated as a joke.[26]

Mere assertion and the quotation of a theological or pastoral text are not satisfactory proofs. One cannot perhaps adequately prove any interpretation of literature, but if the words of the text are taken as of primary importance, there is always a court of appeal. With sixteen meanings for the peacock, who is to decide between them?

Finally, the assumption of the organized use of the symbolic method in medieval literature is essentially simplistic. It imposes a nonhistorical order and system on what was in fact disordered and unsystematic. The theologians of the high Middle Ages were saddled with a theory of levels of meanings from early Christianity and had to give lip service to the principle, but actually there was never any consistent application of that theory anywhere at any time, except for particular biblical passages, in Christian medieval exegesis and, above all, in literary composition.

I would like to conclude with the words of Roger Bacon:

> In sensu litterali jacet tota philosophiae potestas, in naturis et proprietatibus rerum naturalium, artificialium et moralium; ut per convenientes adaptationes et similitudines eliciantur sensus spirituales. Ut sic simul sciatur [sociatur?] philosophia cum theologia. . . .[27]

[26] Cf. the words of the greedy friar in Chaucer's "Summoner's Tale."
> "Glosynge is a glorious thyng, certeyn,
> For lettre sleeth, so as we clerkes seyn"
—*Canterbury Tales*, ed. F. N. Robinson (2nd ed., III, 1793–1794).

[27] *Opus tertium*, 24, ed. Brewer, p. 81. Cf. "Freedom of thought was not repressed in the Middle Ages. It was fostered by the allegorical method of interpretation, whereby the philosopher could connect his private theory with established truth" (E. K. Rand, "Medieval Gloom and Medieval Uniformity," *Speculum*, I [1926], 267). Cf. also Erasmus' attacks on the method in his *Praise of Folly*.

6. Episodic Motivation and Marvels in Epic and Romance

The clearly sensed distinction between early and high medieval narrative has been summed up in the terms "epic and romance." Although it is by no means easy to give a fixed date to the change, it is patent that an early epic like *Beowulf* of the eighth century is very different in technique, content, tone, and style from a romance like Chrétien de Troyes' *Ywain* or *Percival* of the twelfth century. *Chansons de geste*, most of which are commonly considered epics, continued, however, to be written as late as the thirteenth century; and the great Old Icelandic sagas which are clearly not romances were copied down if not composed in the same century. As one might expect, there is a chronological overlap between these two types of medieval narrative. Nevertheless one can speak of the twelfth as the dividing century, and the rise of romance can be considered one of the features of the renaissance of the twelfth century, which saw a new growth of culture and institutions and an interiorization of life and religion.

There have been various attempts to define and explain this change in narrative form, the most widespread of which attributes it to the profound social changes between the early and high Middle Ages, summed up in the concept of an heroic age giving way to a chivalric one. Epic is considered the characteristic long narrative form of the heroic age, and romance that of the chivalric age. There is no doubt that these two forms reflect a different age and a different sensibility. In subject matter, love is a driving force and a source of fascination in the romance, an element if not lacking, at least subordinate, in the epic. War and combat are the main concerns of epic, whereas in romance this subject of perpetual interest is supplemented by love intrigues, especially in a courtly love context. Since the time of the Romantics and particularly Hegel, another feature of romance was felt to be the notion of "aventure" and a sense of the marvelous. To the Romantic period, the element of the mysterious, of magic, of marvel was what gave medieval narrative its charm. The "blue flower," the unattainable ideal, the quest, all appealed to romantic minds unhappy with the developing industrialism around them and bourgeois acquisitiveness. Romance provided an escape to a finer and nobler world.[1]

[1] Although Hill ("Romance as Epic," *English Studies*, XLIV [1963], 95–107) makes a good point in stressing the continuities between epic and romance, few I

97

A more satisfactory and objective method of distinguishing romance and epic would be structural.[2] The purpose of this paper is to look more closely at the narrative fabric of some characteristic epics and romances to see whether a distinction made on structural grounds cannot be found and, if found, to try in some measure to account for it.

Narrative and drama differ from lyric and exposition in the emphasis they give to sequence and sequential action. Their plots occur through time and consist of episodes or events which follow one another.[3] Episodes may occur in lyric and exposition, but they are not of the essence of the form. Sequence links narrative to history since both move through time. Narrative in either dramatic or non-dramatic form is also more like the scientific view of the cosmos than other literary modes. This perhaps accounts for the mode of early Greek science which tends to present "natural science as a kind of epic poem, with beginning, middle and end." [4]

The problem of what is an episode is troublesome, but it need not

---

think would wish to go so far as to deny any fundamental distinction between the two forms. The classic treatment of the distinction between the two is to be found in W. P. Ker, *Epic and Romance: Essays on Medieval Literature* (London, 1896). Cf. the cultural approach in R. W. Southern, *The Making of the Middle Ages* (London, 1953), chap. v, "From Epic to Romance," pp. 219–257. On the love element in some epics, see A. Robert Harden, "The Element of Love in the *Chanson de Geste*," *Annuale Mediaevale*, V (1964), 65–80. On the epic as a reflection of the heroic age, see H. Munro Chadwick, *The Heroic Age* (Cambridge, England, 1912) and *The Growth of Literature*, I (Cambridge, England, 1932).

"The whole of this transformation into romance may be regarded as the intrusion into narrative of a spirit which likes to linger on the elegance of life and belongs to a society which tries to make its customs less brutal and its manners less forthright." C. M. Bowra, *Heroic Poetry* (London, 1952), p. 548.

[2] An attempt first made in the eighteenth century. See Arthur Johnston, *Enchanted Ground: The Study of Medieval Romance in the Eighteenth Century* (London, 1964), p. 234.

[3] I am ignoring the role of the persona if, as he usually does, he appears and makes comments on the action. This action, unlike description, diction, and characterization, is sequential and time-bound, but often in a different time from that of the primary action.

[4] Charles H. Kahn, *Anaximander and the Origins of Greek Cosmology* (New York, 1960), p. 199.

detain us long. Critics may differ as to how many episodes a plot may be divided into, but by and large I suspect there will usually be a large measurement of agreement on the subject. I am using the term in the broad sense, of any natural unit of action, any section into which a plot may be with some reason divided. Episodes may be in other episodes, as clauses may be in other clauses. A knight embarks on a quest and meets a number of adventures and finally terminates his quest. The quest as a whole may be considered as a macro-episode in which episodes are embedded. There may even be, as in some Icelandic sagas, several macro-episodes in a narrative. Episodes may be unusual or decorative or essential; they may be of long or of short duration. Some may consist of dialogue; others of described action; and still others a mixture of both. All sorts of complexity are possible, and the whole topic bears analysis. A narrative, of course, consists of more than episodes, for there are also descriptive passages which may slow down the action, and there may be comments of a persona or teller which punctuate an episode or act as a division between episodes. Episodes do, however, occupy a central role in plot and narrative analysis.

In spite of its sequential element, long recognized, it is surprising how little attention has been given to the analysis of episode, the progressive and basic unit in sequence. Aristotle's *Poetics* does, it is true, devote some attention to episodes in drama and to a lesser extent in epic. In discussing the latter, Aristotle is mainly, although not exclusively, concerned with contrasting episodes in epic and drama and with the role they play in giving each genre its characteristic form.[5] Since his time, episodes have been commented on but usually *en passant* or indirectly.

I have not been able to find any sustained analysis of the nature of episodes in narration. They were commented on—usually briefly —by the Italian Renaissance critics, but they were obviously in most cases a peripheral concern.[6] They were considered in the Renais-

---

[5] *Poetics* 1459a–b (23, 5–7); 1460a (24, 20); 1460b (25, 8). Aristotle conceives of the episode somewhat differently from the definition I use in the following paragraph. He considers it independent of the plot.

[6] See for instance, the various references to episode in Bernard Weinberg, *A History of Literary Criticism in the Italian Renaissance*, 2 vols. (Chicago, 1961). Inasmuch as Aristotle and Horace had touched upon the role of episode, there was a sanction for the Italian Renaissance critics to deal with the subject. Yet they make

sance down to the eighteenth century by many but not all critics, devices of amplitude, decorative means. Hegel has some things of importance to say about them in discussing romance.[7] Georg Simmel, the social philosopher, was fascinated with the nature of narrative and speculated on the sequence of episodes and their relation to each other.[8] In 1928 Propp in his *Morphology of the Folktale*[9] attempted a purely formalistic analysis of the folktale in which episodes were analyzed in terms of their functions in the folktale genre. Propp is concerned with a typological description which will fit all folktales. He also discusses character, movement, conveyance of information, and so forth. A basic morphology of the folktale is his prime purpose. All folktales are variants of one basic type. As is proper with folktales, Propp is not concerned with historical factors. From our point of view, his analysis, though interesting, is not of much help. Very recently, J. Swart has discussed *inter alia* episodic motivation in Layamon's *Brut*.[10]

The notion of *aventure*, a special kind of episode, has been subjected in the past forty years to scrutiny, notably in the work of Elena Eberwein.[11] Some extremely important work on the theory

---

surprisingly little of it. However see Maranta's discussion of episodes (*op. cit.*, I, 162–163); Fabrini's comments (I, 183); those of Ceruti (I, 227); those of Maggi (I, 410–411, 413, 417); those of Giraldi (I, 434–36); etc. In general, Italian critics were bedeviled by a rather narrow, Aristotelian concept of episode, which they regarded as adornment ("amplificatio") and extraneous to the plot. However, there are some exceptions, as for example, Maranta (I, 471 ff.). On eighteenth-century speculation, see H. T. Swedenberg, "Fable, Action, Unity, and Supernatural Machinery in English Epic Theory, 1650–1800," *ES*, LXXIII (1938–39), 39–48.

[7] *The Philosophy of Fine Art*, trans. with notes by F. P. B. Osmaton (London, 1920), II, 367 ff. (Part II, §III, Chap. III$_2$.)

[8] See Rudolph H. Weingartner, *Experience and Culture: The Philosophy of Georg Simmel* (Middleton, 1962), pp. 116 ff.

[9] Ed. Svatava Pirkova-Jakobson, trans. Laurence Scott, Indiana University Research Center in Anthropology, Folklore and Linguistics. Publications 10 (IJAL, XXIV [1959], Part III) (Philadelphia, 1958).

[10] "Layamon's *Brut*," *Studies in Language and Literature in Honour of Margaret Schlauch*, ed. M. Brahner, S. Helsztýnski, and J. Krzyzanowski (Warsaw, 1966), pp. 431–435. Swart also discusses somewhat the problem of the relation between epic and romance. Two recent structural analyses of narrative may be found in *Communications*, VIII (1966) by A. J. Greimas and Claude Bremond. The work of Elli-Kaija Köngäs and Pierre Maranda should also be noted. All these analyses have much wider structural goals than the study of the motivation of episodes.

[11] *Zur Deutung mittelalterlicher Existenz (Nach einigen Altromanischen Dich-*

of romance, with recognition of the role of adventure, has been carried out by Max Wehrli.[12] There have been other treatments of the subject, but as far as I know, none of them concentrates on the role of the episode. Even those works I have signaled out make the episode part of some other approach. The episode as a structural element tends to be ignored.

I shall be concerned with the interlocking of episodes, in particular the means whereby one episode is made to follow another: in short with the narrative motivation of episodes. The mere fact that one episode rather than another follows upon an episode is of great aesthetic significance. Simple juxtaposition can have a powerful effect, and barren juxtaposition produces barren effects. But this aspect—the effect of one episode or episodes on neighboring episodes—however important and closely related to my subject, will not be my concern. It requires the close analysis of particular narratives, critical assessments of a work of art. I am concerned here, however, with a broader task belonging to the theory of literature, not to literary criticism—the degree of motivation of episodes. Nor shall I be concerned with setting up a taxonomy of different kinds of episodes. For folktale, the motifs of episodes have been classified in a monumental manner by Stith Thompson,[13] many of which turn up

---

tungen), Kölner Romanistische Arbeiten 7 (Bonn and Cologne, 1933), esp. chap. ii. Cf. also Erich Auerbach, *Mimesis: The Representation of Reality in Western Literature*, trans. Willard Trask (Doubleday Anchor Books A107 [New York, 1957]; original in German, Berne, 1946), pp. 117 ff., and Erich Köhler, *Ideal und Wirklichkeit in der höfischen Epik, Studien zur Form der fruhen Artus- und Graldichtung*, Beihefte zur ZRP, XCVII (Tübingen, 1956), chap. iii, pp. 66 ff.

[12] See for instance, "Strukturprobleme des mittelalterlichen Romans," *Wirkendes Wort*, X (1960), 334–345, and "Roman und Legende im deutschen Hochmittelalter," *Worte und Werte, Bruno Markwardt zum 60. Geburtstag*, ed. Gustav Erdmann and Alfons Eichstaedt (Berlin, 1961), pp. 428–443.

[13] *Motif-Index of Folk Literature*, 6 vols. (Bloomington and Helsinki, 1932 ff.). Cf. also Tom Peete Cross, *Motif-Index of Early Irish Literature*, Indiana University Publications, Folklore Series No. 7 (Bloomington, 1952), and Gerald Bordman, *Motif Index of the English Metrical Romances*, FF Communications 190 (Helsinki, 1963). The classification of folk tales is even farther from my purpose than motif classification.

It should perhaps be emphasized that I am not using the term "motivation" in this paper in a psychological or character sense, but in a structural sense, which may on occasion include character as motivation. The motivation itself is not necessarily given in the first of two episodes but may be given in the second, often at the beginning of the second.

in epic and romance. But the motif is normally a smaller unit than the episode, and medieval narrative embraces more than folklore. A taxonomy of episodes would be more than a lifetime's task, however desirable it may be.

In order to characterize the motivation of episodes in the epic, let us look at some of them. *Beowulf* is unique in its length and early date and provides us with a good opportunity to examine the motivational interlocking of episodes in early epic. It is a tale of wonders, possibly even preserved because of its emphasis upon marvels,[14] but its mood is very different from that of the typical romance and its use of the marvelous. Perhaps one can sum up the mood or tone by calling it rational. At first sight "rational" may seem a curious and inappropriate word to apply to *Beowulf*, but I think the adjective is well chosen. The events in *Beowulf* may be unreal, but they are all properly and rationally motivated and presented *within the narrative*.[15]

Hrothgar is plagued by Grendel and needs help. Grendel as a descendant of Cain is naturally malevolent toward normal humanity. Beowulf, eager for fame, hears of the Danish dilemma, comes and destroys the monster. The monster's dam seeks revenge and is ultimately killed in her undersea lair by Beowulf with the help of a magic sword. After fifty years, Beowulf goes out and defeats a dragon whose treasure has been disturbed. Except for his trusty retainer Wiglaf, his picked *comitatus* deserts him. He dies in the combat and is properly buried. All is completely sensible within its own premises, allowing for the giants and the dragon. Every action has its proper motivation and is capable of rational explanation.

We can make a similar analysis of *Waltharius*, "a plain narrative proceeding from event to event without the creaking of machin-

---

[14] See W. W. Lawrence, *Beowulf and Epic Tradition* (Cambridge, 1928), pp. 14–15, and Kenneth Sisam, "The Compilation of the *Beowulf* Manuscript," *Studies in the History of Old English Literature* (Oxford, 1953), pp. 65 ff. (reprinted from *RES*, X [1934]).

[15] See J. Leyerle, "Beowulf, The Hero and King," *MAE*, XXXIV (1965), 89 ff. "For every action [in *Beowulf*] a sufficient motive may be assigned," Walter Morris Hart, *Ballad and Epic: A Study in the Development of the Narrative Art*, Studies and Notes in Philology and Literature, Harvard University, XI (Boston, 1907), p. 184. See the chart on p. 127 for a closer motivational analysis of *Beowulf*.

ery": [16] hence with rationality. This tenth-century Latin epic provides us, in spite of the language in which it is written, with one of our few early Germanic long narratives and bears comparison in theme and dignity if not in aesthetic merit with *Beowulf*. Except for occasionally stretching the long arm of coincidence and for the miraculous strength attributed to Walter in his combats, this epic is a perfectly clear-cut and rational story. Motivations and reasons are embedded in the narrative level itself. It contains many pleasant realistic touches and dialogues. Although emphasizing unnaturally Walter's piety as well as his strength, a moral purpose which is easily explicable when we remember the clerical or monastic profession of the author, the story is otherwise, allowing for a few miraculous powers already alluded to, a most natural tale within the rhetorical mould of the time.

Like *Beowulf*, *Waltharius* gives us no sense of mystery or the inexplicable; but unlike *Beowulf* it gives us no sense of fate or destiny which controls the action. Even in *Beowulf*, however, this fate is not mysterious but the given, the matrix in which a man must work out his predestined pattern. Fate is *within* the poem; it is not suggested or adumbrated; it is part of the point of view of its characters as well as, presumably, of its author.

The *Chanson de Roland* also belongs to this group of rational poems. We have prophetic dreams, a day miraculously prolonged, wicked incredible Saracens, religious sentiments, and a whole world of knighthood; but we do not have unmotivated or seemingly unmotivated action. The characters may betray immoderation and pride, but they act from explicable motives. Most medieval narrative claims in one fashion or another, occasionally even facetiously, historical validity, but the *chansons de geste* are even more sternly historical in claim than most.[17]

The older Norse sagas and the Irish sagas present certain difficulties in terms of our analysis. Both are extremely sparse in detail, and episodes tend to be rather short. The *Njalssaga*, which has certainly a historical basis, with its tragic story of Gunnar and Njal, gives a

[16] F. J. E. Raby, *A History of Secular Latin Poetry in the Middle Ages* (Oxford, 1934), I, 263.

[17] On this claim, see Morton W. Bloomfield, "Authenticating Realism and the Realism of Chaucer," *Thought*, XXXIX (1964), 335–358 (below pp. 175–198).

strong sense of complete plausibility in its motivation. The short episodes, told usually with a stark simplicity and restraint, all grow naturally out of each other in terms of the values of Old Icelandic society and culture.[18] The mysterious is not absent, but its center is within the story and involves various folk superstitions. Although the simplicity of the telling may occasionally make us wonder about its meaning, the story line is clearly rational throughout.

Much more complicated and difficult to analyze in these terms are the Irish sagas. First of all, the form of the tales in their fullest and most authentic manifestation is difficult to establish. Texts are incomplete and often late. Mangled and interpolated versions are not unknown, and much hypothetical reconstruction is necessary. Many consist of only one episode or macro-episode, clustered around various recurrent figures. Second, the brevity of the tales is frequently so great that episodes may seem unmotivated for that very reason. It has been suggested that this brevity was merely a reflection of the manner of their preservation and that the early written versions were mnemonic aids rather than the full tale as recited.[19] Third, the great antiquity of these works also leaves us with greater gaps in our knowledge than is the case with narratives of later times.

Nevertheless, "epic and romance go hand in hand in Irish literature."[20] There is much emphasis on marvel and strangeness in these Irish tales.[21] Fairyland is alive in tales of the mythological cycle. Above all in the *echtrae* (adventures) we find much unmotivated action and mystery. We find here an atmosphere close to the fairy tale and most of the fascinating strangeness for which the Irish imagination is famous.[22] The sagas proper on the other hand are on the whole rationally ordered and possess an atmosphere very differ-

[18] For a recent structural analysis of the Old Icelandic Family Sagas, see Theodore M. Andersson, *The Icelandic Family Saga: An Analytic Reading* (Cambridge, 1967).

[19] See, e.g., Gerard Murphy, *Saga and Myth in Ancient Ireland* (Dublin, 1955), pp. 7 ff.

[20] Myles Dillon, *Early Irish Literature* (Chicago, 1948), p. 1.

[21] "The ancient belief in magic, which notoriously has never died out in Ireland, pervades every form of Early Irish literature, corrupting the realism of the sagas and completely overwhelming the saints' lives." Vivian Mercier, *The Irish Comic Tradition* (Oxford, 1962), p. 12.

[22] See below p. 117 for more on the fairy-like atmosphere of these Irish tales.

ent from that of the *echtrae*. The marvels in the former like those in *Beowulf* and the *Waltharius* are, for the most part, rationally motivated and centered *in* the tales themselves. They are less realistic perhaps than their Germanic equivalents but no less rational. What we do not find or at least cannot ascertain is a more or less strict chronological division between epic and romance.

When we call epics "rational," we do not mean that they are "realistic." None of these early stories is realistic or naturalistic. They all deal with mythologized history not history. They claim historicity, but they are not historically exact. They reflect a movement from myth to history. "The episodes which had served a corporate, anti-individualistic bias [in myth] had to be brought into intellectual consonance with a less primitive vision of experience." [23] They are matter-of-fact in their approach to the unknown. There is an unknown, of course, to which we are all subject, but it does not usually take onto itself the meaning of the actions and events. The world is unmanageable or manageable on its own terms; it is not arbitrary or mysterious to the human observer of its irrationalities. Its actions however dark in their ultimate meaning are yet open in some fashion to human understanding and planning and some kind of control of them is possible. The hero may go down to defeat, but we know the steps and causes of his decline.

These epics have their symbolic dimension, of course, but at least on their primary level there is little doubt how to interpret them. We may be puzzled by the poet's attitudes toward his figures, but they encounter and endure explicable opposition of a natural or marvelous sort. The motivation within the story is usually clear; the motivation of the author may not be. We are, however, concerned with narrative not the authorial motivation. The latter will always be open to debate.

As Professor Greenfield has written of *Beowulf:* "The poem gives no sense that Beowulf moves through his heroic deeds in accord with a higher will. Rather, Beowulf's is an *historic* destiny, as are all the doom-laden movements of the poem." [24] Behind epic is the notion of following a pattern, *serving* one's destiny (overtly or

[23] Phillip Damon, "Myth and the First Plot," *Specirum*, VII (1963–64), 16.
[24] "Geatish History: Poetic Art and Epic Quality in Beowulf," *Neophilologus* (1963), p. 216.

covertly presented), and making use of all the clues and advantages the world offers us. The basic notion is serving and doing one's duty, not worshiping or wondering. Life is the framework of a man's destiny and within its limits manipulable; it is not, as in the romance, a dialogic encounter.[25]

In short, what is lacking in the typical epic is "aventure," the opening out to the unexpected, the encounter with the unknown. One point, however, must be made plain. The matter-of-fact attitude of typical epic never entirely died out; there is indeed much of it particularly in the later medieval romance. Unless a story is to be completely irrational, it must have some motivated episodes. Most episodes in romance fall into this category, but there are some, often of the highest importance, which seem unmotivated or weakly motivated within the story—inexplicable events which seem to have their center above and beyond the poem. There is a difference too in this matter between popular and courtly romance. Popular romances have fewer unmotivated episodes than their aristocratic or courtly sisters.

The differentiating quality of romance episode, however, is just the absence of rationality and its replacement by irrational or unmotivated episodes. It is these episodes which are properly adventures and which give romance their particular flavor from the point of view of narrative technique. In other words, romances tend to have apparently unmotivated episodes in them, often episodes of crucial importance to the development of the story.

The irrational episode, the adventure, when properly used, reinforces the sense of mystery which is often inherent in the subject matter of the tale. Unlike the mystery and marvel of the epic, the mystery of the romance is truly a mystery in terms of the narrative line. Something is happening about which we cannot be clear. In the eyes of God, in another dimension, all these episodes are no

[25] See Maria Bindschedler, "Die Dichtung um König Artus and seine Ritter," *DVJLG*, XXXI (1957), 100. Cf. "Nous pouvons constater en effet que, dans la *chanson de geste*, l'événement épique résulte de la decision de heros, tandis que, dans le *roman Arthurien*, il naît d'une constellation fortuite, bien qu'ayant une signification cachée, de plusieurs accidents que le chevalier isolé rencontre sur son chemin et que lui seul peut rencontrer," Hans Robeit Jauss, "Chanson de geste et roman courtois . . ." *Chanson de Geste und höfischer Roman, Heidelberg Kolloquium 30 Januar 1961*, Studia romanica 4 (Heidelberg, 1963), p. 72.

106

doubt explicable, but to human eyes, in the human dimension, something puzzling is going on. The center of the story is not within the tale but beyond it. The "meaning" of the action is not self-explicable but dependent upon the unknown. "Everything we see or read about is part of a wider canvas, of a work still unwritten, to a design still unfulfilled." [26] It is the victory of grace over reason, Augustinianism over Pelagianism, of the supernatural over the natural. The psychology of the ordeal,[27] the throwing of one's self on God, the "tempting of God" [28] (as was said of the ordeal), became victorious for a brief period of narrative glory.

The sense of mystery in the romance lies in many elements but a major one is the unmotivated episode. It creates or strengthens a feeling of strangeness and irrationality. One is forced to ask why and to find no answer; or one must acquiesce in the inexplicable. The mind seeks in general for reasons; and when none is found, one tends to attribute the event to an unknown power. One feels that some fundamental knowledge is lacking. Possibly the matter will be cleared up later or possibly never. If one were to be given some special information all would be clear. If this information never comes —and in medieval romance this is frequently though not always the case—one is driven to assume that if he were to see events from above or from another center the inexplicable would be explicable.

[26] Eugene Vinaver, *Form and Meaning in Medieval Romance*, The Presidential Address of the Modern Humanities Research Association 1966 (Leeds, 1966) p. 15. In this address Professor Vinaver is mainly concerned with the effect of "interweaving" or "entrelacement" in later medieval romance (the use of the macro-episode often in a most complex way), a subject not unrelated to ours.

[27] There is an extensive literature on the ordeal to which reference to the following will perhaps suffice: Karl von Amira, *Grundriss des germanischen Rechts*, 3rd ed., Grundriss der germanischen Philologie, ed. Hermann Paul 5 (Strassburg, 1913), pp. 269–280; W. J. Buma, *Het Godsoordeel in de Oud-Friese Literatuur* . . . (Groningen, 1949); Henry C. Lea, *Superstition and Force: Essays on the Wager of Law— the Wager of Battle—the Ordeal-Torture*, 3rd ed., rev. (Philadelphia, 1878); Jacob Grimm, *Deutsche Rechtsalterthümer*, 4th edition by Andreas Heusler and Rudolf Hübner (Leipzig, 1899), II, 563 ff.; A. Esmein, *Le ordelies dans l'eglise gallicane au IXe Siecle* . . . Ecole practique des hautes études, Sections des sciences religieuses (Paris, 1898); Frederico Patetta, *Le ordalie* (Turin, 1898); and Hermann Nottarp, *Gottesurteil-studien*, Bamberger Abhandlungen und Forschungen II (Munich, 1956).

[28] ". . . to attemte God overmuche I holde hit not wysedom," Sir Thomas Malory, *The Works*, ed. E. Vinaver (London etc. 1954), p. 176. The ordeal was often condemned, as early as the pontificate of Nicholas I (858–867), as tempting God, i.e., forcing God to render judgment.

In this sense of the mysterious other, life itself is reflected, life in its fundamental mystery. Life is both rational and irrational. The typical epic stresses the first, the typical romance the second.

Closely related to this sense is the notion of vocation—the call to action which comes from the unknown. The Judeo-Christian tradition has always emphasized the notion of vocation. One is called by God to perform an action and one must listen. The prophetic task is not chosen; it is forced on one. The prototype of all the faithful is perhaps the offering of Isaac story, the *akedah*, wherein Abraham humbly obeys the dire order coming from above. The mysterious, unmotivated to human reason, order must be obeyed if a man is to be true to himself. A man lays himself open to the instructions of a higher power. Man is tested by the unknown, and his quality is measured by his reaction to this test. A sense of vocation in diluted form runs through the noblest of the romances.

This sense of the mysterious never completely vanished from the romance, but it became debased as time went on and led ultimately to the piling up of episodes and contributed heavily to the disorganization and looseness of the later manifestations of the genre. Yet in some sense the power of the mystery persisted; and the genre through the use of the rogue, the "divine trickster" (as in the picaresque novel) and in satire (as in *Don Quixote*) was capable of self-regeneration. Then later the Gothic romance was able, in however degenerate a form, to continue the tradition. Kafka and Borges in our time are practitioners of the *aventure* type of narrative. The irrational side of life must take its revenge on the rational in literature as well as life.

This vertical rather than horizontal motivation needs further analysis, and perhaps by looking at a few romantic narrative themes briefly we may understand better the role of these mysterious episodes. In this paper we cannot unfortunately analyze closely one romance from this point of view. Unmotivated episodes are of various types. Some are completely unmotivated, others are inadequately motivated and still others are motivated backwards, sometimes adequately and sometimes not.

As an example of the first type we may take the mysterious combat so characteristic of medieval and particularly Arthurian romance. The hero meets an unknown knight and fights with him.

When we are later given an explanation, the mysterious quality vanishes; but when not, we are left with a sense of dissatisfaction and mystery. Playing on this sense will, of course, after a while bring a diminished return, but if used with skill, the unmotivated episode can arouse genuine interest and attention. Episodes like a maiden mourning over a headless knight, a night in a mechanical bed, a questing beast, mysterious ladies, can all enhance the appeal of a story.

The musing of Perceval over three drops of blood on snow is a good example of a weakly motivated episode. The explanation given in Chrétien de Troyes' *Perceval* is that they reminded the hero of his lady's fair complexion. Why the power of these drops should be so great as to put the hero into a long daydream is not adequately explained. We must accept it as a mysterious given. Yet an attempt is made to explain, however unsatisfactorily, this strange conduct.

Gawain and the Green Knight affords a good example of the backward motivated episode (in this case, a macro-episode) in the Green Knight's behavior, which is explained as due to Morgan le Fay's hostility to Guinevere and her desire to shame Arthur's court. As the scholarly debate on the subject reveals, this explanation leaves much unexplained. It raises more questions than it answers. One feels here a kind of compulsion to provide some kind of motivation without too much concern that it be adequate. It is a kind of gesture to rationality without any real commitment to it.

This gesture to rationality is often found—in the Grail procession and Perceval's repudiation, in the Arthurian sword in the stone, in Ywain's lion. Sometimes parodic rationalization is used as in *Flamenca* and *Aucassin and Nicolette*. Rationalization of episodic motivation may become mechanical, problematic, or vanish in some romances. The characters are more at the mercy of chance than in epic, and control over events within the framework of destiny or human limitation can become lost. The movement of the story tends to become more arbitrary. Things happen, things come to (*advenire*) one. Life may be a series of surprises at crucial points. Surprise and wonder has, as Wehrli has put it, become functional.[29]

[29] "Das Abenteuer ist sozusagen das im Roman funktionell gewordene Wunder, ein Wunder, das problematisch, der erlebt, das fruchtbar geworden ist." Max Wehrli,

Once again, I do not wish to suggest that there is nothing but surprises or unmotivated or poorly motivated episodes in the romance. Much of medieval romance is perfectly motivated, but at key points (as for example the beginning or within the tale when a turn in the action comes) we often find episodes of this type, especially before mechanization of action set in.

In classic romance, the rationality of the narrative tends to become suspect. Meaning is often moved out of the realm of experience and put into the unknown. Human action is no longer completely explicable within the limitations of human power, knowledge, and assumptions [30] but contains much that is inexplicable. This element of mystery which was introduced into narrative is best seen in the late twelfth and thirteenth centuries, for as time went on the mystery, as we have seen, became attenuated or mechanically manipulated. In later romances, we often have merely poor organization or mechanical surprises. However, throughout the Middle Ages, we find romances of a genuine power, conforming to the great early romances. As we have said above, the mode, even before its Renaissance transformation, never lost entirely its capacity of self-regeneration. England in particular shows this power notably in Malory. While none of the great early romances were written in English, from about 1350 on we find a number of remarkable romances the like of which are hard to find on the Continent. The alliterative *Morte d'Arthur* and *Sir Gawain*, and some of the *Canterbury Tales*, *Sir Orfeo*, and the stanzaic *Morte Arthur* are all worthy of the hey-day of romance. And in Malory's *Morte d'Arthur* we find a great and enduring masterpiece as late as the mid-fifteenth-century. Vida Scudder recognizes in the *Morte* the tone one of whose structural bases I am endeavoring to identify. She writes,

---

"Roman und Legende im deutschen Hochmittelalter," *Worte und Werte,* ed. Gustav Erdmann and Alfons Eichstaedt (Berlin, 1961), p. 434.

[30] "Epic narrative, in other terms, is a series of adjustments between the hero's capacities and his limitations." Thomas Greene, *The Descent from Heaven: A Study in Epic Continuity* (New Haven and London, 1963), p. 16. "The wonders a hero [in epic] might encounter could not appear too numerous or too farfetched." Gerald Bordman "Folklore and the Medieval Romance," *Folklore in Action: Essays for Discussion in Honor of MacEdward Leach*, ed. Horace P. Beck, Publications of The American Folklore Society, Bibliographical and Special Series XIV (Philadelphia, 1962), p. 38.

"Through the early part of the *Morte* a sense of hidden meaning is intermittent. It is conveyed largely through omens, prophecies, and hints of under-rhythm in the events. As the work goes on, the impression grows, till the whole story seems to move to some unheard music from secret places." [31] The Elizabethan regeneration of romance in Spenser and Shakespeare is another story.

Marvels and the unusual are part of both epic and romance; but they are handled differently in each. Besides their greater frequency,[32] the marvels of the romance are more truly marvels and their irrationality is emphasized and exploited artistically. This exploitation is partly obtained structurally by deliberately neglecting in one way or another motivation in episodic action at crucial points. This neglect helps to create a sense of the mysterious and to suggest another realm of meaning beyond human ken. The marvels of the epic are of this world. Nature is not the object of observation and discovery nor to be finally conquered and surpassed, but an active force under the control of fate or the unknown, part of an endless meaningless meaning. In romance, nature, especially the woods, is often the source of the strange. It is to be encountered and defeated in whatever form it appears. It can bring fulfillment and real success, or it can blight and destroy almost unwittingly.[33] It is opposed to the settlement or city as darkness is to light, as disorder is to order. It is the shadowy underside of life, and out of it

[31] *Le Morte Darthur of Sir Thomas Malory and Its Sources* (New York and London, 1917), p. 399. Cf. "Also characteristic of romance is the notion, frequently stated or implied, that the events in the world of the play [*Comedy of Errors*] are subject to forces other than those of normal cause and effect; that there is some magical reason for the errors of the action." Stanley Wells "Shakespeare and Romance," *Later Shakespeare*, Stratford-on-Avon Studies (London, 1966). pp. 58–59.

[32] "Dragons, giants, monsters of all kinds, hauntings, shape-changings, and sorcery are to be found in all medieval tales; *Beowulf* and the Old Norse sagas use them as much as the romances. But the romance writers probably exploit the marvellous more untiringly than any other medieval writers, and . . . they add ones less terrifying, and, when well treated, more subtle . . ." Dorothy Everett, "A Characterization of the English Medieval Romances" (1929), reprinted in *Essays on Middle English Literature* ed. Patrician Kean (Oxford, 1955), p. 10.

[33] See Marianne Stauffer, *Der Wald, zur Darstellung und Deutung der Natur in Mittelalter*, Studia romanicorum, Collectio turicensis X (Berne, 1959). pp. 9 ff. *et passim*; Robert W. Hanning, *The Vision of History in Early Britain from Gildas to Geoffrey of Monmouth* (New York and London, 1966), p. 158; and Jacque Le Goff, *La Civilisation de l'occident médiéval*. Les grandes civilisations (Paris, 1964), pp. 169 ff. ("Elle [la forêt] est l'horizon inquiétant du monde médiéval," p. 171).

comes all that is numinous, good as well as evil, hermits as well as dragons, salvation as well as damnation.

Because of its attitude toward the unknown, romance is more open to allegory and symbolism than epic. The symbolism of the epic is rather simple and does not normally suggest layers of meaning. Direct Jungean archetypes, if we want to look for them, do very well for epics. Good and evil, rebirth, regeneration symbols can be easily found. The allegory and symbolism of the best romances is much more complex and demanding and adumbrates more mysterious and often Christian levels. I do not wish to imply that romance is necessarily heavily symbolic and epic necessarily lightly symbolic, but there is a tendency in these directions. The symbolism of some epics is shallow, similar to that of comic books and grade-B movies, while that of the greatest romances approaches the depth of Shakespeare. Man is more naked and exposed in the romances than in the epics; he is in a liminal situation where the unknown hovers threateningly over him. He is in need of Christianity and of the merciful powers. He cannot rely on his own strength or on the rationality of the world as the epic hero can. Romance then is more naturally allegoric than the epic.

The hero of the romance is then typically called, has a vocation, unlike the hero of the epic who acts because he wants fame or renown. The hero of romance fights for himself; at a lady's mysterious command; at his king's order; because he has to. The hero of the epic fights for a rational object, a tangible return.[34] The motivational structure of the romance is often deep and below or above the surface; the motivational structure of the epic is shallow and on the surface.

If we look at this subject chronologically an interesting fact comes to light. The earliest of our long Western medieval narratives are more realistic motivationally than the later ones. The romances join in spirit and mood the fairy tales and märchen of the

[34] See Antoinette Fierz-Monnier, *Initiation und Wandlung, zur Geschichte des altfranzösischen Romans im zwölften Jahrhundert von Chretien de Troyes zu Renaut de Beaujeu,* Collectio turicensis V (Berne, 1951), pp. 13–15.

Western world which reflect in however obscure a fashion the values of a preheroic society or a society untouched by heroic values. The world of the supernatural, of the inexplicable which we find in the märchen emerges again in the romance. The romance shows certain similarities to the saints' lives, which we shall touch on below, but their closest and probably earliest narrative parallels in terms of structure (as well as of other elements not our main concern) are to be found in the märchen with its unmotivated or poorly motivated key episodes.

The assumption that fairy tales reflect a preheroic society or a society untouched by heroic values needs some discussion. The wide distribution of folktale motifs argues for a lengthy time of diffusion, even though we know that motifs can be borrowed and worked into tales. Yet the ubiquity and universality of motifs argue against this explanation in all cases. The presence of motifs in America and Australia tend to prove an earlier period of unity. The world of these tales reveals in tone if not in narrative detail a somewhat early period of time. Animism and certain types of magic must reflect in large measure an early society. Folktales are not inviolate and are upgraded to later times in realistic detail—by inns, houses and palaces, noblemen, towns, and so forth—but the existence of "precivilized" attitudes in them cannot be explained by contemporary life.

We are hampered by the fact that many folktales were not collected until modern times, yet medieval exempla of märchen quality and fairy tales do exist to testify to their age. The only reasonable explanation for the presence of magic and mystery in folktales is that in these matters at least they reflect a preliterate society and in some measure indicate a society unaffected by heroic values.

It is true that fairy tales often take a most matter-of-fact attitude toward life and marvels. They may often be, as Lüthi has observed,[35] one-dimensional. Yet this one-dimensionality of the märchen has often been remarked in the romance and in a way adds to the horror or strangeness of the eruptions of the supernatural into ordinary life. The strangeness and wonder of märchen is untouched by the

---

[35] See his *Das europäischen Volksmärchen*, 2nd ed. (Berne, 1960) and *Volksmärchen und Volksage* (Berne, 1961). Lüthi tends to think the märchen is fulfilled in saga or epic. I should say it is fulfilled in romance.

notion of divine control, but it has its own mystery. The notion of the divine center is probably the contribution of the saint's life and Christianity to romance.

Folktales and folk motifs are common in romances. We may observe them in such well-known English romances as *Sir Launfal* and *Sir Orfeo*,[36] not to speak of countless others. Perhaps this affinity argues for a similarity of tone and organization. But in any case it is this tonal and structural similarity that I am arguing for here, not the numerous specific borrowings. The similarity argues for some kind of basic return to an earlier (if we may assume the greater age of the märchen) point of view on the part of the romance.

Let us look at Grimm's "The Gold Children" (*Die Goldkinder*) which may be taken as a typical fairy tale.[37] A poor man out fishing pulls in a gold fish who promises to transform the man's hut into a magnificent mansion stocked with food and wine if he is thrown back into the water and if the source of the fisherman's good luck is not revealed to a single soul. The transformation takes place, but the inquisitiveness of the wife succeeds in turning their good luck to nought. The same fish is caught again, and the same routine follows. On the third occasion, the fish suggests a way of avoiding yet another disaster. He suggests that he be cut up in six pieces, two of which are to be given to the wife, two given to his horse, and two to be buried in the ground. The wife gives birth to two gold sons, the horse to two gold colts, and the ground produces two gold lilies.

The two children when grown go off into the world on the two gold horses and tell their father that if the lilies flourish they are well, if they wither they are ill. One of the boys could not stand the ridicule of the people and went back to his father. The other persists and outwits robbers by wearing a bearskin. Shortly after, in a village, he falls in love with a girl who agrees to be his wife. During the wedding the bride's father suddenly appears (where he had been before, we are not told) and in anger at the bear-skin-covered son-in-law wishes to kill him. With difficulty he is persuaded to de-

---

[36] B. K. Martin, "*Sir Launfal* and the Folktale," *MAE*, XXXV (1966) 199–210, esp. p. 205 and Dorena Allen, "Orpheus and Orfeo: The Dead and the Taken," *MAE*, XXXIII (1964), 102–111.

[37] I am using the version and translation in *The Grimms' German Folk Tales*, trans. Francis P. Magoun Jr. and Alexander H. Krappe (Carbondale, Illinois, 1960), pp. 307–311 (#85), in spite of its relative sophistication.

sist. Next morning to his joy he discovers a gold son-in-law, not a ragged beggar, in his daughter's bed.

The gold child had dreamed he was hunting a stag, and on waking determined to carry his dream into reality. Against his wife's advice and urging, he goes out to hunt the stag. He finds it as in his dream, but he cannot catch up with it to shoot it. In the evening the stag vanishes, and the gold child is left standing in front of a witch's house. Irritated by the witch's dog, he threatens to shoot it. The witch answers by transforming him into a stone, and his poor wife waits in vain for his return.

The drooping of one of the lilies reveals the danger he is in to his brother back home. The brother rescues him by threatening to shoot the witch when he finds her. After the retransformation, the groom goes back to his bride, and his brother to his father. The drooping gold lily straightens itself out.

It is hard to convey the tone and spirit of a märchen in paraphrase, almost as hard as doing it for a poem, but I think the unmotivated episodes do stand out clearly here. The gratuitous kindness of the fish, especially the third time, the meaninglessness of the quest out into the world, the irrationalities of the wedding, especially the appearance and actions of the bride's father, the motiveless quest of a stag and threatening of a dog, the inexplicable discovery of the witch's abode by the stay-at-home brother, all are unmotivated or poorly motivated. On the other hand, certain episodes are, within the magic framework, very well motivated. The changing of the fisherman's hut into a well-stocked mansion is properly if incredibly motivated by magic. Magic, it must be remembered, can be a satisfactory motivation. The golden lilies can theoretically spring from pieces of golden fish. Children want to leave home when they grow up. Yet there are also mere juxtaposed episodes where proper motivation is lacking.

As we have noted, romances contain märchen motifs [38] and share a proclivity for unmotivated episodes, but they also differ from märchen. Although many romances share the lack of psychological interest of the fairy tales, some romances do have a psychological element. In the fairy tale, we rarely have any sense of vocation in

[38] See, e.g., Lucy Allen Paton, *Studies in the Fairy Mythology of Arthurian Romance*, Radcliffe College Monograph 13 (1903).

the chief characters; and although it has a supernatural element, the action is rather one-dimensional. The supernatural in spite of its ubiquity is played down. Episodes are more developed in romance. In fairy tale, the episodes tend to be briefer. "Die Märchenhandlung schreitet rasch und entschlossen von Abenteuer zu Abenteuer." [39] Peasants take a more prominent role in fairy tales than in romances. Yet in a sense of the unknown, in a certain timelessness, and in the structural construction of episodes, romances and fairy tales share a very strong common bond.

The timelessness of the romance is frequently created by placing it in the far-distant past. The epic has a historical or pseudo-historical dimension. Even when romance uses a historical character like Charlemagne or Richard the Lion-Hearted, these are effectively moved out of time. Charlemagne in the *Song of Roland* or Beowulf are treated historically, as if their deeds really took place in a specific location or time. In romances, such characters retain only their names. In fairy tales, not even a bow is made to history. Their proper time is once-upon-a-time.

To return now to our problem. What accounts for the deviation of narrative from the spirit of primitive narrative and its kind of Hegelian return to it? Needless to say, there is no simple answer to this question, but I think some legitimate speculation is in order. What Germanic "literature" was like before the seventh or eighth centuries is unknown directly. That it existed and was carried on orally is quite clear. None of these performances has been preserved. We must only guess at their nature although we do have something to go on.

Beowulf itself tells us of scops singing or composing poems in royal halls. The scop appears as a persona in a number of poems such as *Widith, Deor,* and *The Wanderer,* which tell us about his life and something of his manner of composition.[40] References to Germanic oral poetry are found in Tacitus, Priscus, and Jordanes. Old Norse poetry preserves a good many references to these singers.

[39] Lüthi, *Das europäschen Volksmärchen*, p. 15.

[40] For a collection of material on the scop, mainly of Anglo-Saxon provenance, see L. F. Anderson, *The Anglo-Saxon Scop*, University of Toronto, Philological Series 1 (Toronto, 1903).

Most of this aristocratic oral literature has been lost, but we have written epics and other poems beginning in the eighth century which preserve some of its spirit and technique. Germanic heroic poetry with its historical and rationalistic bias may well have been called into existence by the crisis of the *Völkerwanderung* and the Germanic military drive of the early Middle Ages.[41] It might well have been a literary response to the challenge of the great migrations, performing all the social functions of early epic literature. Among the folk we may surmise a more popular poetry and literature, also oral, which appears much later in the form of märchen, fairy tale, and ballad. No doubt other types of literature flourished —victory, praise and procession songs, riddles and charms, wisdom literature of various sorts—but these are not my concern here.

The Celtic peoples during this period were more or less stable. Their migration period had taken place much earlier. It is possible that the fairy-tale element in early Irish narrative such as we have seen is due to this very factor. The Celts were not expanding against a harsh reality but rather contracting. Their higher level narrative was probably less clearly separated from its lower märchen level. They passed into their stable period before the Germanic peoples did. However, there were no doubt other factors involved including cultural traditions which make any simple answer impossible.

Perhaps the gradual settlement of the Germanic peoples and the decline of their expansionist drive led to the decay of this heroic poetry, allowing the more popular stream once again to have its head by entering into courtly circles and the romance. When it appeared in writing it was, of course, much changed by its class environment and by more sophisticated forms like romance and by ideals like social grace and courtly love.

The rise of the romance is a notable feature of twelfth century life. In some fundamental way the epic was no longer felt to satisfy the world-view of the European center. It continued to flourish at the periphery—in Iceland, Scotland (whose *The Bruce* and *The Wallace* are really retarded epics) and possibly Ireland—and persisted in debased form in France and England and Germany themselves. But it could not satisfy the deep needs of the age of Bernard

[41] This was suggested to me by Professor G. Storms of the University of Nijmegen.

and Anselm [42] nor of the Crusades. To trace the literary and ideational influences on this change is a complex task and only a few remarks, suggestive, it is hoped, can be made here.

The chain between pre-epic narrative and romance was of course carried on by the folk itself. But there was a written literature which had earlier made use of the fairy tradition: the saint's life. To this genre we must now briefly turn.

Because the genre is so heavily didactic and exemplary, saints' lives have more moralizing comments in them than the usual epic or romance. Because the truth element is so important, authenticating devices are more heavily stressed [43] in order to obtain as much credibility as possible. Because they are ideological, they are extremely selective in their details and episodes, with clear criteria for the inclusion or exclusion of matter.

Although the saints' lives of the later Middle Ages become closer and closer to romance in their expansion and treatment, nevertheless they never really lose their fundamental characteristics. Marvel is of course the stock in trade of the saints' lives. All their heroes are "called" and have their vocation. The realm of grace controls the realm of nature and even diminishes it; God's mighty acts are gratuitous and inexplicable to human reason. The motivating center is clearly out of this world, and human action testifies to a superior meaning of existence accessible in the Church.

The heroes are *milites Christi* just as some of the heroes of romance are.[44] Some saints are even warriors.[45] Even those romance

---

[42] See R. W. Southern, *The Making of the Middle Ages* (London, 1953), pp. 221 ff. The Crusade Wars were different in quality from the *Völkerwanderung*. They were ideological and had a national element in them. The peoples were more or less settled and went into the wars as Frenchman, Englishmen, and so forth with a local habitation.

[43] On this point, see M. W. Bloomfield, "Authenticating Realism and the Realism of Chaucer," *Thought*, XXXIX (1964), 344 (below p. 183).

[44] See Max Wehrli, "Roman und Legende im deutschen Hochmittelalter," *Worte und Werte, Bruno Markwardt zum 60. Geburtstag*, ed. Gustav Erdmann and Alfons Eichstaedt (Berlin, 1961), p. 435; Werner Braun, *Studien zum Ruodlieb, Ritterideal, Erzählstruktur und Darstellungsstil*, Quellen und Forschungen zur Sprach- und Kulturgeschichte der germanischen Völker NF 7 (Berlin, 1962), pp. 28 ff.; E. Delaruelle, "La pietà popolare nel secolo XI," *Storia del Medioevo*, Vol. III of Relazioni del X Congresso Internazionale di Scienze Storiche (Florence, 1955), p. 324; Paul Zumthor, *L'inventio dans la poésie française archaïque*, Leçon inaugurale . . . à

heroes who do not fight for Christ are sometimes "called" and respond to an inner or divine demand or urge. The atmosphere of both romance and saint's life can be very similar, and both far from the rationality of the epic.

And of course we find in saints' lives the same kind of motiveless episodes that we have discovered in epic. As Wolpers in his recent magisterial survey of English medieval saints' lives points out, causal and temporal relationships between episodes are often lax. "Sie [saints' lives] sind Teil eines höhern Zusammenhangs, gleichsam unmittelbar and vertikal mit der Überwelt verbunden, ohne allzu dichte horizontale, logische oder zeitliche Verbindüng miteinander." [46]

The similarities between saint's life and romance have been explored in some detail. [47] "Indeed, in the high Middle Ages, when

---

l'Université d'Amsterdam . . . (Groningen, 1952), pp. 6 ff.; also St. Bernard *De laudibus novae militia* PL 182:921–927.

[45] See M. Gyóni, ' Les variantes d'un type de légende byzantine dans la littérature ancienne-islandaise," *Acta antiqua, Academiae scientiarum hungaricae*, IV (1956), 293–313. Oswald of Northumberland is a good example of the heroic Christian warrior, at least as he is portrayed by Bede in his *Ecclesiastical History* III. Oswald is beloved of God; his piety and religion were exemplary; miracles were wrought in the place where he was slain; and a light from heaven guarded his relics the night the monks of Bardney hesitated to admit his bones to their monastery. Many other warrior saints and near-saints could be mentioned, as for example Odo of Cluny's *Vita Geraldi* printed in PL 133:639–704.

On the post-Carolingian resurgence of interest in saints, their lives and their roles, see Hanns Leo Mikoletzky, "Sinn und Art der Heiligung im frühen Mittelalter," *Mitteilungen des Instituts für Österreichische Geschichtsforschung*, LVII (1949), 83–122, who sees it as a reaction against the Carolingian Enlightenment and discusses some of its political implications.

[46] *Die englische Heiligenlegende des Mittelalters, Eine Formgeschichte des Legendenerzählens von der spätantiken lateinischen Tradition bis zur Mitte des 16. Jahrhunderts*, Buchreihe der *Anglia* X (Tübingen, 1964), p. 33.

[47] Notably by Josef Merk, *Die literarische Gestaltung der altfranzösischen Heiligenleben bis Ende des 12. Jahrhunderts*, Abhandlung . . . der Universität Zürich (Affoltern am Albis, 1946). See also Ludwig Zoepf, *Das Heiligen-Leben im 10. Jahrhundert*, Beiträge zur Kulturgeschichte des Mittelalters und der Renaissance ed. W. Goetz (Leipzig and Berlin, 1908). Almost all treatments of saints' lives (such as those by Wolpers, Gerould, Günter) touch on the subject. H. Sparnaay (*Verschmelzung legendarischer und weltlicher Motive in der Poesie des Mittelalters* [Groningen, 1922]) had earlier dealt with the subject at some length. See also Alfred Adler, *Rückzug in epischer Parade, Studien zu Les Quatre Fils Aymon* . . . Analecta romanica, *Beihefte zu den Romanischen Forschungen* 11 (Frankfurt am Main,

the legend and romance reach their fullest development, it is often very difficult to draw the line between them, as witness the more mystical portions of Malory's handling of Arthurian legend in the thirteenth to seventeenth books." [48] Throughout the whole medieval period, we find cross influences between the lives and various popular literary genres. There are epic, romance, exemplum, and courtesy-book types of saints' legends. At the same time, the legends differ among themselves. Some are more solidly historical than others, but most are to some extent based upon miracle and marvel.

It seems hardly necessary to illustrate the numerous examples of unmotivated (that is, by human standards) episodes in saints' lives. They are written over every page. Very frequently, especially in the earlier Middle Ages, the point is made descriptively, and we are specifically told that God has intervened on behalf of His champion. Yet the motivation of many episodes is left to the imagination of the reader—with the proper inference to be understood. The vertical pull so to speak in the saints' lives overwhelms the horizontal pull and orients the legend toward God's rather than man's realm.[49] In structural terms, this reorientation was largely effected by the treatment of motive. Motives and initiative come from above rather than from the environment and deepen the sense of mystery.

The allegorical or symbolic tradition of the early Middle Ages reinforced this orientation. Characters and actions are explicable in terms of an overarching realm of meaning, which is Christian and which directs everything to above. The meaning of events and episodes is found in an overhanging layer of significance which tends to isolate them in terms of the sequence of history and nature.[50]

1963), p. 19; and Ojars Kratins, "The Middle English *Amis and Amiloun:* Chivalric Romance or Secular Hagiography," *PMLA*, LXXXI (1966), 354.

[48] Helen C. White, *Tudor Books of Saints and Martyrs* (Madison, 1963), p. 21. For a specific example, see Joseph Szövérffy, "Deux Héros fédodaux: Perceval et Saint Christophe, Une légende médiévale et la poesie courtoise," *Aevum*, XXXVI (1962), 258–267.

[49] These pulls also operate, of course, in motivated episodes as well, but the vertical pull is always weaker when a rational motive is present.

[50] Inexplicably, Auerbach, *op. cit.*, p. 101, explains this isolation of events, especially in the Old French life of St. Alexis (*Chanson d'Alexis*), as due to the figural tradition. But the figural tradition as he himself has so notably pointed out in his essay "Figura," in *Neue Dantestudien* (Istanbul, [1944]), pp. 11–71), pulls hori-

Romance is more "naturally" symbolic and allegoric than epic. In a symbolic or ideological tale, the meaning can often be assumed, and bridges in the form of forward motivation or linking episodes may be omitted, creating gaps which give rise to a sense of isolated episodes or even jerkiness in development.

Ordericus Vitalis in his *Historia ecclesiastica* VI 2 and 4 gives us evidence that saints' lives could, in the late eleventh century, entertain knights as romances were to do later. He tells us of Gerald of Avranches, a clerk in the household of Hugh of Avranches, who had been invested with the Earldom of Chester by William the Conqueror. He was unhappy with the worldly life of Hugh's courtiers and tried to call them to God. "He drew both from the Old Testament and the more recent Christian records copious accounts of holy warriors who were worthy of their imitation. He described with eloquence the combats of Demetrius and George, Theodore and Sebastian, of Maurice, tribune of the Theban legion, and Eustachius, the illustrious commander of the forces, with his comrades, who obtained heaven by the crown of martyrdom." He also tells us in VI 3 of a story in verse concerning St. William (Courtnez) "which is commonly sung by gleemen." (Translations by Thomas Forester in Bohn Library version.) Ordericus disapproves of this popular version of St. William's life and contrasts it with a sober monkish *vita* of which he approves. These stories at the very least show that saints' lives were entering aristocratic circles in the period before the birth of the courtly romance and preparing the way for the new genre.

The two main literary sources of the romance in structural terms then are the fairy tale and the saint's legend. A possible third—the late classical romance such as *Apollonius of Tyre* which was well-known throughout the whole Middle Ages—must be discarded as a source for the unmotivated or poorly motivated episode. Although

---

zontally not vertically. A character or event points forward in time to another character or event which fulfills it. It connects events and characters along the line of history or action; it does not disconnect them. It is allegory or symbolism which does that. In saints' lives, the allegorical habit was demanded by the ideological and didactic aim of the work. It was no doubt early medieval Biblical exegesis which provided the pattern. For a useful little book on the Bible in this period, see Robert E. McNally, *The Bible in the Early Middle Ages*, Woodstock Papers, Occasional Essays for Theology 4 (Westminster, Md., 1959).

these romances are full of marvels, we find their episodes rather well, if not realistically, motivated. No doubt the odd unmotivated episode can be found in them, but on the whole as far as I can see it is rare. It is unlikely that, although they may share some episodes and motifs,[51] these rationally motivated tales were of much influence on the romance in this regard.

A number of other elements are part of the changes in narrative structure and atmosphere I have been discussing. I can do no more than briefly allude to them here. The Biblical notion of vocation and of the divine erupting into the world was always present to exert an influence when the world was ready to receive it. On occasion, Biblical narrative itself (especially in later books like those of Esther, Jonah, Tobias) could provide examples of abrupt episode for romance writers. The influx of Celtic material is probably a further influence.[52] The Bernadine revolution with its Song of Songs mysti-

---

[51] Although Faral's contention (in *Recherches sur les sources latines des contes et romans courtois du môyen âge* [Paris, 1913]) that the sources of the romance are to be found in classical narrative in general may or may not be correct, as far as episodic structure is concerned, one may well be dubious. Neither Ovid nor Virgil uses the mysteriously motivated episode even when the gods intervene in the world. A much better case can be made for the influence of Biblical narrative—but on this I shall touch only briefly.

An example of a probable influence of an event from classical romance, in this case *Apollonius*, on medieval romance may be seen in Isolde's falling in love with her tutor Tantris (Tristant) in Thomas' *Tristan*. For a recent important study of the classical romance, see Ben Edwin Perry, *The Ancient Romances: A Literary-historical Account of Their Origins* (Berkeley and Los Angeles, 1967).

[52] The subject-matter influence has of course been extensively investigated, especially by Roger Loomis. The structural element much less. Besides the unmotivated episode, the popularity of the "enfance" narrative may well be due to Celtic influence. In the *Táin Bó Cúailnge*, (The Cattle-Raid of Cooley) we have an interruption in the Tale of Cú Chulainn's exploits to tell us of his mac-gnímrada ("boyhood deeds"). The early Celtic saints' lives also stressed the boyhood of their heroes—an emphasis found in English and continental saints' lives, especially of the tenth century and later. See Charles Plummer, *Bethada náem nÉrenn*, Lives of Irish Saints, Edited from the Original MSS . . . 2 vols. (Oxford, 1922), especially Lives of Maedoc of Ferns (II, 177 ff.), of Coemgen (I, 121 ff.), Bairre of Cork (II, 11 ff.), of Mochuda (II, 282 ff.), Ciaran of Saighir (II, 99 ff.). For a twelfth-century Norman example, see Gaufridus de Fontibus, *Liber de infantia Sancti Eadmundi*, ed. Th. Arnold in *Memorials of St. Edmund's Abbey* RS (London, 1890), I, 93–103. See also H. Günter, *Psychologie de la legende: Introduction à une hagiographie scientifique, Formes antiques* . . . Traduction de J. Goffinet, Bibliothèque scientifique (Paris, 1954) (Translation of *Psychologie der Legende*, 1949), pp. 96 ff. This section (pp. 94–151) discusses the notion of election or vocation in saints' legends.

122

cism and its emphasis upon grace and the mystery of God's power is no doubt also part of romance background. A resuscitation of interest in Boethius and a re-evaluation of *Fortuna* also contributed to the narrative revolution of the twelfth century.

Howard Patch has pointed out that *Fortuna* even in classical times had a two-fold meaning—fate and chance.[53] The chance notion was dominant at the end of the classical period. As we might expect, the earlier Middle Ages reversed the emphasis, as we can see in King Alfred's translation of Boethius and elsewhere. Fortune was inveighed against and when accepted was assimilated to Christian providence. It is only in the high Middle Ages when romance began to flower that the submerged meaning of fortune—chance—again emerged, and the fickleness of the Goddess is emphasized again and again. It is hard to say what is cause and what is effect. The shift in the notion of fortune may reflect the same change in attitude that created the romance or it may have been a cause. Probably there were mutual influences, but the facts themselves reveal nicely that the arbitrariness of life which appears in both the figure of fortune and in the genre of romance is once again being emphasized.

At the beginning of this paper, we discussed briefly other changes —the growth of mysticism, the decline of semi-Pelagianism, the emphasis on grace—in the intellectual climate which reflected or produced a new/old type of motivation in the structure of narrative. A full treatment of these subjects would require a new book on the Renaissance of the twelfth century. I think it is sufficient here merely to have indicated some of these forces making for change.

A fascinating example of the shift may be seen in the Latin narrative *Ruodlieb*, which was written after 1050 in Germany. This work, which is incomplete, provides an excellent example of the impingement of fairy tale upon epic. Ruodlieb, a young nobleman, leaves his home because of ill-treatment to seek his fortune. Aided by a hunter, he meets a king who is noble in character and deed. He wins his confidence and with courtly grace defeats for his new master an enemy margrave. The king is as magnanimous as Ruodlieb, and peace is re-established. Ten years later, Ruodlieb receives a letter from his homeland begging for his return. The king gives him

[53] See *The Goddess Fortuna in Mediaeval Literature* (Cambridge, 1927), pp. 10 ff.

123

two loaves of bread, stuffed, unknown to the recipient, with treasure and tells him not to break them until he arrives home. He is also given twelve pieces of wisdom exemplified by adages such as don't trust a red-bearded man, don't ride through cultivated fields, and don't stay with an old man married to a young wife. By observing these odd bits of wisdom, Ruodlieb arrives home safely and finds his treasure intact.

The tale is full of marvels like clever blackbirds, trained bears, a dwarf, an intelligent jackdaw. Yet the story of the war is relatively rational and well motivated. The hero has many traits of the Germanic hero, but the total impression is that of romance. Yet it is romance with a difference. Some critics have also seen in *Ruodlieb* the influence of the saint's life.[54] This early narrative, written down sometime in the period when epic was shifting to romance, is a most revealing mixture of the various elements which were working to create the romance. F. J. E. Raby rightly calls it a "romantic epic." [55]

❧

The structure of Western medieval narrative as revealed in the motivation of episodes seems, then, to have developed chronologically in the following way. We assume on the basis largely of fairy tale and märchen, a prewritten oral period in which unmotivated or

[54] Recently, notably Werner Braun, in *Studien zum Ruodlieb: Ritterideal, Erzählstruktur und Darstellungsstil*, Quellen and Forschungen zur Sprach- und Kulturgeschichte der germanischen Völker, NF 7, 1962.

[55] *A History of Secular Latin Poetry in the Middle Ages* (Oxford, 1934), I, 395. Since writing this essay, I have read "The Definition of Romance" by Nathaniel E. Griffin in *PMLA*, XXXVIII (1923), 50–70, who though noting some differences, such as the historicity of the epic and lack of interest in credibility by the romance writers, between the two genres finally comes down to a social explanation of the distinction. "The epic is the characteristic product of a people that has lived an isolated existence cut off from contact with other peoples. . . . The romance, on the other hand, is the characteristic product of a people that has come into contact with an alien civilization and that has allowed its ancestral traditions to be contaminated, if not altogether undermined, by the infiltration of new ideas" (p. 57), a highly dubious theory. He also tends to favor a masculine as opposed to the feminine or mixed audience theory to explain some of the differences, a more likely point certainly. In many studies of the matter, the distinction between formal and substantive differences and the reasons for these differences is not always clearly maintained.

poorly motivated episodes are to be found. This period was probably coterminous with purely mythic narrative, and the literary
forms, though probably separate, overlapped. Then arose the crisis
provoked by the *Völkerwanderung* period of the Germanic peoples,
which produced a new and more sober view of human action and
motivation. Possibly the earlier Celtic expansion had produced
among the Celts a similar literary reaction; but Celtic expansion was
over before the Germanic one began. The German expansion was
primarily directed against peoples of superior civilization and settled
life. This contact produced after various lapses of time a Christian-
ization of the Germanic peoples. From a literary point of view, this
meant taking over a vast body of literature, mainly the Bible and
saints' lives. The more permanent settling of the Germanic peoples,
though hardly ushering in a peaceful period, did allow once again
the more arbitrary view of life of the fairy tale to prevail, but very
much changed by contact with Christianity and its view of vocation and grace especially stressed by the Church beginning in the
twelfth century. Added to these, Celtic materials exercised a new
fascination in Europe and fitted in with the Christian view of God's
overarching power. With the Renaissance of the twelfth century
and all it implied, these forces created the romance—a new literary
genre which could allow room for the mysterious and the arbitrary.

The picture presented above is highly speculative. The facts such
as we have presented are not. There was a change in structural organization between epic and romance. This change may not be explicable at all, but as long as we believe in some kind of historical
meaning to the events in human culture we must attempt some explanation. If it is not acceptable, then we must try again. That episodes were conceived differently in the periods of epic or romance
can, in any case, be hardly doubted. This essay is fundamentally a
contribution to the understanding of these two genres and only sec-
ondarily an attempt to explain them.

APPENDIX

In order to make more precise episodic and motivational analysis,
I should like to propose a system for visually presenting episodes
and their motivation. It is found in the first chart and is applied in

Sigla for Narrative Motivation

M = macro-episode   **e** = episode   **m** = micro- or sub-episode

X = non-episodic materials (pure descriptions, persona comments, etc.)

Line under **M, e, m** indicates subordinate or embedded **M, e, or m**

$\longrightarrow$ = Prepares way for

$\searrow\!\!\!\nearrow$ = Motivates second episode adequately in either of the two consecutive linked episodes though usually in the first

$\searrow\!\!\!\swarrow$ = Motivates adequately backward

$\cdots\!\!\!\nearrow$ = Motivates inadequately or poorly

The absence of links between any two consecutive episodes indicates the absence of motivation.

the second to a good part of *Beowulf*. Several points should be noted as general background, although I think the charts are more or less self-explanatory. First of all, no true gradient of motivation is presented. I have offered only three motivational states between episodes—fully or adequately motivated (either forward or backward), poorly or inadequately motivated, and no motivation at all. At present I do not see how various degrees of adequate motivation can be visually presented. Perhaps in the future a quantitative method or at least a more discriminating method can be evolved. Second, I do have a fourth state called "prepares way for," when no level of motivation seems to apply and yet some kind of introduction to the next episode is being made. A good example is the genealogical opening of the poem (e) which properly prepares the way for the combat with Grendel (e_1).

Third, the sigla M, e, m all represent relative states, for example, a macro-episode (M) can be embedded in an ordinary episode (e) if it contains within itself further episodes. The terms are used relative to the episodes above and below an episode. Usually episodes of greater derivational complexity than normally expected are indicated by underlining. I have listed the siglum X in order to indicate non-narrative parts of narrative, such as comments by the persona or pure descriptions. However, in the sample *Beowulf* chart I have not used it at all. Actually when the interjections and interruptions are as brief as they are in the *Beowulf* narrative, it seems hardly worthwhile to indicate these passages in any "broad" transcription of episode and motivation.

Fourth, when an episode is broken up by another episode the subscripts a and b are used to indicate the connection of the sepa-

126

Chart of Narrative Motivation in Beowulf

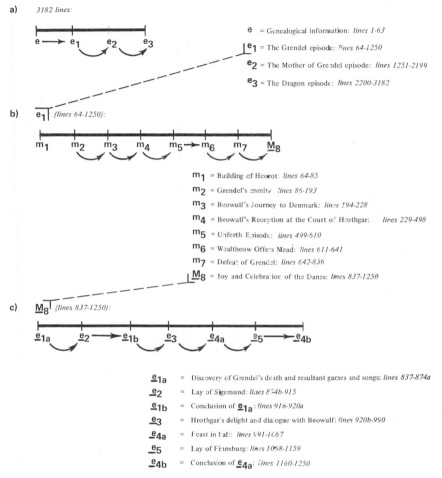

a) *3182 lines:*

e = Genealogical information: *lines 1-63*

e_1 = The Grendel episode: *lines 64-1250*

e_2 = The Mother of Grendel episode: *lines 1251-2199*

e_3 = The Dragon episode: *lines 2200-3182*

b) e_1 *(lines 64-1250):*

m_1 = Building of Heorot: *lines 64-85*

m_2 = Grendel's enmity: *lines 85-193*

m_3 = Beowulf's Journey to Denmark: *lines 194-228*

m_4 = Beowulf's Reception at the Court of Hrothgar: *lines 229-498*

m_5 = Unferth Episode: *lines 499-610*

m_6 = Wealtheow Offers Mead: *lines 611-641*

m_7 = Defeat of Grendel: *lines 642-836*

$\underline{M}_8$ = Joy and Celebration of the Danes: *lines 837-1250*

c) $\underline{M}_8$ *(lines 837-1250):*

$\underline{e}_{1a}$ = Discovery of Grendel's death and resultant games and songs: *lines 837-874a*

$\underline{e}_2$ = Lay of Sigemund: *lines 874b-915*

$\underline{e}_{1b}$ = Conclusion of $\underline{e}_{1a}$: *lines 916-920a*

$\underline{e}_3$ = Hrothgar's delight and dialogue with Beowulf: *lines 920b-990*

$\underline{e}_{4a}$ = Feast in hall: *lines 991-1067*

$\underline{e}_5$ = Lay of Finnsburg: *lines 1068-1159*

$\underline{e}_{4b}$ = Conclusion of $\underline{e}_{4a}$: *lines 1160-1250*

rated parts. See above under M_8 when e_{1a} is interrupted by e_2 and picks up again as e_{1b}. This interjection is the interruption of the games celebrating the death of Grendel by the Lay of Sigemund.

Looking at the *Beowulf* chart, one can easily see the almost universally adequate motivation of the episodes in the epic of whatever location on the chart. Although e_2 and e_3 are not broken down into subepisodes, only m_2, in the overall episodic pattern and in the breakdown of e_1 and M_8, seems not to be motivated vis-à-vis its preceding episode (m_1)—that is, only the enmity of Grendel is un-

127

motivated in my reading of the poem as far as I have analyzed it. There are, furthermore, four links "preparing the way for." In every other case except these five examples we have adequate motivation. In terms of episodic motivation, we may say then that *Beowulf* is well motivated. I wish to point out, however, that in any two consecutive episodes motivation is not always in the precedent episode but may be in the sequent (that is, motivated) episode itself.

It may also be said that this *Beowulf* chart provides an example of tree analysis of narrative, perhaps even with binary oppositions, since, for example, e_1 and e_2 easily unite against e_3 and on the lowest [c)] level we have the total narrative line broken into units. However, in contrast to generative grammar, the lower branches are not due to rewrite rules, but rather indicate the divisions present in the upper branch or trunk relative to each.[56]

[56] Raymond S. Willis, Jr., in *The Phantom Chapters of the Quijote* (New York, 1953), makes an interesting analysis of connection of the chapters in *Don Quixote* in which he finds a variety of means of passage from one to the other. This monograph has just been brought to my attention. Willis does not especially concentrate on motivations.

III. Chaucer and Fourteenth-Century English Literature

7. Sir Gawain and the Green Knight: An Appraisal

The bridge
Lunged over the river into the green chapel.
But the ignis fatuus of a happy ending thawed
The icicle that kept his heart together,
The marrow of despair hissed out of his bones
—Patricia Beer, "Sir Gawain"

In spite of its language which is admittedly difficult and in spite of certain problems of literary history which beset it, *Sir Gawain and the Green Knight* has never been considered hard to interpret as a work of art.[1] The apparent obviousness of its genre and its combination of apparently straight-forward narrative and notable passages of description do not lead one to suspect that complicated problems of intention or meaning are lurking beneath its vivid and attractive poetry. *Piers Plowman*, everyone agrees, is a difficult poem and has, at least since the sixteenth century, been recognized as such. Those who are attracted to it are stimulated to probe its significance and to elucidate its mysteries. No such stimulus comes to the much larger group who enjoy and study *Sir Gawain*, for, although much has been written on it, it has always been considered a relatively uncomplicated, beautifully organized, and masterfully presented obvious poem. Yet the more one studies *Sir Gawain* and ponders on its charms and organization the more one begins to wonder and speculate. Of course in one sense all literary or artistic masterpieces are miracles and occasion for wonder, but above and beyond the pleasure and surprise which come from great achievement and the feeling of perfection, some works create a peculiar sense of intellectual puzzlement as to the author's intention and tone and even on a more prosaic level as to the tie between a work and its milieu: intellectual, artistic, and social.

While I do not wish to suggest that *Sir Gawain* is as much of a problem as is *Piers*, I do contend that it contains many more complexities and puzzles than have hitherto been recognized. One gets the impression that criticism has not yet really come to grips with the romance. The purpose of this paper is to point to some of these difficulties, not all previously unrecognized, to relate them to current and past scholarship and criticism on the poem, and to suggest some possible solutions. Although I may do so later, I do not intend

Reprinted by permission of the Modern Language Association of America from *PMLA*, LXXVI (1961), 7–19.

[1] This paper is a longer version of a speech delivered before English Section I at the MLA convention in Chicago, December 1959. I am much indebted to Professors John Conley, A. L. Kellogg, F. L. Utley, and R. M. Estrich for various suggestions and criticism. I also owe a great debt to the members of a seminar in the romance held in the fall of 1959 at Ohio State University: Sarah Appleton, Louis Sheets, and Robert Hall.

now to develop at any length the suggestions here put forth. At the worst we may get some idea as to where we stand at present in *Gawain* studies, and at the best some suggestions for fruitful future work. Needless to say, my choice of subjects and contributions is selective and is not meant to deny the importance of those which I do not mention here.

Although not considered complicated, *Sir Gawain* has not been neglected by interpreters and scholars in the hundred and twenty years since Sir Frederic Madden rescued it, in his edition of the poem, from the oblivion into which it had fallen for many centuries. On the contrary, since 1839 it has been the subject of much interest to both literary historians and the literate English-speaking public, as the size of a fairly complete *Gawain* bibliography—some two hundred and fifty items not counting numerous incidental references—shows. In recent years, we find, as is general at present, a heavy shift of interest toward criticism of the poem and toward a stress on its meaning and structure.

We are all so busy appreciating poems today that we tend to neglect philology, upon the basis of which everything which may be drawn from literary documents rests. Philology must remain the basis of all sound literary work or we shall end in a morass of subjectivism. It was just this subjectivism and impressionism which led in the late nineteenth century to the application of positivism to literary study. To avoid the swing of the pendulum between a soulless objectivity and a pure subjectivity, we must at present stress the value of philological study, especially of the older literature. However, philology has never been, and especially today, cannot be, a purely mechanical task, although certain mechanical studies are of great help to it. Philology must be guided, especially in translation work, by a feeling for literary values and a sense of rhetorical probability.

The three main philological activities in older literature are the establishment of a text, the identification of the dialect, and the determination of the meaning of the words of a document. As to the former, in the case of *Sir Gawain,* we are pretty much limited to what a close reading and interpretation of the one manuscript which contains the romance—B.M., Cotton Nero A.x—can tell us. In general we may say that unless a new manuscript of the poem turns up little remains to be done. A few reinterpretations of min-ims and letters, a few emendations can still be expected, but as far as an accurate reading of the only manuscript can take us, we have a satisfactory text. In the case of this manuscript, infrared photogra-phy may help us a little, especially to get under blots which disfigure part of the text. It is surprising what a very careful rereading of an original manuscript can do; and a keen eye and keen wit may yet turn up a few new readings. But Cotton Nero A.x has not been neg-lected in the past and to expect too much from this line of endeavor would surely be a mistake.

On the other hand, I think we may hope for a number of pleas-ant surprises from future work on the meaning and identification of the language of the poem. *Sir Gawain* is written in a difficult dialect which is not preserved in many documents. The whole state of Mid-dle English dialect study is in an unsatisfactory position, partly be-cause of factors beyond our control, like the paucity of documents, and partly because of factors under our control, like the absence of adequate tools. The latter is now being remedied, but it will still be some time before the *Middle English Dictionary* is complete, the study of English place names finished, and a linguistic atlas of Eng-land begun. We still need a fairly complete dialect dictionary of English. These difficulties beset all Middle English studies, but, be-cause of the rarity of raw material and its innate difficulties, North West Midland is particularly affected. But, in spite of this, help is on the way, and the *MED* offers the most immediate prospect of relief. We have hardly yet exploited what has been printed there and what lies still unprinted in its files, in elucidating *Sir Gawain*. The wealth of material present and yet to come in the *MED* offers the most promising path for a solution of the number of *cruces* in which the poem abounds.

Even with the material we already have, we have not completely exploited the possibilities. In spite of Mrs. Wright's plea, we still have not made enough use of the *English Dialect Dictionary* [2] for the light it may cast on the vocabulary of the poem. Place-name study and the linguistic atlas are further promised aids. Place-name study, of course, will be primarily important for the contribution it can bring to clarifying Middle English dialects, not for the elucida-

<hr>

[2] "Sir Gawain and the Green Knight," *JEGP*, XXXIV (1935), 161.

tion of place-names in the poem.[3] The linguistic atlas should enable us to localize more exactly the dialect of the poem and explain some of the hard words.

However, the problem is not merely to know the meaning of a large number of unusual words but also to understand properly their connotations. To translate *Sir Gawain* involves, of course, not merely a knowledge of Old and Middle English, Old Norse, Old French, and modern English and Scottish dialects, but an interpretation of the poem and a feeling for rhetorical fitness. The context determines the exact meaning of a word or the choice of alternatives; and this means a knowledge of the semantic environment of that word. The determining of context and texture demand a literary sensitivity and a common sense which have not always been applied to the interpretation of the basic meaning of *Sir Gawain* in modern English.

A good example of this matter may be seen in the question of how to translate "wonder" in line 16 of the poem. There is no problem here as to the basic meaning as the word is well-known. The general sense here is probably, as *NED* puts it, "an astonishing occurrence, event, or fact," but philological scholarship has wavered between taking the astonishment as due to a good or bad cause. In other words should we translate the word as "marvel" or as "crime," both of which are "astonishing occurrences." Both meanings have support in Middle English lexicography.

Following Joseph Hall, Mrs. Wright suggested for the first time in an article in 1935 [4] that it should be translated as "sorrow," "distress," or "crime," instead of as in its modern sense, making the lines read in modern English, "Britain . . . where war, vengeance and crime at times have dwelled therein." Earlier editors read "where war, vengeance, and marvels," etc. She established without difficulty other similar uses of the word and appealed to the whole line to support the rationality of her translation. But Adrien Bonjour in 1951 [5] carried the appeal to context even further and pointed out that the whole stanza contrasts good and bad things and that

[3] We now possess a useful index of names in the four Cotton Nero poems in C. O. Chapman's *An Index of Names in "Pearl," "Purity," "Patience," and "Gawain"* (Ithaca, 1951).

[4] *JEGP*, XXXIV, 349.

[5] *English Studies*, XXXII, 70–72.

line 18 has even the same contrast in "and oft both bliss and blunder." Bonjour enables us to see a basic setting up of oppositions in the first stanza and indeed perhaps in the whole poem. Here philology and literary sensitivity are beautifully united to the enrichment of both.

Thus literary criticism must frequently be combined with philology and even, though I am here offering no examples, with literary history. As each grows or deepens, the other two approaches are bound to be affected. It must be admitted, however, that each study must be considered as independent in its own right and should only come together on certain levels and on certain problems.

I do not wish to give the impression that we shall perhaps some day understand to everyone's satisfaction what the poem means and intends or all the facts of its literary history. Some questions will always remain in doubt. Some lexicographical solutions, in particular, will doubtless never be universally accepted. Some will depend on what interpretation one assumes for the poem or parts of it. Some lexicographical ambiguities will never be removed. Real progress can, however, be made even if only the proper alternatives are understood or if impossibilities are revealed as such. In this sense, with the help of the new tools and a deeper insight into the external history and internal meaning of the poem, we shall make philological advances in our study of *Gawain*.

Literary historical problems in plenty remain to be solved in the study of *Gawain*. The more puzzling of these may be enumerated as follows: Who was the author of the poem? Is he also the author of the other English poems in the Cotton Nero MS? When was the poem written? What is the relation of the poem to the times and to the geography of England? What were the poet's sources? Some of these questions are closely dependent on each other as may be clearly seen. Yet for purposes of analysis we may separate them.

In recent years scholars have been chary of suggesting an author for our romance. There has, on the other hand, been less hesitancy in suggesting possible historical prototypes, especially for the Green Knight. Since the virtual disappearance of that universal genius Huchown of the Awl Ryle and Ralph Strode as claimants for the honor of writing *Sir Gawain*, only three or four possible names have been suggested—John Donne, John Prat,[6] John Erghome [7]—and very recently, Hugh Mascy.[8] Modern scholars are rightly wary of such suggestions, although of course speculation does no harm. Most of the evidence put forth is very slight and often rests upon the unproved assumption that the four Cotton Nero poems are by the same author leading to hypothetical arguments based on a hypothetical assumption. Internal evidence or unproved external evidence forms a very weak basis for any substantial case. I think we may say that, unless new evidence turns up, the problem of the author will remain unsettled.

There were various green knights and green squires running around Europe in the last half of the fourteenth century, and the temptation to identify one of them with Bercilak has been great. Braddy has suggested Ralph Holmes for this role [9] and Highfield has chosen Simon Newton.[10] In none of these cases is there any probability that, even on the basis of internal, let alone external evidence, there could be any good reason for the poet to allude to these men under the mask of Bercilak. The *roman à clef* theory has recently been urged by Henry Savage, a notable scholar of the poem, who sees in the story of Gawain a covert allusion to the fortunes of Enguerrand de Coucy, who married a daughter of Edward III.[11] This too does not seem very probable, and the evidence is of such a hypothetical character that one is rightly suspicious of the claim.

In spite of the widespread acceptance of the theory of a common authorship for *Gawain*, the *Pearl*, *Patience*, and *Purity*, I still consider the case not proved. John W. Clark has in the past twenty

---

[6] For these two, see Oscar Cargill and Margaret Schlauch in *PMLA*, XLIII (1928), 105–123.

[7] Put forward by C. O. Chapman in *PMLA*, XLVII (1932), 346–353. Henry Savage in *The Gawain-Poet, Studies in His Personality and Background* (Chapel Hill, 1956), Appendix K, argues that poet may have had some Chancery experience.

[8] See *Sir Gawain and the Green Knight*, trans. Brian Stone, The Penguin Classics L 92 (London and Baltimore, 1959), pp. 128–129.

[9] In *MLN*, LXVII (1952), 240–242. See also P. A. Becker, "Der grüne Ritter," *Archiv*, CLIX (1931), 275–276, and S. R. T. O. d'Ardenne, " 'The Green Count' and *Sir Gawain and the Green Knight*," *RES*, n.s., x (1959), 113–126.

[10] In *MAE*, XXII (1953), 18–23.

[11] *Op. cit.* Cf. his "*Sir Gawain* and the Order of the Garter," *ELH*, V (1938), 146–149. Dr. Savage does, however, argue his case circumspectly.

136

years been pointing to various weaknesses in the theory, and at the least he has shown how difficult it is to prove.[12] It is not easy to separate dialect from personal linguistic characteristics. I am especially suspicious of arguments for dating and authorship which rely on cross arguments from the other poems. The mathematical probability of an hypothesis based on an hypothesis is very slight.

Attempts to fix *Sir Gawain* in time and space and to relate it to its milieu have largely been concerned with possible historical allusions, with the identity of the scene of the action at the castle and Green Chapel, with the geography of Gawain's journey, and with the relation of the poem to the Order of the Garter. All this, while not unimportant, is certainly rather limited and limiting. There are other problems of milieu to which attention should be given and which have more immediate bearing on *Sir Gawain* as a work of art meaningful to us in our milieu. Before I turn to these new problems, however, I should like to say a few words about the older ones.

For some strange reason, the problem of the dialect of the poem has in general been connected with the location of Bercilak's castle and Green Chapel. Although everyone who has dealt with the philological problem of the dialect puts the poem in Lancashire, Western Yorkshire, Cheshire, or Derbyshire, the exact location within this area is difficult. The present tendency is to favor southern Lancashire.[13] In the minds of some investigators, the location of the dialect seems to be reliable evidence for locating the castle where the Gawain-poet wrote his poem or where Bercilak held court. This does not seem to me to be very soundly based. Why a poet should have to put the scene of his poem and be himself located in the area of the dialect he uses in writing is not at all evident. Yet we find this unsound and dubious assumption made in almost every case when these questions arise. The dialect of a poem certainly tells us something about the place of origin of the writer, if we can be sure that the scribe has not transformed it into his own dialect, but it is not necessarily that of the scene of the poem. A Scotsman could write about Yorkshire, a northern Lancashireman could write

---

[12] See, e.g., *PQ*, XXVIII (1949), 261–273; *JEGP*, XLIX (1950), 60–66; and *MLQ*, XII (1951), 387–398.

[13] See Oakden, *Alliterative Poetry in Middle English* (Manchester, 1930–35), I, 72–87 and 257, and Savage, *The Gawain-Poet*, *passim*.

about southern Lancashire. In all these matters caution is surely necessary.

The attempt to find historical allusions in *Gawain* has also been bedeviled by a paucity of evidence and an enthusiasm for hobby-horses. I suppose as Kittredge has said "thought is free," but one at least should distinguish between facts and hypotheses. Our knowledge of fourteenth-century England is still surprisingly incomplete, and we may yet make some discoveries which will cast light on the historical circumstances behind our romance. We would all benefit in various ways by the publication of various medieval documents and treatises, mainly in Latin and French, still unpublished, and we may even actually turn up something on our poem. As regards documents, however, it must be recognized that official records rarely help us to decide a literary question, for we do not find in the Middle Ages that all-encompassing interest in literary creation which is a mark of a later period. As we all know, the Geoffrey Chaucer of the contemporary records is not once identified as the poet near our hearts.

However, there are several fields of inquiry in the milieu which have hardly yet been studied with our poem in mind. Perhaps we may best indicate them by raising again some questions. What is the meaning of the "alliterative revival" in fourteenth-century England? What is the significance of the later flowering of Arthurian romance in England? To what extent is *Sir Gawain* a poem written in high style? What evidence is there of a baronial opposition to London in this period? What did chivalry mean to the aristocracy of fourteenth-century England? What audience was *Sir Gawain* written for? Was it written to give fourteenth-century noblemen a thrill?

All these questions have a bearing on the relation of *Gawain* to its milieu. Except perhaps for some remarks of Pons,[14] very little attention has been paid to these matters. Hulbert has, of course, looked into the meaning of the alliterative revival in general. Ear-

---

[14] In his edition *"Sire Gauvain et le Chevalier Vert," Poème anglais du XIVᵉ siècle*, Bibliothèque de philologie germanique IX (Paris, 1964), pp. 46 ff. Cf. the few but suggestive remarks of Gollancz in "Chivalry in Medieval English Poetry," chap. VII of *"Chivalry: A Series of Studies to Illustrate Its Historical Significance and Civilizing Influence*, by Members of King's College, London, ed. Edgar Prestage, The History of Civilization, ed. C. K. Ogden (New York, 1928), pp. 175–178.

lier Ten Brink had associated Edwardian nationalism with this movement.[15] But in the past thirty years little, if anything, has been done relating *Sir Gawain* to the wider issues of the century. In short, what exactly is the meaning of *Sir Gawain* in terms of fourteenth-century culture? This question sums them all up.

They all lead too into the whole fascinating subject of the lateness of the medieval English literary flowering. While France and Germany had lost interest in Arthurian legend or at least only treated it in debased fashion by 1350 or earlier, England suddenly at that time begins, if we ignore a few earlier works mainly in Anglo-Norman, to create an Arthurian literature. Why? Perhaps the answer lies merely in language. It was not until the fourteenth century that English finally vanquished Anglo-Norman. This may not be the entire explanation. Compared to France, English culture and literature were *retardataire* in the fourteenth century. England was able to make use of the Italian renaissance before France perhaps because of this very fact. Unlike his French contemporaries, Chaucer was not weighed down by a glorious literary tradition. Just as today Spain, for instance, is in some particular ways more modern and up-to-date than England and France because it was so terribly behind when it came into our century and thus was able to adapt foreign ideas more freely, so perhaps Chaucer and Gower would pick up the new developments in Italy without the burden of a past. The older English literary achievement had been forgotten by the fourteenth century, and English writers perhaps felt that they could create as they liked without a load of great masterpieces on their shoulders.

The rise of English nationalism under Edward III must have been an important factor in this matter. There is evidence that Edward deliberately strove to rehabilitate chivalry and knighthood. The Arthurian legend provided England with a ready-made aristocratic myth of its past glories. Unlike France which could look back to Charlemagne, England could only offer the misty and ambiguous figure of Arthur.

Indeed there were rich ambiguities in the whole Arthurian cor-

---

[15] See J. R. Hulbert, "A Hypothesis Concerning the Alliterative Revival," *MP*, XXVIII (1931), 405–422, and B. Ten Brink, *Early English Literature (to Wiclif)*, trans. H. M. Kennedy, Bohn's Standard Library (London, 1883), pp. 329 ff.

pus. Arthur, Gawain, Lancelot, and the others were both worthy and ridiculous figures. They were to be taken seriously and admired and at the same time to be laughed at for their childishness. And besides, much of it was in conflict with an aroused and serious Christianity which was a strong feature of late medieval life. For all this the romances provide much evidence. Courtesy and courtly love were both necessary to elevate human nature and at the same time silly in their pretensions.

The problem of milieu is much more than finding the exact location of the Green Chapel or discovering who the poet had in mind when he created the Green Knight. The intellectual and ideological feel of late medieval life needs to be related to the poem. The decline of feudalism and the reaction to that decline will help to explain the poem. Of course even in the twelfth century we find laments over the decline of chivalry, and like most ideals it never was on land or sea; but there is objective evidence for a decline in the later Middle Ages, no matter how stylized some of the complaints were.[16] The relation of this movement and counter movement to the English nobility and conditions of life in late fourteenth-century England have yet to be investigated.

Fourteenth-century poetic theory and rhetoric also stimulate difficult questions. What, for instance, was the attitude of the fourteenth-century writer toward his material? To what extent was he dominated by rhetorical theory, especially the theory of styles? That he took them seriously there can be no doubt, but what exactly did high style in English mean at that time? Was high style even pos-

---

[16] On this whole subject, see Raymond Lincoln Kilgour, *The Decline of Chivalry as Shown in the French Literature of the Late Middle Ages* (Cambridge, 1937). This book, of course, concentrates on France. For England, see Gervase Mathew, "Ideals of Knighthood in Late-Fourteenth-Century England," *Studies in Medieval History Presented to Frederick Maurice Powicke,* ed. Hunt, Pantin, and Southern (Oxford, 1948), pp. 354–362 (who uses, inter alia, *Sir Gawain* for evidence). Cf. also Kurt Lippmann, *Das ritterliche Persönlichkeitsideal in der mittelenglischen Literatur des 13. und 14. Jahrhunderts,* Inaugural-Dissertation . . . der Universität Leipzig (Meerane, 1933), and Dietrich Sandberger, *Studien über das Rittertum in England vornehmlich während des 14. Jahrhunderts,* Historische Studien 310 (Berlin, 1937). Sandberger brings much evidence to show how late chivalry flourished in England. "Im 14. Jahrhundert ist dann England so 'ritterlich' wie nur irgendein Land" (p. 241).

140

sible in the mother language? Could comedy and high style be wedded in any way? What is the significance of the narrator in medieval literature? To what extent were ironies possible? The love of decorative detail in *Gawain* and much of the poetry of the period is probably a reflex of the idea of courtesy and chivalric manners. One does not hasten into action but dwells on the form. Furthermore, the poet of *Gawain* stresses the aspect of wonder and suspense in his romance. James V. Cunningham has studied in interesting fashion the relation of wonder to literature in a fascinating chapter in his book *Woe or Wonder: The Emotional Effect of Shakespearean Tragedy.*[17] He is primarily concerned with the role of wonder in tragedy, but it also has its place in comedy. Cicero, he tells us, connected wonder with ornate or figurative diction and a charming style (p. 76). This is a notable feature of our poem. Wonder has various meanings, and that which arises from the unforeseen (*agonia*) seems to fit the mode of its employment in our romance. It is possible that such wonder, as opposed to other types, is appropriate to comedy. In all this our poet may be following a little known rhetorical precept. The whole rhetorical tradition has hardly yet been explored for this and other matters.[18] Much of the material for this work lies in manuscripts unprinted and in Latin, but not all of it is unavailable.

Finally as part of literary history, let us turn to the sources of Gawain. This section will also serve as a bridge to problems of literary criticism as such. In recent years both the mythic and religious elements in *Gawain* have received much attention, not merely as source material or background but as alive in the poem as part of the poet's deliberate intent. John Speirs raised the myth issue in an important article some ten years ago,[19] and several scholars and

[17] (Denver, 1951), pp. 62–105. See also Benjamin P. Kurtz, *Studies in the Marvellous*, University of California Publications (London and Berkeley, 1910), esp. chap. i.

[18] See, however, Derek A. Pearsall's interesting "Rhetorical 'Descriptio' in *Sir Gawain and the Green Knight*," MLR, L (1955), 129–134, which has some very good things to say about the Gawain poet's use of rhetorical devices in descriptions which have long been praised for their naturalism. On this last point, see G. Plessow in *Gotische Tektonik* . . . (Munich, 1931), pp. 144 ff.

[19] In *Scrutiny*, XVI (1949), 274–300 (reprinted with some minor changes in *Medieval English Poetry, The Non-Chaucerian Tradition* [London, 1957], pp. 215–251).

critics have recently made much of the religious element in the poem. On the latter point, Miss Willcock has said, "the poem grows more moral, religious and even mystical with every succeeding editor or commentator." [20]

Until the thirties scholars engaged in source study were for the most part primarily interested in the literary and to some extent the folklore elements in *Sir Gawain*. Miss Weston, in her early treatment of the Gawain figure,[21] suggested that Gawain was originally a sun hero and was related to the Irish hero Cuchulinn. But even she was primarily interested in the literary sources of *Sir Gawain* when she confined her attention to our romance. Sir E. K. Chambers was the first to suggest in 1903 [22] that the green man of the peasantry reappears as the challenger in *Sir Gawain*. Cook a few years later [23] saw the Indo-European tree or vegetation god in Bercilak. In 1912 Henderson repeated Cook's idea that the Green Knight was a tree-god.[24] In 1916 Kittredge wrote a brilliant book on the Irish and Old French sources or analogues of *Sir Gawain*, dividing the narrative into two main themes—the Beheading or Challenge and the Temptation.[25] The immediate source, however, was, he believed, a lost French romance. One has only to read Welsh and Irish sagas to recognize that, although some of the matter of *Gawain* may be Celtic, its literary form approximates that of the great French romances. *Sir Gawain's* immediate source may not be French, it may indeed be English, but it is a poem in the French

[20] YWES, XXVIII (1947), p. 90.

[21] *The Legend of Sir Gawain, Studies upon its Original Scope and Significance*, Grimm Library 7 (London, 1897). Gaston Paris also recognized a mythic quality in Gawain. For a literary history of Sir Gawain in the Middle Ages and later, see B. J. Whiting, "Gawain: His Reputation, His Courtesy and His Appearance in Chaucer's *Squire's Tale*," *Medieval Studies*, IX (1947), 189–234.

[22] *The Medieval Stage* (Oxford), I, 185–186. It may be noted that there is a slight confusion in myth and source study as to whether the dying-rising god is Bercilak or Gawain. Perhap they should be considered doublets.

[23] "The European Sky God VI, The Celts (contin.)," *Folklore*, XVII (1906), 308–348; 427–453, esp. 338 ff.

[24] *Miscellany Presented to Kuno Meyer* (Halle, 1912), pp. 18–33.

[25] *A Study of Gawain and the Green Knight* (Cambridge). Kittredge believed that the two themes were united for the first time by the unknown French romancer who wrote the lost source of the poem, but as Buchanan (see note 29 below) and perhaps Hulbert (see next note) have urged, there is evidence even in the Irish material that the two themes were at least related.

literary tradition. Kittredge had the literary sensitivity to see that. But Kittredge would have no truck with vegetation or other myths. He did not deny their total relevance to the study of the sources of the romances but dismissed them as too speculative to be worthy of much thought.

The problem of the main themes of *Sir Gawain* has been taken as settled once and for all by Kittredge. I am not, however, completely satisfied that this is the case. This is a matter of more than antiquarian importance in source study, for the themes are what determine where one is to look for sources. It is possible, for instance, that the temptation theme might be considered part of the benevolent (or imperious) host theme and best studied as such. Further and other divisions of the story could be made. "The exchange of winnings" theme, for instance, has been suggested. I must admit, however, that the criteria for determining the themes are difficult to establish and partly depend on an interpretation of the poem. We are back to literary criticism again.

At about the same time as Kittredge, Hulbert suggested a mythic theme for the poem [26]—that it or its lost original, like the *Fled Bricrend*, was concerned with a test for winning a fairy-mistress. Morgan le Fay initiated the whole business of the story because of her love for Gawain. Her motives enunciated in the poem by Bercilak—to frighten Guinevere and to test the pride of Arthur's Court—are dismissed as a later addition. Like many commentators wedded to the historical method, Hulbert did not claim that *Sir Gawain*, as at present constituted, presents this theme directly—he could hardly do that—but that the fairy-mistress story accounts for the general organization of the tale and for some of its apparently inexplicable details. He, like most source scholars, was concerned with the evolution of the story not the final product. Often in this approach and in its more modern version—myth analysis—the actual work of art which presumably calls forth the whole investigation is a minor episode in the history of a story or myth which has a disembodied viability of its own. I am not claiming this neglect of the work may not at times be justified as a method, but its limitations should be recognized. Hulbert's particular interpretation of the source of this Gawain tale has only been taken up with any thoroughness by Ott

[26] In *MP*, XIII (1915–16), 433–462; 689–730.

Löhman in 1938.[27] Much more popular has been the vegetation myth theory, adumbrated in Chambers, Cook, and Henderson.

Professor Loomis a few years later in his general explorations of Celtic sources and parallels to Arthurian legend began a series of articles and books which did not neglect *Sir Gawain*.[28] Although he does not deny mythic elements in the background of the main characters and perhaps even the story of *Sir Gawain*, Professor Loomis is primarily concerned with written and hypothetically reconstructed sources.[29]

The whole subject took, however, a new turn in the thirties and forties when, with the rise of myth criticism or, as Jean Paul Sartre puts it, the new mythology of myth, interest shifted to the mythic meaning of the elements in the sources in *Gawain*, as well as in other works. Some of this work was scholarly and some not, depending on whether the main purpose was to stress the ultimate mythic sources of *Sir Gawain* or to stress the vitality of these sources in the finished work of art. In the history of the interpretation of our poem in this light five names may be mentioned—Nitze, Krappe, Coomaraswamy, Zimmer, and Speirs.[30] The first two—Nitze and Krappe—are strictly scholars in their approach. Nitze argues that the root of the *Sir Gawain* story is a vegetation myth best

---

[27] *Die Sage von Gawain und dem grünen Ritter*, Schriften des Albertus Universität . . . 17 (Königsberg & Berlin).

[28] See *Celtic Myth and Arthurian Romance* (New York, 1927), pp. 39–123; *PMLA*, XLIII (1928), 384–396 (a theory somewhat modified later); *PMLA*, XLVIII (1933), 1000–1035; *JEGP*, XLII (1943), 149–184 (revised as "Welsh Elements in *Gawain and the Green Knight*," *Wales and the Arthurian Legend* [Cardiff, 1956], pp. 77–90); *Speculum*, XX (1945), 183–203; and *Arthurian Tradition & Chrétien de Troyes* (New York, 1949), pp. 41 ff.; 146 ff., 278 ff. *et passim*.

[29] Following Loomis' method, the contributions of Miss Buchanan in *PMLA*, XLVII (1932), 315–338, and Roland Smith in *JEGP*, XLV (1946), 1–25, should be noted. Smith shows some important parallels to the poem in the Finn cycle. Before his article, only the Ulster cycle had been used in source work on the poem. An important recent discussion of the sources of the poem may be found in Albert B. Friedman, "Morgan le Fay in *Sir Gawain and the Green Knight*," *Speculum*, XXXV (1960), 260–274. Friedman makes some very telling points against the theories of both Buchanan and Loomis.

[30] Nitze in *MP*, XXXIII (1935–36), 351–366; Krappe in *Speculum*, XIII (1938), 206–215; Coomaraswamy in *Speculum*, XIX (1944), 104–125; Zimmer in *The King and The Corpse*, ed. J. Campbell, Bollingen Series XI (New York, 1943), pp. 67–95 and Speirs in *Scrutiny*, XVI (1949), 274–300, and some further material in subsequent issues.

preserved in the *Perlesvaus* analogue. Krappe finds the root in a journey to the realm of the dead for the purpose of defeating death. Zimmer and Speirs, on the other hand, are not so much concerned with the nature of the myth at the basis of the romance, although Speirs finds it to be a vegetation story and Zimmer seems to favor a conquest of death interpretation, as with the presence of mythic and ritual elements alive in the poem as we have it now; and Coomaraswamy falls somewhere in between. The latter gives us new analogues to the beheading episode but stresses the powerful psychic appeal of the myth as present in the poem. He fits it into his great synthesizing view of life and story wherein myth gives perpetual meaning to both. Speirs' work, however, has been the central event of modern scholarship for our poem. His position is argued with such vigor and dogmatism that he has given new life to *Gawain* scholarship. In a sense he has set the terms for most work on the poem since 1948 to move in. Even those who write on the poem from a different point of view feel constrained to place their contribution in relation to his. He has certainly made the mythological theory the dominant frame of reference for subsequent critical work, most of which does not, however, accept his theories.

Charles Moorman recently has criticized both Speirs and Zimmer [31] for neglecting *Sir Gawain* as a poem and argues that as literary critics we may accept the myth element as in the poem, but we must emphasize what the *Gawain*-poet did with the myth in the particular work of art he created. A myth critic must not merely identify the *genus* of the myth the poet chooses but also the *differentia* as developed in the poem. How is the source or pattern used in the poem? Moorman himself argues that the *genus* is a variety of the *rites de passage* ritual and myth and tries to show how it lives in the poet's hands. He also stresses the Christian element in the finished poem. Gawain's *rite de passage* serves to test the whole Arthurian court and to teach them the value of chastity and loyalty. Guinevere, who incidentally is a very minor character in the poem, in particular is being shown up. "What the critic can say . . . is that the myth of the hero's journey from innocence to knowledge

[31] "Myth and Mediaeval Literature: *Sir Gawain and the Green Knight*," *Mediaeval Studies*, XVIII (1965), 158–172.

145

underlies the poem and to a large extent determines its specific structure and theme."

This whole question of myth is a complicated one. Part of the problem is a difficulty in knowing what these critics and scholars claim. If a scholar is arguing that the original story behind *Sir Gawain* is a myth or partly a myth, one surely cannot object. If a scholar or reader is claiming that in order to understand the poem in its deepest sense today one should interpret it in mythic terms or relate it to subconscious archetypes, one again surely cannot object if he prefers to think that way or if he can only be happy in the subconscious or on the pre-Christian mythic level of meaning. If, however, the claim is being made that the author of *Sir Gawain* is deliberately conscious of the mythic or ritual element in his poem and is using it for deliberate effect to an audience which would understand it then one has a right to raise questions. The whole problem is concerned with historical actuality. Is our task to discover what the *Gawain*-poet was trying to do? If so, then whether myth is consciously alive in Sir Gawain is a problem which can be tackled by the historical method—at least theoretically.

The proponents of the mythic interpretation of *Sir Gawain* in this sense find very little in the poem itself to support their hypotheses. Speirs, to take one example, gives us the phallic towers of Bercilak's castle; the word "ver" (1. 866) which may or may not mean "spring" as Spiers would like to have it; the holly branch and big beard of the Green Knight; the pentangle; the importance of the Christmas-New Year season in the poem; the old woman (Morgan) and the young woman; [32] the presence of a chapel "in the earth"; by some curious argumentation the hunts; and I suppose the beheading game itself. This is not a very impressive list, especially if we remember that all castles have phallic features, that New Year is the usual time for the beginning of Arthurian adventures, that comparing a beard to a bush is a well-known metaphor, that old and young women are pretty common in life and so forth.

There is no doubt that pagan rituals were still alive in the four-

[32] Mrs. Laura Hibbard Loomis in "*Sir Gawain and the Green Knight*," chap. XXXIX of *Arthurian Literature in the Middle Ages, A Collective History,* ed. R. S. Loomis (Oxford, 1959), p. 535, suggests that Bercilak's wife is a double of Morgan as an analogue in the *Vulgate Lancelot* seems to show.

146

teenth century, as they are today, but there is much doubt that the participants had any notion of their meanings. And besides, these ritual relics were to be found among the folk. *Sir Gawain* is one of the few undoubtedly aristocratic poems of the English Middle Ages extant. It would be surprising if in this courtly and Christian atmosphere of a poem perhaps written entirely or partly in high style, we could find alive mythic and ritualistic elements. Of Moorman's attempt to save both the poem and the myth we may say that, however satisfactory his theory may be, it is hard to find in practice any specific evidences of a "rite de passage" ritual in *Sir Gawain* unless all testing is to be regarded as a type of *rite de passage*. Gawain is perhaps humbler at the end of his adventure than at the beginning, but just what has he been initiated into? He has perhaps learned that all human beings including the best are weak, but this lesson is not the purpose of the usual *rite de passage*, even a Christianized one. If he had been a good Christian, he should have realized this from the beginning; it is not secret knowledge. Then too the Court, as Moorman himself indicated, for which the whole affair was managed, is no better or wiser; and besides *rites de passage* are for individuals not institutions. To me at least Moorman has fallen into the trap he has so carefully delineated and whose dangers he has so vividly portrayed. Without being specific as to what a *rite de passage* means, without, in other words, establishing his *genus*, he makes the *differentia* he discusses lose the characteristics of *differentia*. Not only this; he has to force the plain meaning of the text to fit it into his theory. The shade of the golden bough [33] obscures the poem for one reader at least.

The Christian and moral elements in the poem on the other hand are obvious from beginning to end. The ethical and religious interpretation of the poem is not new. W. P. Ker in 1912 made this point clear in his excellent little book in the Home University Library on Medieval English literature. I am sure that he was not the first to do so,[34] and he was certainly not the last. In recent years the

[33] See M. J. C. Hodgart, "In the Shade of the Golden Bough," *Twentieth Century*, CLVII (1955), 111–119, esp. 116–117. Hans Schnyder in "Aspects of Kingship in *Sir Gawain and the Green Knight*," *English Studies*, XL (1959), 289–294, considers the romance to be, at least in part, a rebuke of Arthur as a bad king.

[34] Cf. ". . . all this art [of the *Gawain*-poet] is in the service of moral ideas." B. Ten Brink, *Early English Literature (to Wiclif)*, (London, 1883), p 347.

Christian element and aim of the poem have received increased emphasis. There have been strong differences of opinion on various topics, as for instance whether the purpose of the temptation of the lady is to test Gawain's loyalty or chastity or whether the poet emphasizes Gawain's failure as a Christian or his nobility of character while admitting he is not perfect or whether the sources of the temptation scene are secular romances or saints' lives.[35] Yet there has been a continuing interest in this approach.

The poem is fairly and squarely Christian. Pride is the great sin, the Virgin Mary helps humanity, the characters are continually going to Mass and confessing. Recently Ackerman has discussed [36] the Christian significance of the pentangle and the association of the various quintuplets mentioned in the poem at this point with the sacrament of penance. As he writes, "the stress in the sixteen-line interpretation of Gawain's pentangle falls on the hero's deeply religious devotion, even when one takes into account the five chivalric virtues. Moreover, the poet chose, for the most part, to express this fundamental aspect of Gawain's character in language made familiar to his audience by the confessional" (p. 265). A sermon by Thomas Bradwardine delivered just after the victory at Crécy has very recently been published [37] in which he claims that victory in battle comes from God alone and refers to seven erroneous theories which claim to explain military prowess. One of these is that sexual virility accounts for military success. Bradwardine takes some

[35] Else von Schaubert, "Der englische Ursprung von Syr Gawayn and the Grene Kny3t," *ES*, LVII (1923), 330–446, is the foremost exponent of the latter in her attempts to posit an English rather than a French lost original for the poem. It may be of some interest here to point out that the temptation of a good man by a woman would probably suggest to medieval man, certainly before some of the tales in the Golden Legend, the story of Joseph and Potiphar's wife, a connection not hitherto made as far as I'm aware. On this Biblical story and legend in the Middle Ages, see F. E. Faverty, "The Story of Joseph and Potiphar's Wife in Mediaeval Literature," *Harvard Studies and Notes in Philology and Literature*, XIII (1931), 81–127.

[36] In *Anglia*, LXXVI (1958), 254–265. I am not convinced that Ackerman has completely proved his case. The five wits are associated with sin, true; but they are also associated with the origin of all knowledge good or bad. Another discussion of the penance theme in the later part of the poem may be found in John Burrow, "The Two Confession Scenes in *Sir Gawain and the Green Knight*," *MP*, LVII (1959–60), 73–79.

[37] Heiko A. Oberman and James A. Weisheipl. "The *Sermo epinicius* ascribed to Thomas Bradwardine (1346)," *Archives d'histoire doctrinale et littéraire au moyen âge*, XXV (1958), 295–329. The passage referred to occurs on pp. 323–329.

148

pains to refute this explanation. This part of the sermon shows us that some men in the fourteenth century believed that there was a connection between lechery and courage. Perhaps like Bradwardine, the author of *Sir Gawain* is also trying to combat this idea by showing us a hero chaste as well as courageous.

I think in the coming years we will find further and deeper religious aspects and significances in the poem.[38] Yet I am inclined to agree with George Kane when he writes that the success of our poem does not fundamentally arise "from the concepts of conduct upon which the characters act. These are, to be sure, noble and gracious enough, and reflect a good knowledge of human behaviour. . . . The exceptional success of this romance comes from other sources than the principles of behaviour upon which its action is based." Kane, however, finds its success in the acute visualization of the action and setting.[39]

This religious and ethical dimension, as well as the mythic dimension, still seems to me to leave unanswered the question of the poet's primary intention. Here we pass over completely into the problem of literary criticism, although we have already been deep in it, a circumstance which shows how difficult it is to separate background from foreground in literary analysis.

A third possibility which has been much ignored, although suggested by a few,[40] is a comic or humorous intention. John Conley in

[38] George L. Engelhardt's "The Predicament of Gawain," *MLQ*, XVI (1955), 218–225, also makes an important point about the religious element in the poem. It emphasizes the weakness of Gawain and his moral predicament, the significance of which is revealed only because of Gawain's apparent integrity. His strength is his weakness. "Actually it [*Sir Gawain*] is a humane and sympathetic presentation designed to reveal how human and imperfect is even a supposedly perfect knight such as the pentagonal Gawain" (pp. 224–225, note).

[39] *Middle English Literature, A Critical Study of the Romances, the Religious Lyrics, Piers Plowman* (London, 1951), pp. 73–76. The quotation above is from p. 76. Professor Baugh makes the same point: "Though it [*GGK*] exemplifies the knightly virtues of courage and truth, it is in no sense a story told to enforce a moral." *A Literary History of England* (New York, 1948), p. 236. On the *Gawain*-poet's descriptive and visual powers, see the article by Alain Renoir, "Descriptive Techniques in Sir Gawain and the Green Knight," *Orbis litterarum*, XIII (1958), 126–132.

[40] See Elizabeth M. Wright, "Sir Gawain and the Green Knight," *JEGP*, XXXIV (1935), 157–158, and G. H. Gerould in "The Gawain Poet and Dante: A Conjecture," *PMLA*, LI (1936), 31. Mrs. Wright in the above article (pp. 158–161) also suggests that in the beheading theme we have a description of a feast-day dra-

an unpublished paper on the romance, which he has been kind enough to show me, argues that *Sir Gawain* is fundamentally humorous, although by no means unserious. The beginning tells us that the subject of the poem is marvels and the treatment throughout is touched, often strongly touched, by humor. Laughter and smiles are frequently referred to in the text. The vividness of the language, the subtleties of the lines, the extraordinary lightness of tone, all bespeak a sophistication, an irony, a sense of humor which illuminates the whole thing from beginning to end. Not only, however, do we find within the poem the humor which arises from the author's attitude toward his characters and their involvements but another kind of humor in his attitude toward his audience and readers. The author is playing a game with us just as Morgan is playing a game with Arthur's court. He is keeping us in a state of suspense, holding back information, and fooling us.

Humorous romances are not unknown in the Middle Ages, and this genre can contain such tensions and oppositions. None of them of course treats these matters in exactly the same way as our poem does, and few if any equal our author's literary virtuosity. But not all romances are straightforward tales of adventure, or rich pageantries of chivalry, or even religious quests, but some indeed are at one and the same time witty, ironical, and religious. Such a one is, I believe, *Sir Gawain*.

Two writers, Francis Berry and William Goldhurst,[41] have

---

matic entertainment. She stresses the dramatic and theatrical elements in the two meetings between Gawain and the Green Knight. Eagen, in "The Import of Color Symbolism in *Sir Gawain and the Green Knight*," St. Louis Univ. Studies, Series A, Humanities I, 2 (1949), pp. 11–86, sees the romance, at least on one level, as a satire against the average contemporary romance with its glorification of adultery and a decadent chivalry. "The Gawain-poet wished to write a genuinely Christian poem to glorify true Christian chivalry in which the virtue of chastity held the foremost place" (p. 62). One gets the impression that Father Eagan falls back on satire to extricate him from the difficulties that this highly Christian interpretation of the romance gets him into.

[41] Berry, "The Sublime Ballet: An Essay on Sir Gawain and the Green Knight," *Wind and Rain* (Winter 1949–50), 165–174, (which I have not been able to consult), and "Sir Gawayne and the Grene Knight," in *The Age of Chaucer*, A Guide to English Literature I, ed. Boris Ford, Pelican Books A290 (London, 1954), pp. 148–158, and Goldhurst, "The Green and the Gold: The Major Theme of *Gawain and the Green Knight*," CE, XX (1958–59), 61–65.

stressed the tension in the poem between the civilized and courtly element and the primitive and vitalistic element. Berry writes of the many contrasts in the poem which may be classified under these two headings—getting and spending, begetting and dying, humanity and nature, and so forth. These contrasts are beautifully seen in the person of the Green Knight, who is both civilized and amoral at the same time. "He testifies to an assumption that moral behaviour, though of vast importance, is subservient to and dependent on something even more primary—creative energy. In the poem Gawain and his 'society' humbly come to terms with the Green Knight. They had been in danger of forgetting their own *sine qua non*. . . . The poem involves the divine and the human, the natural and the magical and presents a pattern of these categories in which potential antagonisms between them are conciliated, and this in a partly comic temper."

Goldhurst makes the same point, perhaps less subtly, but stresses this paradox and tension as it appears in the style of the poem "which combines the qualities of straightforward vigor with a suggestiveness and a subtle, almost elegant, lightness of touch." Each of the characters is a combination of antitheses. The Green Knight is a beheader and a civilized courtier. Gawain is a rugged warrior and capable of delicate and refined reactions. Bercilak's wife possesses both refinement and sex appeal. Elements in the poem betray a similar ambivalence—the mound is a chapel, the girdle is an ornament and a sexual symbol. "The poem suggests that at best life is but a truce between natural impulses, and allegiances to the virtues which civilized creatures are pledged to uphold."

That these antithetical forces are present in *Gawain* cannot be doubted, but it is a large question whether any poet could be a kind of Bergson in the fourteenth century. This opposition between the untamed forces of nature and human civilization which precariously opposes it seems extraordinarily unmedieval to me. It sounds too much like nineteenth- and twentieth-century romantic thought to be a satisfying interpretation of the poem.

Nor is there much in the poem itself to bear out this interpretation. The same throbbing meter which Berry and Goldhurst find in *Sir Gawain* is also to be found in *Purity* and *Patience* and *Piers Plowman* where it hardly indicates any life force. I do not sense any continual struggle between civilization and barbarism in the poem, although both elements are certainly present. The Green Knight, who is subdued by Gawain's courtesy and loyalty,[42] is hardly the amoral life force blindly striving ever onward. He was given a task and the gift of re-heading himself by Morgan le Fay, but other than this gift and other than an ability to act like a scornful bogey-man when necessary, he possesses a perfectly moral and civilized human character. As for contradictions in the characters, we may say that all characters are contradictory. Lear is a child and a hero; Hamlet acts and does not act; Becky Sharp has her moments of remorse; Leopold Bloom is both lecherous and civilized. We may say of almost any work of art that it combines opposites of this sort. The problem is whether the point of the work is to set these antitheses into sharp relief and whether it is basically built around them. I cannot see that *Sir Gawain* is constructed along these lines.

In more sober wise, Markman has argued from genre—that our poem falls into the category of romance, a narrative which concentrates on testing a hero.[43] The primary purpose of the poem "is to show what a splendid man Gawain is" (p. 575). Gawain is pitted "against a marvelous, unnatural man" with the intent of discovering "what a perfect knight can do when he is forced to face the unknown" (p. 575). Magic not mythology directs the marvelous occurrences within the romance. Gawain is, however, a man and has his weaknesses, but the poet is on his side. Gawain's courtesy and loyalty are fundamental to the meaning of the poem and are part of the poet's vision of life which stresses decorum.

Markman has emphasized the genre of the poem with its hero, its testing, and its atmosphere of the marvelous. All this is to the good. I would suggest, however, that romance is not a simple genre but a highly complex one and that there are many varieties of romance. The important point is to specify more precisely to what subtypes or types *Sir Gawain* belongs. There are comic as well as serious, religious as well as amorous, psychological as well as objective, episodic as well as tightly organized, romances. The romance

[42] Note that the problem of who subdues whom in the encounter between Gawain and Bercilak is not easily answered. Berry argues that Gawain comes to terms with Bercilak.

[43] "The Meaning of *Sir Gawain and the Green Knight*," PMLA, LXXII (1957), 574–586.

genre is by no means a unified monolithic type. Much more needs to be done on this matter.

Miss Dorothy Everett has also stressed the testing element in the poem.[44] Like Markman and many other earlier critics, she underlines its ethical content. She writes "the first concern of the poem is thus with conduct; that is, it is moral in the true sense of the word" (p. 77). As I have mentioned above, this view is gaining much ground today and is more or less widely accepted. With perhaps the exception of Kane, who specifically denies that the conduct of the hero is the main concern of the poet, most scholars and critics, even those who are strongly addicted to the mythological interpretation, seem to agree on the importance of this element. I think it cannot be denied, but the question is how central is this matter. What is the poet's first intention? Although I do not agree with Kane that it is the decorative and visual which the poet wishes to elevate I think he is making an important point—that the ethical side can be overvalued. I do not believe the poem was written fundamentally to present us with a good man who emerges somewhat stained or humbled from his encounter with the world of evil or of the supernatural. The humor, suspense, and tone of the poem belie the centrality of this interpretation.

If we look closely at the narrative structure of our romance, we find that the poet uses suspense as his organizing principle. We pass from ignorance to knowledge after the suspense has been built up to an agonizing climax. If we examine the formal divisions of the poem, those in the manuscript, to which Mrs. Hill has called our attention,[45] we may, I think, see this. Madden in his edition ignored, in dividing the poem into its major parts, all but four of the nine large initials with which the text is adorned. All editions since have followed his predilections in the matter; but there is a good case for dividing the work into nine divisions of which only the first corresponds to our present system. It is surprising that this suggestion has not been taken up by literary critics of the poem. In fact, the whole subject of formal divisions in medieval poems, including

---

[44] *Essays on Middle English Literature*, ed. P. Kean (Oxford, 1955), pp. 68 ff.

[45] "Madden's Divisions of *Sir Gawain* and the 'Large Initial Capitals' of Cotton Nero A.x," *Speculum*, XXI (1946), 67–71 I am indebted in the details of my interpretation here to the investigations of Miss Sarah Appleton.

those of Chaucer, has frequently been ignored. The ninefold division corresponds to points of new suspense. The descriptive technique of the poem is also guided by this principle. I cannot go into this subject here in the detail it requires, but if the romance is analyzed in terms of suspense and wonder the formal and stylistic principle of the romance becomes clearer.

This ignoring of the manuscript divisions in *Sir Gawain* seems to me to be characteristic of the refusal of much scholarship and criticism to come to grips with our poem. As I implied earlier, *Gawain* seems to cast a spell on its commentators. There have been few if any close investigations of the structure and diction of the poem, if we except the positivistic studies of earlier days when such investigations were undertaken in a very mechanical fashion. The poem has to be looked at closely.

I regard the poem as an aristocratic romance reflecting a many-faceted solidity which is both comic and serious. It is meant to entertain and to some extent teach a sophisticated audience. Its style is probably mixed and part of its humor lies in the juxtaposition of high and medium style. It is a combination of secularism and religion, of the marvelous and the real, of the subjective and the objective, of the decorative and the direct, of the vague and the clear, of courtesy and horror, of the elevated and the plain. There is a solidity about *Sir Gawain* which encompasses a variegated world.

The treatment of time in the poem is most interesting. We have a beginning and an end in the distant past. The story itself is laid in the closer past. The poet as narrator-character suggests that he is in our presence telling us of what happened long ago in Arthur's days. These events are, moreover, the outcome of a much longer history going back to the Trojan War and the earliest ancestors of the race. Even Aeneas, we are told, was found wanting.[46] Moreover we get the building of the poem on the passage of a year. Cyclic time or the time of nature is superimposed on linear time or the time of history, in order to contrast the two and to point up Ga-

[46] I cannot accept the suggestion of Gollancz and Day in their EETS edition of the poem (London, 1940) that "þe tulk" who was tried (or distinguished) for his treachery was Antenor, who would hardly be called "the trewest on erthe." The introduction to this edition by Miss Day contains an excellent summary of the problem of *Sir Gawain's* sources.

154

wain's dilemma. The winter to come is not merely the same as last winter but different. Further, when the author writes of the temptation scenes, he tells us of the hunting activities going on at the same time.[47] Against the very nature of narration, we are plunged into two events happening simultaneously. The Gawain-poet is one of the first poets in English to handle the difficult problem of simultaneity in narration.

Besides all this, we have an inner or psychological time represented on occasion, when the narrator speaks of events occurring inside Gawain's head.[48] Events are sometimes seen as subjective duration.

All this seems to be reflected in the poet's curious use of tenses which should be studied—especially his shifting between past and present and occasional use of the subjunctive. *Sir Gawain* is soaked in time in all its aspects, and this rich chronological perspectivism is one of the strongest elements in the sense of solidity we get from reading the poem. It, along with the rhetorical descriptions, is part of the richness against which these strange, tense, and comic events of the plot play themselves out. These many dimensions of time are part of the bulwarks of life; they give security and strength. They are the framework of the human universe into which fantastic and puzzling irrationality penetrates and which it seems to wish to destroy. Here we have a cosmic humor in which the fragility of life and honor are threatened against a solid and rich background akin to the density of reality itself.

Except when he deliberately violates the illusion, the poet endeavors to maintain a distance between his poem and the reader which is necessary to true comedy. Time is functional to this purpose. It helps to create the impression of another world both similar to and different from our own which keeps the reader away from

[47] Bercilak may have some features of the "wild huntsman"; see R. S. Loomis in *JEGP*, XLII (1943), 170–181, where similarities of GGK to the Welsh mabinogi of Pwyll are pointed to.

[48] See Everett, *op. cit.*, pp. 78–79 *et passim*. The alternation throughout the poem of inside and outside is a most significant feature and helps to create the sense of solidity I find in the poem. I am indebted to Mr. Robert Hall for an awareness of this feature of organization, Mrs. Loomis suggests somewhat this point in *op. cit.*, p. 539. The romance is at its densest during the temptation scenes, when action goes on in the castle and out of it, in Gawain's bedroom and elsewhere, and within Gawain's soul and without, all at the same time.

155

the events taking place. They are far enough to preserve their integrity and strangeness and near enough to interest us. If the reader were to get too closely involved, he might find a tragic horror too great to be borne. The wonder would turn to fear and the delight and curiosity which are always a product of objectivity would be lost. Occasionally, however, especially in the temptation and journey scenes, we are deliberately brought into the poem by being told what the hero is thinking. These passages are, I believe, deliberate and are justified by the circumstances. We get close to tragedy for the heart of Gawain's predicament. But on the whole, life in *Sir Gawain* is "apprehended in the form of spectacle rather than in the form of [inner] experience." [49]

The pastness of the whole poem makes a major contribution to its ideal and aristocratic as well as its comic nature. Things, however, are not quite what they seem. Gawain, the perfect knight, is also a human being, and the Green Knight is really only a mask. His wife only seems to be unfaithful. The old harmless lady is really a witch. The court is silly and yet capable of honor. Nature is both horrid and benign. Life is a tissue of contradictions, even in its most aristocratic and idealized form.

Time also serves to bind and order the poem just as its stanzaic form does. The timeless but clearly segmented present as revealed in the cycle of the year is firmly embedded in the vaguely known past. Time functions as a part of the decorum and restraint of the poem which are dominant features of its background. This decorous, calm, and aristocratic world is menaced by the indecorous, wondrous, and mysterious, but only for a while. Order and decorum re-establish themselves with a laugh after we have been both held in thrall and amused. The rich irony and humor of the whole situation are suddenly revealed, but then we return to the stability time

[49] Maynard Mack, in the introduction to his edition of Henry Fielding's *Joseph Andrews*, Rinehart Editions 15 (New York and Toronto, 1948), p. xv.

On the mixture of jest and earnest in medieval literature, see Appendix IV to Ernst Robert Curtius, *European Literature and the Latin Middle Ages*, trans. W. R. Trask (London, 1953), pp. 417–437. There is a long tradition connecting the realm of the erotic with comedy which suggests a comic side to the temptation scenes. See Walter Pabst, *Novellentheorie und Novellendichtung: Zur Geschichte ihrer Antinomie in den romanischen Literaturen*, Universität Hamburg, Abhandlungen aus dem Gebiet der Auslandskunde, Band 58, Reihe B, Band 32 (Hamburg, 1953), p. 25.

perspective can give. The jewel has been seen in a strange light but then it is put back into place—somewhat different but still recognizable.

As I suggested above, the ambiguities of the Arthurian legend in the fourteenth century perhaps give us a clue to all this. In an age and a country which deliberately tried to keep the fading aristocratic ideals alive by tournaments and the founding of chivalric orders, we find a poet striving to present both the serious and the comic side of this aspect of his times. *Sir Gawain* both praises and belittles the past and the ideal. It tries to come to terms with the political and ideological tensions of its age by the dissolving force of humor and clarity, and it definitely assumes the importance of loyalty and Christianity. Life is perhaps at bottom such a suspenseful and wondrous game. By means of an art so vivid and so rich that many have been tempted to regard it as life itself, the *Gawain*-poet has created a new world which both beckons to and laughs at our own. The great charm of the poem perhaps is due to this curious mystery which both amuses and sobers, delights and frightens us at the same time, as it teeters on the edge of tragedy and defeat but at last safely brings us back to the solid ground of a happy ending. It all happened long ago and the past is after all both unreal and solid, and certainly far from us, and even slightly comic just because it is the past.

8. Piers Plowman *as a Fourteenth-Century Apocalypse*

Professor C. Vann Woodward, the distinguished authority on American history, in an address on the necessity of interpretations and analyses of new historical problems and issues by his fellow-historians, makes, toward the end of this interesting talk, the following point about our own times:

> The new age bears another and more ominous gift for the historian, one that has not been conspicuous in historical writings since the works of the Christian fathers. This gift is the element of the catastrophic. The Church fathers, with their apocalyptic historiography, understood the dramatic advantage possessed by the storyteller who can keep his audience sitting on the edge of eternity. The modern secular historian, after submitting to a long cycle of historicism, has at last had this dramatic advantage restored. The restoration, to be sure, arrived under scientific rather than apocalyptic auspices. But the dramatic potentials were scarcely diminished by placing in human hands at one and the same time the Promethean fire as well as the divine prerogative of putting an end to the whole drama of human history.[1]

Mr. Woodward is here stressing the advantages which our age offers for the writing of dramatic history. For the first time since the Middle Ages, historians as a whole can with justice be convinced of an appalling catastrophe hanging over the world and may use this threatening possibility to write with a fervor and sense of doom such as the Church Fathers possessed when writing of human history. Since the sixteenth century or even earlier, only a few historians could write their histories as if an end of human history could soon be expected.

This is a good point, and I hope modern historians may give heed to this advice from one of their number and inject more life and vitality into their work. Other professional scholars could also benefit by this advice. It seems to me, however, that there is another advantage, if such is the right word, to be gained from the history of our own time—a new ability to understand literary works and hu-

Reprinted by permission from *Centennial Review*, V (1961), 281–295.

This paper is based on a lecture first given at the Modern Language Association convention in Philadelphia, December 1960.
[1] "The Age of Reinterpretation," *AHR*, LXVI (1960–61), 19.

man beings of the past, obsessed or deeply concerned with the imminence of the end of human history by divine intervention. In short, we may now begin to understand anew the apocalyptic and eschatological element in the past.

There is evidence indeed that such is happening. Modern existentialistic theology is much concerned with the apocalyptic and eschatological. The apocalyptic interpretation or reinterpretation of Jesus' teachings and of early Christianity has by now almost become a commonplace. The discovery of the Dead Sea Scrolls has revealed the apocalyptic views of a Jewish sect, probably the Essenes, which flourished around the period of Jesus' life. Other Jewish apocalypses are also known. Christianity seems to have arisen out of a similar small Hebrew apocalyptic sect or at least found favor at first among those who believed that the end of the world was near and that a Messiah would come to prepare the elect for the Day of Judgment. This new knowledge explains much in the New Testament and earliest Christian writings.

As a result of all this, we can now reread certain apocalyptic writers of the past in a new light. All thinking men have been forced to consider the possible end of human existence on earth. In the past, since the Renaissance, this concern was always limited to the few. We can now better understand the implications of the Day of Judgment in the older Judeo-Christian tradition. The apocalyptic and catastrophic is not merely evidence of human aberration or eccentricity but a continuing and serious aspect of the human story. It is true that today it may be science and human nature rather than God which will destroy us all, but God may be working through science, and in any case the destruction of the world, if it comes, will be the same, whatever the cause.

It is true, of course, that apocalyptic thinkers were often eccentric and even mad, but we can at least see them as concerned with certain fundamental problems of humanity, no matter how wild their theorizings and beliefs may have been. The apocalyptic thinker is convinced that God's judgment hangs over the world and that it is his task to warn people because he can see correctly the signs of coming catastrophe, not always necessarily the end of the world.

In the Judeo-Christian tradition, the apocalyptic view of the world is enshrined in the dogma of the Resurrection and the Day of Judgment, but it also appears in other concepts and key notions such as those of the Kingdom of God, the Messiah, and Antichrist. The latter will lead the forces of evil and will be opposed by the Messiah or his representatives. In fact, all of history may be seen as a struggle between various Antichrists and various representatives of the elect and the chosen. The tradition, as we may even see in the New Testament (for example, 1 John 2:18 and 2 John 7), admitted the possibility of various Antichrists. In the latter part of the Middle Ages, this belief in a plurality of Antichrists was widely held, and, at the end of time there would be the greatest Antichrist of all. This period in history was especially rich in apocalyptic thinking of various sorts with paradoxical attitudes. We find in the fourteenth century a strong belief both in the imminent end of the world and in a great coming future after a time of troubles, a new age. In all this, some scholars have tried to find the medieval antecedents of the Renaissance.

As we pass from one age to another, there are persecutions of the righteous, widespread sin, and the advent of Antichrists; a time of troubles comes upon the world. But all for the ultimate purpose of renewal. The very sufferings of the age and of the church were proofs of the coming new age or of a profound reformation.

This apocalyptic current is not the only one in the later Middle Ages, but it is an important one. It is in its terms that I think we can best understand the work of the fourteenth-century William Langland, who wrote a very long poem in three versions called *Piers Plowman* between 1363 and 1386, usually designated A, B, and C. His apocalypticism, however, was centered around the ideas of order, moderation, and temperance. It was through these virtues practised by all groups in society, but above all by the friars, that he believed the crisis of his own time could be solved, so that a new age could dawn for humanity.

Piers Plowman is divided into two sections, the first called the *Visio* and the second the *Vita*. It relates the dreams of a rough, uncouth but yet self-conscious man named Will about the world around him, who seeks the meaning of the Christian life in this world. The *Visio* presents a picture of a corrupt society dominated by cupidity (personified as Lady Mede, that is Lady Reward) but which is attempting in a confused way to find the right way to God. Piers Plowman, a mysterious figure (who later in the poem turns out to be the human aspect of Christ), tries to help the world but fails. After this depressing picture, Will begins again in the *Vita* to search for an answer to his problems, in other words, for Christian perfection. The *Vita* is divided into three subsections, the life of Do-good, of Do-bet(ter), and of Do-best. "Do-good" deals with Will's search for an authority within himself or in the world to answer his questions about Christian perfection and he is shunted from one authority to the other, but finally arrives at the answer that Do-good is to lead a life of humble poverty. In "Do-bet," we are presented with the three Christian virtues of faith, hope, and charity; this section culminates in a treatment of the scene of Christ liberating the saints of the Old Testament from Hell, an event usually known in the tradition as the Harrowing of Hell. Here Christ appears in His majesty. "Do-best" returns to the society of Langland's own time, with which the poem began. Here we see the forces of Antichrist rife, and all seems to be in a state of hopeless corruption. After various vivid descriptions, the poem ends on Conscience's setting out to find Piers Plowman again so that pride may be destroyed and the friars may have enough for their maintenance. Needless to say, as the above outline shows, this poem is difficult to interpret, and there have been various attempts to do so.

In recent years there has been a tendency to find in *Piers*, which is built around a quest by the hero Will, the journey of a mystic toward God, and perhaps in one sense this is true. But *Piers* is first of all socially oriented—that is, apocalyptic in its view of Christian perfection. History and society must come first as both the beginning and final sections of the poem show very clearly. The journey of the individual soul to God is perhaps also implied, but it is not central. It is Piers, not Will, who starting as a simple peasant becomes the human aspect of Christ. Piers, not Will, is deified. Will's quest is for the three "Do's"—Christian perfection—and he grows old in it, but he knows that Piers Plowman must be found by Conscience and returned to Holy Church, that is, the society of Christians, before he can find his answer. He must, by a quest, cooperate with the grace which Piers represents and the Christ he stands for. But Piers is sought to save Holy Church, not primarily to save Will. And it is this which makes the poem basically an apocalyptic, not a mystical, poem. *Piers* is not fundamentally the story of the journey to God of the individual, and the three "Do's" of the *Vita* section are not fundamentally the purgative, illuminative, and unitive ways of the mystic but belong to an older tradition, a monastic one originally, of the states of Christian perfection which involve fundamentally the Kingdom of God.

Moreover, the fundamental symbol of the poem, Piers, and its attendant agricultural imagery, together with other important classes of images in the poem like those of food and clothing, all reinforce the apocalyptic point. Any poem thus organized must at the very least in a Christian society have eschatological aims in mind. Both in the Old and New Testaments, agricultural, food, and clothing imagery has a basic apocalyptic dimension.

Jesus' parables are full of these images. Jesus, interpreting his own parable of the tares, says: "He that soweth the good seed is the Son of Man; the field is the world; the good seed are the children of the kingdom; but the tares are the children of the wicked one; the enemy that sowed them is the devil; the harvest is the end of the world; and the reapers are the angels" (Matthew 13: 37–39).

The harvest is paradise or salvation, and those who tend it lead man to his proper end. Christ is the supreme harvester or plowman, and all plowmen to some extent are symbols of his true followers—priests, religious, or even laymen, who are creating or bringing in the harvest. The plow is the tool whereby He prepares the field of the world for His harvest of souls. Do-best, the concluding section of the poem, begins with a description of Pentecost, and Pentecost is the feast of the Church, of the mission of the Holy Ghost, and also the feast of the end of time, of the Church Triumphant.

Throughout the poem, we also find particular apocalyptic passages. The prologue of the *Visio* with its picture of a corrupted society which holds promise of renewal sets the tone from the beginning. Evil has corrupted Christian society and the church militant; yet out of evil good may come, for God allows evil to flourish and the Church to suffer while He plans for its rebirth and regeneration.

Conscience in her great speech before the king—who is also an apocalyptic figure—breaks out into an apocalyptic vision (B III, 282 ff.). Langland's predilection for prophecies, usually of the most difficult kind for us, is further evidence of his apocalyptic frame of mind. Obscure prophecies are the stock-in-trade of all those who are convinced that history is soon about to undergo a profound change. They satisfy the love of the obscure and are a delight to those who look for self-justification and religious reform. To those convinced of their truth, they make sense out of the current miseries of history. They are also difficult to disprove and may be applied again and again *ad libitum*, not to say *ad nauseam*. Above all, they prove the superiority of redemptive to secular history. In a time of crisis, such as the later Middle Ages, they were very popular, especially with those concerned with the writing of history. These enigmatic prophecies are of the essence of the apocalyptic view of life.

Closely related to the prophetic frame of mind is the tendency to find eschatological signs in natural phenomena, especially those of weather and the sky. These are not wanting in *Piers*, but to Langland contemporary social phenomena were his main signs. The current social evils provide the main evidence that a new or reformed age is about to dawn. The evils of his time afford the best proof to Langland that, if God and His Church are realities, and to him there could be no doubt on these matters, good was to come out of evil. The persecution of the just and of the true church was a fundamental proof of their coming rehabilitation. Fundamentally, Langland, like all millenarians, was an optimist.

Omitting for lack of time the many other apocalyptic passages, or passages which have an apocalyptic dimension in the poem, I should like to point out that the culmination of the poem from Passus XVIII in "Do-bet" to the end is openly apocalyptic. The Harrowing of Hell scene is a forshadowing of the Last Judgment. Here Christ is seen in His majesty, not in His suffering on the cross. The section beginning "Do-best," following on this scene contains a long discussion on Christ the King. In the apocalyptic vision, it is the triumphant, ruling Christ who is to conquer. Then Langland goes on to picture the coming of Antichrist to whom he felt his own time and society had given allegiance.

Just as Satan and his minions were overcome in the Harrowing of

Hell, so finally will Antichrist and all his hosts be subdued—when Conscience finds Piers Plowman and when the religious orders will be able to take over their fundamental task of transforming the world. The Antichrist scene which ends the poem on a realistic note is the anti-vision to the vision of the Harrowing of Hell—the present reality as opposed to God's reality. The concluding vision of "Do-bet," however, foretells the true end to the Antichrist vision of "Do-best." The very presence of Antichrist is, to thinkers like Langland, actually evidence for the imminence of renewal and fundamentally a hopeful sign.

Piers Plowman is thus deeply immersed in the apocalyptic vision of the world and its history. The ideal Pope or spiritual leader is seen in Piers, who is a multidimensional symbol, and the saviour-emperor or ideal king appears *in propria persona* in several of the more notable apocalyptic passages. These two figures of late medieval apocalypticism—the angelic pope and ideal king—are united in the figure of Christ in His majesty Who harrows Hell and Whose power and dignity are carefully described in "Do-best." "Do-best" concentrates on Jesus as Conqueror, King, and Judge. Individual perfection becomes in the last analysis a problem of social perfection, and social perfection to a convinced Christian means the Kingdom of God.

Piers Plowman begins with a vision of society, a fair field full of folk, and ends with a similar vision but with the forces of Antichrist unleashed against the true church and the society of the elect, *Unitas*. In between we witness first the problems of society and of the proper distribution of earthly goods, the desire for salvation which is frustrated, and finally the journey of the self toward enlightenment in perfection which leads inevitably back to society. But the only answer is the help of God and His inscrutable will which ordains in this time of *Heilsgeschichte* that sufferings be undergone, so that the just and the merciful may finally come into their own and a great social renewal may take place on the road to the Kingdom of God.

The greatest difficulty in seeing the basic apocalyptic quality in *Piers* is the strong and violent criticism of the friars which runs through the whole poem. This satire reaches its culmination at the very end of the poem when Conscience sets out to find Piers Plowman or Christ for two reasons—to destroy pride and to provide a minimum sustenance for the friars. The solution to the whole problem of the world for Langland turned to a great extent on the reform of the friars. How can we relate this violent attack on the friars and the conviction of the centrality of their role in the attainment of perfection with the apocalyptic frame of mind which informs the whole poem? If friars are merely one group in society among many, it is difficult to see why Langland should consider their reform the crucial problem for the solution of the problem of the world.

The answer to this question is complex. The greatest source of evil in his time, Langland thought, lay in the violation of their natural roles by all groups in society. Of these, the religious are the highest class in society, and their betrayal is the worst just because so much is demanded of them. The wickedness of the clergy is the classic case of all wickedness and the true symbol of the current debasement of society. Within the religious, the monks, or friars, represent the highest group. Monasticism is the quest *par excellence* for Christian perfection. Monasticism in its ideal form is the foreshadowing of the Kingdom of God. Monasticism is the eschatological element in history. These views are commonplaces of the monastic point of view. I believe that Langland was profoundly influenced by this point of view and that he felt the activities of the friars were the most blatant violation of the monastic ideal possible. In this, he was no doubt partly influenced by the quarrels between the monks and friars in his own time, but fundamentally he was sincerely concerned with the violation of trust involved.

Langland's attitude toward the friars was ambiguous. He honored them as types of monks, but he despised them for betraying their ideals. Of all classes of society, their betrayal was the worst just because they, of all groups, had the most to offer society as the exemplars of the Kingdom of God. They were most debased because they should be most elevated. Their debasement, Langland thought, was founded primarily on their view of the nature of poverty which they equated with mendicancy. The recognition of legitimate need on the part of the friars is the first step in the reform of the friars. If they abandon their erroneous concept of poverty and realize that the quest for perfection requires a minimum of food and clothing which can be obtained by legitimate labor, they can then give up their concern for wealth with the inevitable corruption which attends upon it and truly become, as their status on the highest level as religious demands, genuine seekers for perfection. They would then presumably set an example for all other estates and lead the way to a regeneration of society. If they could be reformed, then all society could be reformed. They are crucial to the salvation of Christendom. We may then, in some sense, all become monks, as Joachim of Flora, a medieval thinker of the twelfth century, had predicted.

❦

In discussing literature, it is not enough to be concerned with what it says; we must also be concerned with how it is said. The how must also be related to and reinforce the what. Literary form is what makes literature in the last analysis literature; otherwise, there is no fundamental difference between a series of notes or a loose discourse on a subject and literary endeavor. Form makes matter memorable; it lifts what is being said to the heights of art.

Now in dealing with older literature in especial, we must endeavor to find out what tradition the writer was working in. In the Middle Ages, the writer was considered a craftsman who knew his business and not merely someone inspired by his own psyche, although there were medieval theories of inspiration, especially connected with the role of the prophet. No doubt Langland and Dante worked under what we would call inspiration, but this did not mean that they could neglect the traditions of their craft.

Among the literary traditions available to these writers and others was the concept of genre. A literary work was thought to belong properly to a genre, an overall literary form, which controlled in general the aims and organization of the attempted work of art. There were other traditions too of style and figurative language, but we shall not concern ourselves with them here. If we can identify the genre or genres which dominated Langland's work, we may get valuable clues as to his intentions and understand better his artistic goals.

Let us now turn to the form of *Piers*. Is there such a genre as an apocalypse? Is *Piers* not only apocalyptic in content but also in form? Here we run into difficulties. What was the literary tradition in which Langland conceived his vast poem? I think part of the difficulty with the work lies in its confusion of genre. *Piers* is a combination of several genres, and in fact there is even a certain clash between them. The restlessness of Will's search for perfection is reflected in his author's uncertain sense of genre.

This is not the place to enter into a discussion of the importance of genre as one of the literary boundaries for the artist. Some have denied its validity in assessing and understanding art, but without committing myself on other periods, I think it is perfectly obvious that the medieval writer was very conscious of the kind of form in which he chose to present his artistic vision and that it is against the customary lines of this form that we can best understand his innovations and his uniqueness. And with a certain form went certain expectations which the writer felt he must at least satisfy.

It is also true that genre analysis is not free of difficulties, great difficulties, especially of definition. What is one man's genre may be another man's theme or motif. Genres also overlap. I think, however, one must only accept as genres, literary forms defined as such before the time of the composition of the work being considered, for some forms are esoteric and others are so broad that they lose the distinguishing marks of a genre—a literary type which has a certain general organization and arouses certain definite expectations in its readers or listeners.

This problem of definition comes to the fore in connection with the quest around which *Piers Plowman* is mainly organized. The literary quest has been a most popular unifying principle in literature in all ages, but in the later Middle Ages it reached its zenith. But it seems to me that it is a theme or dominant image rather than a genre. If then *Piers Plowman* cannot be classified as a quest in regard to genre, what form is it cast in? One of the possible answers is that it is an apocalypse.

Is the apocalypse a literary genre? There are conflicting answers to this question. It is now recognized how indebted Jewish and Christian writings of the period just before, during, and after the life of Jesus are to Greek literary forms and rhetoric. In particular, the influence of the genre called the aretalogy and of the eulogistic biography on the New Testament and early Christian writings such as the *Shepherd of Hermas* have been recognized.[2] The aretalogy is similar in many ways to some of the early apocalypses. Aretalogies were connected with Hellenistic mystery religions and developed alongside the Greek novel. They are narrations of the theophany of a god among men with emphasis on his miracles.[3] No doubt the Semitic prophetic vision is another element in the apocalyptic form. The Books of Daniel and Second Esdras provided models here for Revelation and early Christian apocalypses. The characteristics of the early apocalypses include a vision form and direct revelations by God or angels. Yet I agree with Father Musurillo when he writes: "The form known as 'apocalypse' creates a problem, and perhaps no useful purpose is served in making the term a technical one applicable both to the Revelations of St. John and the so-called *Shepherd of Hermas*." [4]

The confusion implicit in the use of the term is seen in the fact that Klingner calls Boethius' *De consolatione*, the great philosophical work of late antiquity, an apocalypse like *Poimandres* and the *Shepherd of Hermas*, earlier works of an apocalyptic cast, while Northrop Frye sees it as a Menippean satire or anatomy.[5] It is clear that it can also be called a *consolatio*, that is a work written to console someone on a loss.[6] While there is no rule that a literary work

[2] On the aretalogy, see R. Reitzenstein, *Wundererzählungen* (Leipzig, 1906), esp. pp. 7 ff; Moses Hadas, *Hellenistic Culture, Fusion and Diffusion* (New York, 1959), pp. 170 ff; and Georgius Manteuffel, *De opusculis graecis aegypto e papyris, ostracis lapidibusque collectis*, Travaux de la Société des Sciences et des Lettres de Varsovie, Classe 1 (1930) (Warsaw, 1930). On the pagan encomium and biography and their influence on saints' and martyrs' lives, see Herbert A. Musurillo, *The Acts of the Pagan Martyrs, Acta Alexandrinorum* (Oxford, 1954).

[3] I am indebted for this definition to Herbert Musurillo, "History and Symbol: A Study of Form in Early Christian Literature," *Theological Studies* XVIII (1957), 357–386.

[4] *Op. cit.*, p. 365. Cf., however, R. L. P. Millburn, who writes that ". . . this type of imaginative novel-writing [stories about the Virgin] not seldom took the specialized form of apocalypse, perhaps the most influential of these compositions, though its fourth-century date makes it a fairly late one, being the *Apocalypse of Paul*" *Early Christian Interpretations of History*, The Bampton Lectures of 1952 (London, 1954), p. 190.

[5] See Fritz Klingner, *De Boethii consolatione philosophiae*, Philologische Untersuchungen 27 (Berlin, 1921), pp. 112 ff., and N. Frye, *The Anatomy of Criticism* (Princeton, 1957), p. 312.

[6] On the *consolatio* as a literary genre, see Charles Favez, *La Consolation latine chrétienne* (Paris, 1937); Michele Coccia, "Le 'consolatio,' in Seneca," *Rivista di*

must be written in one genre, and indeed deliberate mixing of genres is characteristic of many medieval literary works, it is true, I think, that one genre must be thought as somehow dominant in a work or the whole point of the genre as a controlling device is lost.

If the apocalypse is not a literary genre, it is true that it possesses certain characteristics, although not unique ones: it is cast in a vision form, it contains a revelation from on high, or at least a superior guide, and it is severely critical of contemporary history. In general it is oriented toward man's and mankind's final destiny and often contains prophecies under enigmatic figures. *Piers Plowman* possesses all of these elements with possibly the exception of a divine or angelic guide, although *Lady Church* does briefly perform that function in Passus I of the *Visio*. Part of the problem of Will is actually to find an authority, and his quest is not only for perfection but for someone who can lead him to perfection, until finally he realizes that only Piers himself can.

There are differences too. The bitter and explicit satire of *Piers* is rarely to be found in the older apocalypses. Perhaps here we have some influence of the parodic medieval apocalypse such as the twelfth-century Latin *Apocalypse of Golias* where Pythagorus serves as a guide to the dreamer and which is a violent attack on religious abuses.[7] This work was exceedingly popular in England and may have originally been written there.

Rather than set up a genre called the apocalypse which can only be very vaguely established, I prefer to think of *Piers* rather as an amalgam of the allegorical dream narrative as in certain French

---

cultura classica e medievale, I (1959), 148–180; Sister Mary Edmond Fern, *The Latin Consolatio as a Literary Type*, Dissertation . . . of St. Louis University . . . Typewritten MS, 1931; Alfred Gercke, "De consolationibus," *Tirocinium Philologium*, Sodalium Regis Seminarii Bonnensis (Berlin, 1883), pp. 28–70; Carolus Buresch, *Consolationum a graecis romanisque scriptarum, historia critica*, Leipziger Studien zur classischen Philologie IX (Leipzig, 1887), 3–170; Edouard Boyer, *Les Consolations chez les Grecs et les Romains*, Thèse . . . La Faculté de Théologie Protestante de Montauban . . . 1887 (Montauban, 1887); Constant Martha, "Les Consolations dans l'antiquité," *Etudes morales sur l'antiquité*, 2nd ed. (Paris 1905), pp. 135–189.

7 Ed. Karl Strecker, Texte zur Kulturgeschichte des Mittelalters 5 (Rome, 1928). I owe this suggestion to Professor John Conley.

works; the vertical dialogue, *consolatio,* or debate [8] as in Boethius' *De consolatione;* and the encyclopedic (or Menippean) satire as in Nigel Wireker's *Speculum stultorum,* a twelfth-century poem about an ass who is looking for his lost tail and which is a satire on the church. These genres are not mutually exclusive, and genetically some are related. The *consolatio* in its classic medieval form is, for instance, also a dream vision. Even when this is admitted, however, it is still true that in the Middle Ages these forms were distinct in tradition, had a definite organization, and were designed to satisfy certain expectations in an audience.

These three genres are all related in medieval times to the quest for perfection to which Langland was committed artistically and most certainly personally. In order to dramatize his complex theme, with its mixture of quest, debate, and satire, Langland found himself, so to speak, in the midst of three literary genres which were well-established before his time; and from their conventions he attempted to weave together a unified work of art, a work which would reveal his basic perplexities, dramatize, and objectify them. He was perhaps attempting too much and this alliance was not always successful. And beyond all this hovers the apocalyptic urgency which must have been the driving force in his character.

The reform of the friars is to be the main task of his age, as Langland saw. Not scientists working in laboratories, not the proletariat, but monastic ideals as lived by monks and friars were to be his agent for the reform of the world, and their guidance would lead the world into the golden age awaiting it, hid in the womb of time. This was Langland's answer to his quest for perfection.

In spite of his propensity to ramble, to develop, to divagate, Langland is firm and single-minded in his essential point—in A, B, and C from beginning to end. The expansions and changes in the different versions do no more than add more material to build up the essence of what he has to say; they all reveal the hard struggle for Christian perfection. The basic answer, though, the answer Langland never doubted is set out in Passus I of the A-text—moderation in self and society, victory over the betrayal of ideals especially by the clergy, the need for love and justice. In these essen-

[8] On the adjective *vertical* here see Stephen Gilman, *The Art of "La Celestina"* (Madison, 1956), pp. 159–160.

tials Langland never wavers. *Piers Plowman* is a monument to the struggles of a perplexed but hopeful, sensitive, fourteenth-century Englishman for a solution to the problems of his time and of all time in the attainment of Christian perfection which must, to his apocalyptic mind, be a social solution which would involve the setting up of the Kingdom of God on earth, very much as his master Jesus had Himself promised in the New Testament.

9. Authenticating Realism and the Realism of Chaucer

Whenever anything looks like what it is not, the resemblance being so great as nearly to deceive, we feel a kind of pleasurable surprise, an agreeable excitement of mind, exactly the same in its nature as that which we receive from juggling. Whenever we perceive this in something produced by art, that is to say, whenever the work is seen to resemble something which we know it is not, we receive what I call an idea of imitation. . . . Now two things are requisite to our complete and most pleasurable perception of this: first, that the resemblance be so perfect as to amount to a deception; secondly, that there be some means of proving at the same moment that it is a deception.—John Ruskin, Modern Painters I, *iv*

In all probability, no subject in literary theory has been more quarreled over, argued about, and commented on than that of realism. Yet in spite of certain recurrent themes and a good amount of repetition, new aspects of this eternally fascinating subject do appear at times and a more precise understanding of the nature of art becomes possible. In the past decade, Charles Muscatine's *Chaucer and the French Tradition* (Berkeley, 1957) has enabled us to look at Chaucerian and medieval realism in a new, or perhaps I should say old, way. He has made us see that it is a style and not merely a reproduction of life. Realism, in other words, has a strong conventional element in it, going back in large measure to French models. A medieval writer writes realistically not merely by observing and selecting materials from life around him but also by imitating the features of the realistic style. Realism in Chaucer, and in other medieval writers, is not merely an imitation of life but also of the characteristics of certain kinds of literature. As Muscatine writes, "The literature of the [medieval] bourgeois [1] tradition is 'realistic' or 'naturalistic' but it neither attempts nor achieves the reportorial detail of the modern fiction describable by these labels. It is based, even more clearly than the realism of the novel, on a circumscribedly conventional style. It is full of exaggeration, of caricature and grotesque imagination" (p. 58).

The great Chaucerian critics of the past half century were unconsciously under the influence of the contemporary climate which saw realism as a vivid slice of life and as the highest expression of literary art. They tended, therefore, to see the dramatic and circumstantial element in Chaucerian narrative to the exclusion of the conventional and stylistic element—the details themselves rather than how they were used. No doubt recent criticism is also under the influence of the contemporary climate which stresses the symbolic and meaningful aspects of experience and in which Kafka has replaced Zola. But we can deny our own time and our own historical situation only at a great cost to our judgment and our honesty.

Reprinted by permission from *Thought*, XXXIX (1964), 335–358.

[1] Although there is a realistic French style, mainly in the fabliaux, it is no longer clear that it is actually a bourgeois creation. Per Nykrog argues cogently that the fabliaux arise in the same social circles as the courtly romances and were written basically to mock the bourgeois. See his *Les Fabliaux: Etude historique littéraire et de stylistique médiéval* (Copenhagen, 1957).

There is good reason why realism in general is such a popular subject in literary theory and criticism, for in one way or another one might say that it is central to any discussion of literature or even art. As the ancient theory of imitation or mimesis testifies, art must claim to be real in some sense if it is to be taken at all seriously. The whole problem lies, of course, in what sense or senses art is real. In an immediately obvious sense, it is patently not real. Art objects are not natural, and all art objects are human creations of some sort. They are made up. Yet in another sense, they must be real if they are worthy of engaging the attention of human beings. And art has engaged and continues to engage the attention and endeavors of men in various capacities. Art is in some way both real and unreal at the same time. The sharpness of the real-unreal dichotomy comes out very clearly in Gilbert Murray's comment on the *Iliad* written over fifty years ago. "If you take up the Iliad as a record of history, you will soon put it down, exclaiming, 'Why, this is fiction!' But if you read it as fiction, you will at every page be pulled up by the feeling that it is not free fiction." [2]

Two hundred years ago, David Hume wrote more vigorously, "Poets . . . though liars by profession, always endeavour to give an air of truth to their fictions; and where that is totally neglected, their performances, however ingenious, will never be able to afford much pleasure." [3] The irony of this statement turns ultimately against Hume, for poets are liars only in order to be true to life in its deepest sense. That life is more than sense experience, more than the "fact," is a principle all great writers have subscribed to. They have understood, as Hume did not, that one must lie in order to get at the truth.

Yet Hume raises a very fundamental issue here. Why in order to deny mere sense experience must writers pretend that what they are

[2] *The Rise of the Greek Epic* (Oxford, 1907), p. 158.

[3] *Treatise of Human Nature*, I, iii. 10, ed. L. A. Selby-Bigge (Oxford, 1928 ed.), p. 121. Cf. Henry James's shock in "The Art of Fiction" (ed. Morris Roberts [New York, 1948], pp. 5–6) at the fact that Trollope admits in his novels that "the events he narrates have not really happened." Cf. also *ibid.*, pp. 59–60. Of course, the problem of lying in art was not first raised by Hume, but goes back to a long tradition beginning with Plato and was much discussed in Renaissance criticism. Cervantes writes in his *Viaje del Parnaso* VI ". . . falsehood satisfies when it looks like truth and is written in a delightful way," quoted in E. C. Riley, *Cervantes's Theory of the Novel* (Oxford, 1962), p. 19.

writing is true? Why this "air of truth"? In attempting to answer this question, we must discriminate among realisms,[4] as we have been taught to discriminate among romanticisms. In order to make use of such a protean word as "realism" at all, we must give it, as we must to all general words in the humanities, many meanings if appearances are to be saved. My main purpose is to look into one of the meanings of this word as it may be applied to narrative, especially Chaucerian narrative.

A basic realism in narrative is concerned with the establishment of an air of truth or plausibility to a tale. In part, narratives are strategies to avoid the accusation of lying. This type of realism may be called "authenticating realism" and is to be found in one way or another in almost all narratives. It is fundamentally concerned with the truth-claim of the narrative and although related to it, is very different from ordinary realism. This realism of truth may be achieved in various ways, not all incompatible with each other. Frames of various sorts are popular for this purpose. Benjamin Constant's *Adolphe* opens with a fake publisher's foreword in which the publisher explains how the hero's story fell into his hands when he met him in Calabria. Stendhal tells us, in an address to the reader at the beginning of *The Charterhouse of Parma*, how the story which he is about to tell was told him in Parma toward the end of 1830 by the nephew of a friend of his, a canon of Parma. *Gulliver's Travels* opens with a letter from Captain Gulliver to his cousin Sympson the publisher, followed by Sympson's address to the reader. We also find more elaborate framing devices used in whole or in part to authenticate a narrative or narratives as in the *Decameron*, the *Arabian Nights*, and the *Canterbury Tales*, to the last of which we shall return.

More frequently, however, we merely find an "I" in the story, the presumed narrator who may or may not bear the author's name. In medieval narrative, the "I" is usually the literary equivalent of the author. Sometimes the "I" may participate in the action of the

[4] See Wayne C. Booth, *The Rhetoric of Fiction* (Chicago, 1961), pp. 53 ff. *et passim.*

story which he is presumably narrating, and sometimes he is merely an observer. If there is a frame, he may appear in it—as in the *Canterbury Tales*. This authorial "I" is a creation of the author and serves, among other things, to give "an air of truth" to the tale.

There are also other methods of authentication used by writers. Sometimes authentication may be obtained by the tone of the authorial voice alone. This method too is not inconsistent with the others we have discussed but is, on the contrary, always an accompaniment of every narrative. As Mons. Georges Blin has said, "The narrator has supposedly been, directly or as confidant of a witness, the witness of the facts which he is reporting" (Le narrateur a censément été, directement ou comme confidant d'un témoin, le témoin des faits qu'il rapporte").[5] In some narratives there is neither a frame nor an "I" but merely a voice. Dr. Anne Ferry has recently shown how the authenticating voice operates in *Paradise Lost*.[6] Here the narrator establishes his authority by adopting the conventional epic invocation (which is, incidentally, a frame of sorts). The narrator "endows us with the power to penetrate the world of the poem." "His tone is controlled by his personal experience of this mortal world and his inspired vision of its contrast with the golden world of Eden before the Fall and of the Paradise to come."

Not all literary works display the virtuosity of decisiveness of the *Paradise Lost* narrator,[7] but in every narrative there is the tone of the narrator's voice which serves as a kind of control and a guarantee of authenticity or on some occasions deliberate inauthenticity.

[5] In the discussion following Albert Henry's "L'Expressivité du dialogue dans le roman," as printed in *La Littérature narrative d'imagination aux genres littéraires aux techniques d'expression*, Colloque de Strasbourg 23–25 avril 1959, Bibliothèque des Centres d'Etudes supérieures spécialisés . . . Université de Strasbourg, Centre de Philologie Romane . . . (Paris, 1961), p. 19. Cf. also "A writer stands in a certain relation to his subject, and that relation must be accounted for and disposed of," review in *Edinburgh Review*, XCII (October 1850), 488–489, quoted in Richard Stang, *The Theory of the Novel in England 1850–1870* (New York and London, 1959), pp. 110–111. Its author was John Conington, Professor of Classics at Oxford. (I am indebted to Professor Walter Houghton for this information.)

[6] "The Authority of the Narrative Voice in *Paradise Lost*," *In Defense of Reading: A Reader's Approach to Literary Criticism*, ed. Reuben A. Brower and Richard Poirier (New York, 1962), pp. 76–93.

[7] The voice may sometimes be difficult to pin down. Paul J. Alpers, "Narrative and Rhetoric in the *Faerie Queene*," SEL, II (1962), 35, speaks, for instance, of Spenser's self-effacing "manner of address" as contrasted with that of Milton.

We read a narrative not only for the story but for the authenticating voice. In one way or another a narrative must not only present a story but an authentication of that story. In other words, a story must also present a solution to its epistemological problem. How are we to know that the story is true or presumably true? The suspension of disbelief is a fundamental process in narrative art. Part of the privilege of reading a narrative is to know in some measure the teller or assumed teller and the claims of his authority.

In much modern literature, tricks are played with the authenticating level. As Stephen Spender writes, "the mode of perceiving itself [in modern fiction] becomes an object of perception, and is included as part of the thing perceived." [8] We find figures such as the author himself in his own name talking about writing the book he is actually giving us or the "unreliable narrator" as in Henry James's novels or those of others. [9] However, tricks on the authenticating level are not unknown in earlier times. Cervantes, for instance, used a mythical Arab historian in *Don Quixote*. The "I" is used in an extremely confusing fashion by Vincente Espinel in his *Relaciones de la Vida del Escudero Marcos de Obregón*, a seventeenth-century novel. [10] Or the obvious parodic realistic authentication of Dickens' *Pickwick Papers* provides another example. However, the deliberate manipulation of the authenticating level to raise problems of perception and truth is largely a modern characteristic. In some cases, we even find the absolute destruction or abolition of a narrator or even "tone of voice." As we shall see later, however, all authenticating devices not only authenticate but also call attention to the need for authentication and hence to the inauthenticity of the work of art.

When an artist plays tricks with his authenticating level, he is not normally giving up the truth-claim of his story but is putting it on to another level—the level of the real world as seen in his title or

[8] "A Short History of the Pers. Pron. 1st Sing. Nom.," *The Struggle of the Modern* (London, 1963), pp. 133–134.

[9] See Wayne Booth, *op. cit.*, pp. 339–374. I doubt whether we can find an absolutely unreliable narrator much before the nineteenth century, although the narrator may be ironical about himself as in the *Canterbury Tales*, as one might be in real life.

[10] See George Haley, *Vincente Espinel and Marcos de Obregón, A Life and Its Literary Representation*, Brown University Studies XXV (Providence, 1959), pp. 65 ff.

chapter headings or preface or what you will. This particular type of authentication raises many difficult problems which need further investigation.

Finally, details of background in the tale itself or in the outside of the inner tale—in the world of the frame or the world of the "I" —may be used to gain authenticity. Localities, names, dates, and so forth may give an air of truth. These naturalistic and realistic details are very characteristic of the nineteenth- and twentieth-century realistic novel, but they may be found at all times in narrative art. Certain periods seem to favor this type of authentication over others, but although it has been most widely and consistently used in the past two hundred years, it is an old device and by no means the invention of modern times.

The authenticating level joins, in a way, the reader to the reporter in a shared intimacy. The reader or hearer is asked to accept the truth of something which is being told to him, and he is left free to accept the tale if he wants and to interpret it as he sees fit. The choice is up to him to accept or reject the plausibility of the tale. When the authenticating level is presented in the form of a presumed experience which has happened to the narrator or the voice telling the tale, as is very common, the narrator is taking the reader into his confidence and allowing him to judge the tale as the narrator judges it. The reader and the narrator are sharing an experience together. This makes for a kind of closeness which comes from allowing someone to speak to you. One is prepared to believe and to suspend disbelief. Since the rise of writing and printing, the greater need to create authenticating intimacy has led to more complicated authenticating devices. The ironies are deep here, for the teller and the reader both know that the story is not true, or at least not entirely true, in the sense of its having really happened, but that if the tale is to be told in a satisfying manner, they must both pretend together.[11]

When stories were oral performances, the whole milieu contained

---

[11] A good example of how unawareness of the authenticating level in narrative may lead to misinterpretations may be seen in Ernest Hoepffner, *Aux Origines de la nouvelle française*, The Taylorian Lecture (Oxford, 1939), pp. 11 ff. (a charming lecture on Marie de France), where Hoepffner argues that Marie de France believed in the magic and supernatural in which her *lais* abound because she says these unnatural experiences really happened.

180

a kind of built-in guarantee of their truth. The teller himself stands before his audience and tells them something which he himself knows and which the hearers probably also know. He is recreating shared knowledge of heroes and gods. Early narrative is supposed history. The whole situation, the speaker's voice, the reality of the audience, the sense of expectation, all contribute to an authentication of the tale. Although some authenticating devices, often merely a statement that the story is true, were used, authentication was not needed to the same extent as later.

When stories gradually moved out from their oral setting, the authentication principle became more important. Just as the development of reproductions gradually destroyed, as Malraux has emphasized, the sacred and social nature of painting and sculpture,[12] so the invention of writing and later of printing gradually brought about the separation of literature and its audience. In fact they were a major factor in creating an audience instead of participants. The social context, the uniqueness of oral performance, the visual reality of the narrator, all were gone. The shared knowledge may, however, have remained. This was, of course, a gradual process, but from that time until very recently when television and radio have begun to make the oral important again, though perhaps in a different way, the literatures of all civilized peoples, except in a few pockets like parts of Yugoslavia, were largely written. The invention of printing was the decisive step in cutting the bond of social participation already weakened by writing.

But the feeling that a tale must be or claim to be true, or if not true, be a special violation of truth, has persisted, and authors have continued to cater to this feeling because it is something absolutely basic to narrative art. Pure fiction, except under very controlled circumstances, is not worth a man's attention.[13] The very strong and

[12] See Joseph Frank, "Malraux's Metaphysics of Art," *The Sewanee Review*, LXX (1962), 620–650, esp. 621 ff. Cf. also Walter Benjamin, "Das Kunstwerk im Zeitalter seiner technischen Reproduzierbarkeit," 1936, reprinted in *Schriften*, ed. T. W. & Gretel Adorno (Frankfurt, a.M., 1955), I, 366–405. "The story of the gradual emancipation of conscious fiction from myth and moral parable has not yet been told." E. H. Gombrich, *Art and Illusion: A Study in the Psychology of Pictorial Representation* (New York, 1960), p. 128.

[13] This feeling is still widespread. Nancy Hale (in *The Realities of Fiction: A Book about Writing* [Boston and Toronto, 1961], p. 8) tells of the shock a clergyman's wife displayed on being told that one of her stories was not true. Yet there

181

deep feeling about this goes back no doubt to the conviction that an imitation which is not faithful to the basic reality of the original deeds, for very early narrative must have been both historical and mythic, destroys the magic power of participation. An art object reproducing a sacred story or being must be true if it is to carry the mana of the original. So a tale should be true if it is to work and enable the audience to participate again in the primal or strength-giving deeds of gods or heroes.[14]

Plays are still performances and social events. The actors carry their own authentication in their actions. Since the reading of plays in the closet is still not the normal procedure, the performance is all. Hence they do not normally need special authentication devices. Narratives have, since the invention of writing, more or less lost whatever built-in authentication they possessed. Narrative was the first of the arts to be detached from ritual and social participation, but it still bears the mark of its origin in this, as perhaps in other ways. Special efforts at authentication were felt to be necessary for narrative though not for drama. By this I do not of course mean that drama does not also have problems of authentication and in authentication, but they have to be approached in a different fashion.

In Western civilization, the Judeo-Christian religious tradition has been another less ancient but nevertheless powerful influence

---

are occasions when an author may deliberately claim that his story is not true (in fact as we shall see later a story must also indicate its untruth too), but except for deliberate violation, the norm on the epistemological level is a truth-claim. The following is of interest in this connection. "They [the Ashanti] tell stories only at night, and they precede each story by a public disclaimer that what is to follow is the truth; the teller will say: 'We don't really mean to say so; we don't really mean to say so.' Under these special conditions subjects ordinarily taboo can be talked about, laughed at, ridiculed." R. S. Rattray, *Akan-Ashanti Folk-Tales* (Oxford, 1930), pp. x-xii. Cf. the irony of Buckingham in *The Rehearsal* II, i, 56 ff. in Bayes's boast, "I despise your Johnson and Beaumont, that borrowed all they writ from Nature: I am for fetching it purely out of my own fancy."

[14] See, for instance, the act of truth in ancient Irish and Indian stories discussed by Myles Dillon, "The Archaism of Irish Tradition," *The Proceedings of the British Academy*, XXXIII (1947), 245–264. See also Erich Köhler, "Zur Selbstauffassung des höfischen Dichters," *Der Vergleich, Literatur und Sprachwissenschaftliche Interpretationen, Festgabe für Hellmuth Petriconi* . . . ed. R. Grossman, Walter Pabst, and Edmund Schramm, Hamburger Romanistische Studien A42 and B25 (Hamburg, 1955), pp. 65–79, esp. p. 65.

for associating authentication with narrative. The basic problem of all revealed religions is just this authentication. If Moses did not actually receive the Law from God or if Jesus really did not live and suffer under Pontius Pilate or, to put it another way, if there is no true history in the Bible, then the whole basis of the religious claim is gone. Sacred history to the Christian is an authentic linear development through time and is naturally presented in narrative form. One can be a Buddhist without insisting on the historicity of Buddha's intuition—all one has to insist on is its truth. But it is not an intuitive truth that Judaism or Christianity offers, but a logical paradox which bears the claim of historical accuracy. This demand for historical truth is woven into the very fabric of Judaism and Christianity and is discussed in the Bible itself. And the presentation of historical truth must be in narrative form. Unlike those of Judeo-Christianity the narratives of Buddhism—say the birth stories—are embroideries, not the fabric of religious belief.

The problem of authentication is very much in the minds of the human writers of the text as a reading of the Pentateuch or the New Testament reveals. The end of Chapter 18 of Deuteronomy frankly discusses the problem of how to distinguish true prophecy from false. So does Matthew 24. The methods of authentication used are most instructive, but we may not delve into them here.

In the really popular literature of the Middle Ages—saints' lives—the problem is faced again and again. Even in the most fantastic of lives, some attempt—and often more than that—to give credibility is made. Circumstantiality, prophecy, witnesses, threats and promises, awareness of the problem, all these and others occur again and again to emphasize the truth-claim of these stories. Oral epic stories are largely concerned with knowledge or belief which the audience already possessed; hence not too much emphasis on authentication was necessary. With saints' lives, however, the epistemological problem is much more difficult and the teller usually could not rely on a shared knowledge; hence the very great effort at authentication. The author or teller of a saint's life faced problems similar to those of a novelist who cannot count on the suspension of his audience's disbelief. He even more than most novelists had to relate logical absurdities. In other words, for the novelist or writer of romances or saints' lives, authentication is a very real problem and not merely conventional. Of course, the religious aim of the writer of a saints' life makes the problem of truth fundamental in a way unknown to a novelist. An oral narrative poet who knows what his audience knows has a much easier task.

One may allow a little embroidery, "pious frauds," but the basic truth of the tales of Jesus and his apostles and saints, their essential historicity, must be established. One reason why pagan narrative forms were accepted and used by the early Christians was that they had "an air of truth" about them and could be used for the real truth. This religious demand for truth reinforced the deeper more primitive truth-claim of ordinary narrative and helped to strengthen the importance of authenticating devices in Western narrative technique.

When we look at Chaucer's authenticating devices, we see that from the very beginning of his literary career he put a great deal of care into them. His favorite device, as with most medieval writers, was the dream. It is perhaps hard today to think of the dream framework as an authenticating device, but as even a superficial study of dream theory shows, dreams, especially "in the morning," that is, late, after the food has been digested, are bearers of revelation and true. The dream frame has been much misunderstood. For much of the past, it served to suspend disbelief and to obtain credence. The dream may be fantastic, but it really happened. The dreamer is also an "I" so that the basic credibility may be maintained. A man telling his own dream usually tells the truth. The dream framework gives us then two authenticating devices per se, the dream itself and an "I." The dream frame has other functions as well, for the tone established and the facts set forth tend to heighten the meaning of the dream itself, ironically or directly, but its chief function is in a very basic sense to establish the presumed reality and truth of the story. In *The Book of the Duchess* the voice speaking the poem tells us of his insomnia and unhappiness (probably from love) and how he read a book "this other night" to "drive the night away." He is presumably telling us about some of his constant problems. The first forty-three lines are in the present tense. Then at line 44 we move into the past. He is telling us of a particular experience—the reading of the story of Ceyx and Alcione—which is to lead into his narrative. The past tense signals this shift to a particular experience. The story of Ceyx and Alcione, which deals with faithful love beyond death, tells us how love can overcome death and prepares us to accept the mourning knight in the story. But it also has the detail and circumstantiality of truth. The tone is intimate—yet with the distance objectivity, irony, and self-awareness can give. The "I" falls asleep as he finishes the tale, and in his dream we are given the story of the grieving knight set in a partially ideal landscape such as we often find in dreams. After he has unburdened himself and the dreamer has asked his famous question and received his answer, the knight rides away.

The dreamer then awakes and tells us that he must "put this sweven in ryme/As I kan best and that anoon." The poem ends with the line "This was my sweven; now hit ys doon." I have completed my task; this was my real dream. These words echo the line just before the dream is introduced "Loo, thus hyt was, thys was my sweven." The last sentence drives us back to the beginning of the dream and the beginning of the poem. The circle comes full close. A circle is a most appropriate organization of a frame for a story about death for the thought of the unceasing round of death for all men is one of the traditional consolations for bereaved humans. All men die, it happens again and again.

The frame then is detailed and quasi-personal. It provides its own rationale as well as authenticating the content of the dream and presenting a counterpointing tale to that of the grieving knight within the story. There are three unhappy lovers in *The Book of the Duchess*: the dreamer, Alcione, and the knight. But the dreamer is speaking to us and telling us of the other two, and his rather indefinite sorrow, as well as the general circumstances of his dream, authenticates the sorrow and story of the others.

The inner story is full of dialogue and circumstantial detail, but it is set in an ideal and somewhat unreal landscape. The ideality of *The Book of the Duchess* lies almost exclusively in this setting. Every other level is presented in as lifelike a fashion as possible, but the inner background with its aroma of timelessness and unreality makes all the difference. The boundary between the frame and the

185

inner story is firm. There is a "real" world and a "dream" world, and each is kept completely separate as a unit from the other, unlike the procedure in *Piers Plowman* where the reader is often haled back into the "real" world. The third world, the real world revealed by the title is, as always, real and direct although only briefly given. The world of the title is real, the world of the frame is presented as real, the world of the inner story is presented as made up by, to use a modern term, the unconscious of the dreamer and contains real and ideal details.

If we turn to *Troilus and Criseyde*, we find a different frame—a frame which distances us from and authenticates the inner story by history and the historical consciousness. Here it is not a dream which separates the frame from the story as in *The Book of the Duchess*, but the past and time of which we are made constantly aware. The "I" of *Troilus and Criseyde* is constantly bringing us into the present, authenticating the story by the pose of the historian. The narrator is bound by history. The contrast between past and present in *Troilus and Criseyde* gives us a feeling of timelessness, of the spatialization of time,[15] while within the world of the story itself we get a lively sense of the passage of time which is a strong realistic device. Time is of the essence of narrative, which is, as Lessing long ago pointed out, sequential, but narrative writers all more or less try to transcend this limitation without at the same time destroying completely the temporality of narrative. Samuel Johnson speaks of diversifying narrative by "retrospection and anticipation." [16] Chaucer knew this secret as all his narratives show.

The setting of the inner story is Troy but recreated with much vividness.[17] Both the frame and the story are equally alive and pre-

---

[15] On spatialization of time, see Joseph Frank, "Spatial Form in Modern Literature," reprinted in revised form from *The Sewanee Review* (1945) in *Criticism: The Foundations of Modern Literary Judgment*, ed. Mark Schorer, Josephine Miles, and Gordon McKenzie (New York, 1948), pp. 379–392. See also Isabel Gamble MacCaffrey, *Paradise Lost as "Myth"* (Cambridge, 1959), pp. 44 ff. The weakness of Frank's perceptive essay lies in the fact that the "neutralization" of time is not only a modern phenomenon. It might also be argued that all art strains against its limitations of form, e.g., temporalization of Western painting and sculpture.

[16] *Lives of the English Poets*, ed. George Birkbeck Hill (Oxford, 1905), I, 170 (Life of Milton).

[17] See John McCall, "The Trojan Scene in Chaucer's *Troilus*," ELH, XXIX (1962), 263–275.

sented with great psychological acuity. There is no ideal level in *Troilus and Criseyde*, although Troilus himself and perhaps even Criseyde are idealistic characters. But the setting of the world of the frame against the world of the story takes us out of time [18] and gives an ideality of immobility to the work. As a result, the naturalism in the inner story set in this contrast gives us a stronger sense of reality than we get from *The Book of the Duchess*. However, both frames are realistic in the ordinary sense of the world, but they present us an individualistic not a social world. Both "I's" are directly responsible for the inner story—one as dreamer, one as historian.

With the *Canterbury Tales*, however, to which we now turn, it is a social as well as a personal world which authenticates the inner stories. Chaucer has moved from dream and past history [19] to a report on the contemporary world and present history, producing thereby yet another variation on the numerous ways of giving a realistic effect. The *Canterbury Tales* has always been considered Chaucer's greatest realistic masterpiece, but I think we should look a little more closely at the way in which Chaucer gains this realistic effect and also ask ourselves whether it is as realistic as is generally assumed. It, like *The Book of the Duchess* or the *Romance of the Rose*, is set in the present, but we are given a social world in the frame, not an individual's problems or attitudes. Part of the sense of vitality and plenitude which comes from a reading of the *Canterbury Tales* is due to the variety and extension of the frame. The stories, as we shall see, vivid as many of them are, do not give us this same sense of fullness. Unlike *The Book of the Duchess* but like *Troilus and Criseyde*, the two worlds of frame and story interpenetrate. Between stories we move back into the firm setting of the

[18] At the very end, Chaucer achieves a complete victory over time by moving Troilus to a pagan heaven and the "I" to the contemplation of the Trinity.

[19] Although, as Ralph Baldwin points out, Chaucer does juxtapose present and past in the General Prologue when, although presumably at the Inn before the journey, he describes the pilgrims as he could have known them only after the journey started. This technique is similar in part to that used more frequently in *Troilus and Criseyde*. See Baldwin's *The Unity of the Canterbury Tales* (Copenhagen, 1955), pp. 54–57. James V. Cunningham, "The Literary Form of the Prologue to the *Canterbury Tales*," MP, XLIX (1951–1952), 172–181, argues with great persuasiveness for the similarity of the General Prologue to the dream-vision prologue, especially that of the *Romance of the Rose*.

frame. And occasionally the frame interposes itself into a story as when the Friar accuses the Summoner of lying after he begins his tale or when a character in the Merchant's Tale alludes to the Wife of Bath.

The frame of the *Canterbury Tales* is in the form of a supposititious pilgrimage to St. Thomas' shrine in Canterbury. The pilgrim's tale of his voyage is a well-known literary genre, although until the later Middle Ages normally in Latin. It is a religious genre which catered to human curiosity about other lands and strange places and which stimulated religious piety. The pilgrimage is also a key metaphor for life from the religious sphere. We are all pilgrims on the way to the heavenly city, and every journey, but especially a religious one, reflects the basic pattern of existence. We are all homeless, exiled from paradise, looking for a return to our true home which is heaven, of which the earthly paradise was the foreshadowing. No doubt Chaucer had this religious dimension in mind when he chose a pilgrimage as a frame. The introduction to the last tale, that of the Parson, makes this quite clear. But a report of a pilgrimage is also a true report of an experience, and it is customary to report it in the first person. The authentication of a real pilgrimage lies in the personal participation of the pilgrim. In the *Canterbury Tales* the reporting pilgrim is the Chaucer figure, and it is on his authority that we must accept the truth of his story about events and tales. As we have already said, the vividness and circumstantiality of the *Canterbury Tales* seem to come largely from both the choice and treatment of this frame, so much so that some scholars have tended to reduce the individual tales of the work to mere appendages of the frame and its characters. Professor Kittredge, for example, writes that "the pilgrims do not exist for the sake of the stories, but *vice versa*. Structurally regarded, the stories are merely long speeches expressing, directly or indirectly, the characters of the several persons." [20] There is good reason for this opinion because it is in the authenticating device of the work, in the frame, that Chaucer's circumstantial and dramatic verisimilitude most strongly appears. In an age which admired realism in narrative art, Kittredge's judgment would be especially welcome.

Let us look at the individual stories. They too individually have

[20] *Chaucer and His Poetry* (Cambridge, 1915), p. 155.

their authenticating devices, but since things are complicated enough we shall not discuss them here but get to the content of the tales themselves. The Knight's Tale is not realistic in any direct sense: the characters are very stylized, as disputes over whether Palamon or Arcite is the more worthy show, and Emily is little more than a bone over which the dogs fight. We are told about her beauty; we do not see it. Conrad and Henry James would be very dissatisfied with Chaucer's art here. The story is laid in the past, and the action has a pageant, tapestry-like quality, with much description and decorative detail. The Miller's and Reeve's Tales, on the other hand, are full of circumstantial detail, and they are laid in contemporary England. Yet as stories, both are so improbable as to be grotesque. The whole scheme of Nicholas in the Miller's Tale is so fantastic that in terms of everyday realism it is absolutely unbelievable. It depends on a remarkable credulity on the part of the Carpenter, on a series of incredible coincidences, and above all on an unreal world in spite of all the detail with which it is recorded. Then too the plan, even if it went as Nicholas had hoped, could only work once. For a pleasant run of adultery, it was the worst possible scheme. Many of these points can also be made concerning the Reeve's Tale, although it is more credible in some ways.

The Man of Law's Tale lacks circumstantial realism and is laid in a vague past and for the most part in strange countries. The Wife of Bath's Tale is set in Arthurian England among characters who never could have existed. But here, as in most of Chaucer's Tales, we get a most lively dialogue. But the tale is fundamentally a fable. The Friar's Tale is a story of the supernatural, while the Summoner's Tale, in spite of its great circumstantial detail, has many of the characteristics of the fabliau as we have presented them in our brief comments on the Miller's Tale, and displays a most grotesque wit.

The Clerk's Tale has strong symbolic overtones, is laid in Italy, and has a most incredible plot. The climax of the Merchant's Tale is extremely unrealistic, it is peopled by figures like January and May, Placebo and Justinus, and is set in Lombardy. Yet it too has much circumstantial detail. The Squire's Tale is set in Asia and is frankly a tale of the supernatural.

The Franklin's Tale is by no means fundamentally realistic. It is set in pagan Brittany and depends on magic for the success of its story. The locale of the Physician's Tale is ancient Rome, and the rather summary story cannot be called realistic in the ordinary sense of the word. The Pardoner's Tale is an exemplum with little characterization and with a supernatural atmosphere. The Shipman's Tale is another fabliau with much circumstantial detail and a fantastic plot. The Prioress' Tale is a miracle of the Virgin, set in Asia. Sir Thopas is a parody of the romances which gains its effect by exaggerating their already incredible events and descriptions. The Tale of Melibee is more or less a string of proverbs and moral apothegms. The Monk's Tale does have some historical realism, but here history is being used for moralizing purposes, not for its own sake.

The Nun's Priest's Tale is a charming beast fable. The Second Nun's Tale is a saint's life. The Canon Yeoman's Tale is perhaps the most realistic of all the Canterbury Tales in the sense that we have been using the term "realism." Yet it is also one of Chaucer's least interesting tales. The Manciple's Tale is a mythological story from Ovid; and finally the Parson's Tale is not a tale at all, but a moral tractate.

As we look over this list, we see that actually none of these tales, with the possible exception of one, can compare in realism, in the sense of a reproduction of the details and events of ordinary life and their credibility, with the frame of the *Canterbury Tales*. It is the authenticating part of the work, the frame, that basically gives us that strong sense of real life that the poem affords. Now it is true that Chaucer's dialogue and characterization in many of the tales do reflect such a sense, but practically none of the tales can stand up in full measure as realistic, as true to perceived life. If some are realistic in one regard, they are apt to be unrealistic in another. At times, they are not even as realistic as Langland's *Piers Plowman*. The feeling of the action in the tale is real, as it is in almost all narrative, but the plot is often improbable either because of its deficient or accidental causality or because of its dependence upon the supernatural. The frame has a strong temporal quality which always makes for realism, but the stories themselves tend to move out of time or to do incredible tricks with it.

The *Canterbury Tales* is, however, realistic in a way that *Piers Plowman* is not because it has an authenticating frame which gives us a strong sense and feel of contemporary English life. It is the frame which creates the fundamental realism of the work. Of the two worlds of the *Canterbury Tales*, that of the frame conveys a strong sense of the workaday universe, that of the stories, in spite of many realistic aspects, really an ideal world which is stylized and patterned. And it is to the frame that Chaucer returns again and again.

Of course, by all this I do not mean to imply that, in a more profound sense, in the sense that all great art is real, the tales, or most of them, are not real too, but in the narrower sense, most of the tales are not as satisfyingly naturalistic as many critics seem to assume. When they are realistic their realism is very much a stylistic matter with skillful use of naturalistic elements in dialogue, diction or subject matter (bourgeois life).

Where did Chaucer get this notion of a realistic authenticating frame? It is hard to find before Chaucer's time consistent circumstantial realism used to any degree in English literature, with the exception of religious literature. The first realistic pictures of English contemporary life in English are to be found in religious literature where the truth of detail in sermon and tractate was necessary to bring the audience to the proper mood. Episodes in saints' lives are perhaps among the earliest examples. The *Ancrene Riwle* of the thirteenth century contains realistic vignettes, especially in similes and metaphors. Yet this and other religious works such as collections of exempla do not use a realistic frame. The realism of the narrative part of the Bible is extraordinary in its power, but it is not a realism of detail. The English romances move more or less in a timeless world of the mythical past, both in the frame when they have one and in the adventures themselves. The histories of England are of course realistic in another sense because they purport to deal with real persons. But the desire to moralize as well as deficient knowledge affect the circumstantiality of these accounts. Besides, the historians were mostly interested in high political action and signs, especially in natural phenomenon. Pseudo-histories, like Layamon's *Brut*, sometimes present an autobiographical introduction, but this is only a mere suggestion of a realistic framework. There were no doubt French and probably lost English fabliaux available. But it is hard to think of them as the sources for the frame of the

Canterbury Tales. The psychological realism of the best French romances and Boccaccian narratives provided some, but not much, "real life."

Some of the Latin satirical works of the Middle Ages are full of circumstantial detail, and we know that Chaucer knew the *Speculum stultorum* with its story of a donkey looking all over Europe for a longer tail. The Goliardic satires also provided pictures of contemporary life. Some would argue, as Professor Levin does,[21] that circumstantial realism always takes its rise in parody of the current literary and worldly conventions. All realism is in some ways offensive.[22] If we consider the important role that satire plays in the General Prologue, and indeed the whole work, it is not unlikely that the satirical impulse was strong in leading Chaucer to realism of this sort. *Piers Plowman* as a satire is full of realistic pictures of England, and it is not unlikely that Chaucer knew it. Yet the realism of Piers is largely within the dreams of the dreamer and not in the frame. Satire as far as I know does not give the kind of realistic frame we are looking for.

Framed stories from the Orient, such as *The Seven Sages of Rome*, usually have a rather slender frame, and collections of saints' lives are usually altogether frameless. In contemporary Spain and Italy, we do find framed collections of tales which use the frame more or less as Chaucer does. Chaucer, however, probably did not know the *Libro del buen amor* or the *Decameron* either of which would have provided an excellent model, at least in some respects.[23] Yet there were Italian collections with some kind of realistic frame which he might have known. John Gower's *Confessio Amantis* may or may not be in the running because of chronology.

Chaucer's realism of detail in the authenticating frame seems to be largely original with him. He no doubt took some suggestions from earlier literature, and possibly the dream-vision prologue as

[21] See "What is Realism?" *CL*, III (1951), 193–199. Cf. also John Lawlor, "Radical Satire and the Realistic Novel," *Essays and Studies* (1955), esp. pp. 74–75.

[22] "Il realismo, quando sia autentico e consapevole, offende la cultura costitutiva." Salvatore Battaglia, "L'essempio medievale," *Filologia romanza*, VI (1958), 79.

[23] The frame of the Decameron actually works in the opposite way from that of the *Canterbury Tales*. Except for the plague, the frame creates a kind of ideal world. The stories on the other hand are for the most part more "realistic" than the Canterbury tales.

Cunningham has suggested,[24] but I suspect that the realistic climate of the later Middle Ages in art and literature and about which Huizinga has written so eloquently led him to his original notion of using elaborate circumstantial social detail without relying on the dream convention as in *The Book of the Duchess* or the historical approach as in *Troilus and Criseyde* to give him what every narrative writer needs—his authenticating realism. In other words, Chaucer's originality from this point of view consists in combining the truth claim of his major authenticating device with a circumstantial realism.

Let us look at the *Canterbury Tales* from another point of view. I wish to stress that background in narrative is much more complex than is commonly realized and that in a way the naturalistic realism of narrative art often lies more in the background properly defined than in the foreground. A narrative must reproduce or indicate the real world at two points—in its extreme foreground of action and in its extreme background, the world of titles, summaries and epigraphs. In between, the levels may or may not be realistic. When we speak of realistic fiction in the normal sense of the term, we mean fiction which is realistic in some of these in-between regions, for the other two levels must be realistic.

What I call the extreme foreground of every piece of fiction is the inner action. I choose action as the extreme foreground because with Aristotle I assume that action is fundamental to both narrative and drama. It may be defined as the movement and contacts of the characters in deeds and words. In any narrative the description of this action must be realistic. The parts may not fit in a probable way or the deeds and dialogue may be untrue so that the plot itself may not be credible, but the *action* itself must be described as if it actually happened. When a personified knight attacks a dragon, both unreal creatures, we must have a description of a real fight, not necessarily with full detail, but the fight must give the impression of a real combat between two beings of some sort. When Don Quixote attacks a windmill, however deluded or unlikely the action may be in its context in real life, it is described in a realistic way as

[24] See note 19 above.

if a man were really attacking a windmill. When K. is taken into custody in Kafka's *The Trial,* the description and dialogue indicate a real arrest. It is in this sense that I believe the extreme foreground of all fiction must be realistic.

However, the sequence of the action—the plot—may not be likely, probable or "true to life." It may be controlled by some tight intellectual scheme rather than by verisimilitude. But what is done is done realistically. The characters too who participate in the action may or may not be like real people or animals. They may have various degrees of reality. They may be real internally, that is psychologically or symbolically, but unreal externally, that is naturalistically, or vice versa. Or they may be unreal in both regards. The locale or setting of the inner story may or may not be portrayed realistically. Some stories are set in the past or the future, both imaginary, some are set in an ideal landscape, some merely suggest a background and some are set in a very natural setting of nature and artifacts or society, or in various degrees of the three. It is the fullness of this natural setting which gives the nineteenth-century novel much of its realistic quality. It is not an invention of the nineteenth century; the kind of detail with its social and class dimension which evokes a special atmosphere was, however, something new which helps to create the feeling of a slice of life.

When we move out of the inner story on to the authenticating level, whether it be a frame, an "I" or merely a voice, one of its main purposes is to give the reader a feeling that the story is true. We have tried to argue that the special quality of the realism of the *Canterbury Tales* lies in the circumstantial realism of its authenticating level. This level often does have circumstantial detail, but it is by no means universal. A tone of voice, for instance, may merely convey authority, not circumstantial surface reality. But the authenticating level of a narrative is concerned with realism in a fundamental way, for it must make possible the suspension of disbelief and is basically though not exclusively concerned with an epistemological question. It must try to validate the story which is being told. However, it may also reinforce the inner story or ironically counterpoint it or be used to shift perspective. Ironically, however, the authenticating level also in a way makes us more aware of the fact that the inner story is a creation which needs authenticating.

Finally, we move out of the story to the level of the author speaking directly to the audience without *persona* or any mask, to which we have already briefly alluded. In most narrative this level is only made known to us by the title of the tale, or by the table of contents, or summaries or chapter headings or divisions if some are given. Here is a man telling us directly or occasionally ironically what he is doing as he sees it. He usually writes in the present tense about his subject, how he is dividing it, and occasionally what he thinks about it. When he is being ironical, he is being ironical to us directly. We are out of the world of the story, listening to the author being as objective as he can be about his intentions.

Chaucer in the *Canterbury Tales* complex makes more use of this level than most readers are aware of.[25] At the beginning of the work he tells us "Here bygynneth the Book of the Tales of Caunterbury," even before he breaks into that famous description of the showers of April. Before every tale and every section and subsection, mostly in English, but occasionally in Latin, he tells us directly what he is doing or sometimes what he has done, as, for instance, "Here endeth the Wyf of Bathe hir Prologe." Occasionally these comments are more than merely neutral, as, for instance, "Bihoold the murie wordes of the Hoost to the Shipman and to the lady Prioresse." Note, incidentally, the immediacy of the imperative "behold." Finally at the very end of the work, we have Chaucer's retraction in which, in two or three paragraphs, he, following a long tradition, asks God to remember those works of his which lead to virtue and to forgive those "of worldly vanities" and his "lecherous" lays. Here is the voice of the Christian man, Chaucer, speaking in dead seriousness.

In each case, Chaucer takes his readers out of the work of art back into the real world where he is speaking to them quietly and directly, in the present time. He uses no persona here beyond the natural personae of all human beings when speaking publicly, and continually reminds us in these titles and comments that the poem is his creation and his world and that he is master of both. Some-

[25] These titles may be the work of scribes. It is impossible to prove that they are Chaucer's, but I am making this assumption here. I owe the germ of the notion of the world of the title to Dr. Käte Hamburger, *Die Logik der Dichtung* (Stuttgart, 1957); see Roy Pascal, "Tense and Novel," *MLR*, LVII (1962), 6ff.

times he tells us how to divide one of his stories into parts; sometimes he tells us what he wants us to call the work or its parts; sometimes he directs our attention to some point. The creator of these titles and comments is not the pilgrim who is reporting the Canterbury pilgrimage, although he is related to him very closely. He is speaking to us from another part of his being.

I have up to this point been stressing for the most part how Chaucer gave his *Canterbury Tales* a sense of reality. Now it is necessary to backtrack a bit and argue that he is also showing us its unreality and untruth. For Chaucer in the *Canterbury Tales* by means of various devices which we have discussed brings us into a real world and then transcends it by his art and his presence. His art and his presence distance his readers or audience from their own world so that they can see its meaning as he interpreted it. Yet because his subject was set in the contemporary world on the authenticating level, he is in a profound sense satirical. The first step, the precondition of all satire, is objectivity. But in order to create an objectivity in his readers toward his story, he must also establish the unreality of the real world. The dialectic between real and unreal is handled in a masterly fashion and creates one of the fascinations of the *Canterbury Tales.*

Professor Wolfgang Clemen in a stimulating address to the Fifth Triennial Convention of the International Association of The University Professors of English in Edinburgh in August 1962, in speaking of Chaucer's early poetry said that he created there a "new realism of the unreal." This, at least as it applies to *The Book of the Duchess*, is perhaps overstating the case, but it contains much truth. I would urge that in the *Canterbury Tales* Chaucer's problem was just the opposite. He had to create a new unreality of the real so that the real could be brought into art in a manner proper to the illusion of art. This task he accomplished in various ways—by his individual stories, by his selection of the facts, by his comments on his poem. But it is also achieved by the elaborate structure he made of the different levels of the work so that the reality of the world of Chaucer and of the authenticating level is balanced by an unreality in the tales and by the unreality of constantly shifting us back into various levels because this movement makes us aware of the manipulating role of the artist.[26]

The tales themselves have subtle meaning, and often have strong realistic elements, but in practically every case they have a strong ideal base of some sort. They are meaningful in themselves in various ways and in their relation to the frame. The authenticating frame, however, except for its suggestion of life itself and for its authenticating power, has little narrative meaning by itself. It exists for the characterization of the tellers and for the tales they tell. This is generally true of authenticating devices. They do not exist for themselves. Although we may delight in the authenticating level, as we certainly do in the frame of the *Canterbury Tales*, from the point of view of narrative we read it for the inner story or stories and for the relation between the frame and the story. We cannot reduce the tales to the characters of the frame as Kittredge suggested without killing the work as narrative art. The experience of reading the General Prologue is not for its narrative itself but for what is to come. If we read it for itself, as we do in many college courses, it is for the portraits, the humor or the expressive power. Yet ironically as I hope I have shown, it is the frame which gives a strong sense of ordinary circumscribed reality to the whole work as narrative.

The *Canterbury Tales*, unfinished as it is, is a complex work of art, and by looking at its variety of realisms and unrealisms we gain a deeper sense of its profundities. We demand illusion and reality, but illusion which seems real and, of course, which reflects reality. We see through things in the *Canterbury Tales*. Panofsky has shown that in the Middle Ages *perspectiva* was connected with "seeing clearly," but in the Renaissance it is used in "the sense of seeing through something." [27] In this perspectivism of Chaucer we have an

---

[26] The need to de-realize very realistic narratives is by no means limited to the *Canterbury Tales* or any of Chaucer's narratives, but is widely found. The end of Thackeray's *The Newcomes* (I owe this example to Professor Stephen Gilman) or the philosophical disquisition at the end of Tolstoy's *War and Peace* provide excellent examples, and others are not far to seek.

[27] *Early Netherlandish Painting: Its Origins and Character*, 2 vols. (Cambridge, 1953), I, 3–4. I wish to thank my colleagues Professors Stephen Gilman and Larry Benson for their helpful criticisms of this paper, some of which I have adopted.

early foretaste of the Renaissance as well as delight in the skill of his realistic artificiality.

The interplay of real and real, of unreal and unreal, one of the basic tensions in the *Canterbury Tales*, provides part of its greatness and an awareness of this dialectic brings us to closer grips with Chaucer's great masterpiece.

10. *Distance and Predestination in Troilus and Criseyde*

For we are but of yesterday.—Job viii.9

In *Troilus and Criseyde* Chaucer as commentator occupies an unusual role. It is indeed common for authors to enter their own works in many ways. Writers as diverse as Homer, Virgil, Dante, Cervantes, Fielding, Thackeray, and George Eliot all do so. Sometimes, as with Fielding, the author may keep a distance between himself and his story; sometimes, as with Dante, he may penetrate into his story as a major or the major character; and sometimes, as with Homer, he may both enter and withdraw at will. When Homer directly addresses one of his characters, he is deliberately breaking down, for artistic reasons, the aloofness to which he generally holds.

Chaucer also frequently appears in his own works, usually as one of his dramatis personae, and participates in the action.[1] Although he is not always an important or major character, his actions or dreams within the work frequently provide the occasion for, or give a supposed rationale to, his literary creations. Chaucer the character's decision to go on a pilgrimage to Canterbury provides the ostensible justification for the *Canterbury Tales*. His dreams as a character, following a great medieval literary convention, give rise to the *Parlement of Foules* and the *Hous of Fame*.

In *Troilus and Criseyde* Chaucer plays his artistic role with a striking difference. Here he conceives of himself as the narrator of a history, of a true event as the Middle Ages conceived it, which happened in the past; and as historian he meticulously maintains a distance between himself and the events in the story. His aloofness is similar to and yet different from Fielding's in *Tom Jones* or Thackeray's in *Vanity Fair*. In these works the authors look upon their puppets from their omniscient, ironical, humorous, and at times melancholy point of view and make comments on them or their predicaments, using them as excuses for brief essays or paragraphs on different subjects. In *Troilus* Chaucer does not look upon his characters as his creations. His assumed role is primarily descriptive and expository. Though we are continually reminded of the presence of Chaucer the historian, narrator, and commentator,

Reprinted by permission of the Modern Language Association of America from *PMLA*, LXXII (1957), 14–26.

[1] On this point in connection with the *Canterbury Tales* see Donaldson's stimulating "Chaucer the Pilgrim," *PMLA*, LXIX (1954), 928–936. I am indebted to Professor Donaldson for several suggestions made orally to me which I have woven into this article—notably the root idea of note 14 below.

at the same time we are never allowed to forget that he is separate from the events he is recording.

Troilus is not a dream vision nor is it a contemporary event. It is the past made extremely vivid by the extensive use of dialogue, but still the past. Chaucer cannot change the elements of his story. As God cannot violate His own rationality, Chaucer cannot violate his data. Bound by his self-imposed task of historian, he both implies and says directly that he cannot do other than report his tale.

If we assume that Chaucer is a painstaking artist—and it is impossible not to—it is clear that the nature of the role he assumes has an extremely important meaning in the economy and plan of the poem. Why, we must ask, does Chaucer as character-narrator continually remind us of his aloofness from and impotence in the face of the events he is narrating? A historian takes for granted what Chaucer does not take for granted. A Gibbon does not tell us constantly that the events of the decline and fall of the Roman Empire are beyond his control. That is an assumption that anyone reading a true history makes at the outset. Chaucer introduces just this assumption into the body of his work, continually reminding us of what seems, in the context of a supposed history, most obvious. What is normally outside the historical work, a presupposition of it, is in the history of Troilus and Criseyde brought into the poem and made much of. This unusual creative act calls for examination.

We must also wonder at the quantitative bulk of Chaucer's comments on the story. Frequently, even in the midst of the action of the inner story, we are reminded of the presence of the narrator— sometimes, it is true, by only a word or two. We cannot dismiss these numerous comments merely as remarks necessary to establish rapport with the audience under conditions of oral delivery. The few remarks of this nature are easy to pick out. If we compare the simple comments made by the narrator in, say, *Havelock the Dane* or any other medieval romance with those made by the *Troilus* narrator, I think the difference is plain.

Although many stanzas belong completely to the commentator *in propria persona* and others pertain to the events of the tale, so many are partly one or the other, or merely suggest the presence of a narrator, that a mathematical table which could reveal the actual percentage of commentator stanzas or lines would be misleading and inaccurate.[2] Anyone who has read the poem must be aware of the presence of the commentator most of the time; one is rarely allowed to forget it for long. And even more impressive than the number of comments are the times and nature of the author's intervention. At all the great moments he is there directing us, speaking in his own person close to us and far from the events of the tragedy which he is presenting to us within the bounds of historical fact.

This sense of distance between Chaucer as character and his story is conveyed to us in what may be designated as temporal, spatial, aesthetic, and religious ways, each reinforcing the other and overlapping. For the sake of clarity, however, we may examine each in turn as a separate kind of aloofness.

The aspect of temporal distance is the one most constantly emphasized throughout the poem. Chaucer again and again tells us that the events he is recording are historical and past. He lets us know that customs have changed since the time when Pandarus, Troilus, and Criseyde lived. The characters are pagans who go to temples to worship strange gods and are caught up in one of the great cataclysms of history. Their ways of living are different from ours. Their love-making varies from the modern style. They lived a long time ago, and Chaucer, to tell their story, is forced to rely on the historians. In order to understand their actions, we must make an effort in comprehension. Yet, says Chaucer, diversity of custom is natural. At times, it is true, Chaucer is very anachronistic, but he still succeeds in giving his readers (or listeners) a feeling for the

---

[2] For what they are worth, I give the following statistics on the first book. All Chaucer quotations are from the edition of F. N. Robinson (Boston, 1933). The following passages seem to me to belong wholly or partially to the narrator as commentator: ll. 1–56 (proem), 57–63, 100, 133, 141–147, 159, 211–217, 232–266, 377–378, 393–399, 450–451 (a direct rapport remark), 492–497, 737–749 (doubtful), 1086–92. Excluding ll. 737–749, we find that 141 lines out of 1092 may be said to be comments by the author as commentator. Roughly 12 percent of the lines of the first book (one line in 8⅓ lines) belong to the commentator. Even allowing for subjective impressions, 10 percent would certainly be fair. This is a remarkably high percentage I should say. The proem I shall analyze below. The other remarks bear on his sources, moralize, establish a mood of acceptance, indicate distance and pastness, and refer to fate and destiny. For overt references to fate and providence in the poem, see the list in Eugene E. Slaughter, "Love and Grace in Chaucer's *Troilus*," *Essays in Honor of Walter Cyde Curry* (Nashville, 1955), p. 63, n. 8.

pastness of his characters and their sad story and for what we today call cultural relativity.[3]

Throughout, Chaucer tries to give us a sense of the great sweep of time which moves down to the present and into the future and back beyond Troy, deepening our sense of the temporal dimension. He tells us that speech and customs change within a thousand years (II.22 ff.) and that this work he is writing is also subject to linguistic variability (v.1793 ff.). Kingdoms and power pass away too; the *translatio regni* (or *imperii*) is inexorable—"regnes shal be flitted/Fro folk in folk" (v.1544–45). The characters themselves reach even farther backward in time. Criseyde and her ladies read of another siege, the fall of Thebes, which took place long before the siege of Troy (II.81 ff.). Cassandra, in her interpretation of Troilus' dream (v.1450–1519), goes into ancient history to explain Diomede's lineage. We are all part of time's kingdom, and we are never allowed to forget it.

Yet, as I have already mentioned, Chaucer vividly reconstructs, especially in his use of dialogue, the day-by-day living of his chief characters. This precision of detail and liveliness of conversation only serve to weight the contrast between himself in the present and his story in the past, to make the present even more evanescent in the sweep of inexorable change. It is the other side of the coin. These inner events are in the past and in a sense dead, but when they occurred they were just as vivid as the events that are happening now. The strong reality and, in a sense, nearness of the past makes meaningful its disappearance and emphasizes paradoxically its distance. If there are no strong unique facts, there is nothing to lament. We cannot escape into the web of myth and cycle; the uniqueness of the past is the guarantee of its own transience. This is the true historical view and this is Chaucer's view. For him, however, even unique events have meaning, but only in the framework of a world view which can put history in its proper place.

Not frequently used, yet most important when it is, is the sense of spatial distance which Chaucer arouses in his readers. The events of the poem take place in faraway Asia Minor. Chaucer creates a sense

[3] See Morton W. Bloomfield, "Chaucer's Sense of History," *JEGP*, LI (1952), 301–313 (see above pp. 13–26).

of spatial distance by giving us a shifting sense of nearness and far-ness. At times we seem to be seeing the Trojan events as if from a great distance and at others we seem to be set down among the characters. This sense of varying distance is most subtly illustrated in the fifth book when Chaucer, after creating a most vivid sense of intimacy and closeness in describing the wooing of Criseyde by Di-omede, suddenly moves to objectivity and distance in introducing the portraits of the two lovers and his heroine (799 ff.)—a device taken from Dares. With the approach of the hour of betrayal, as we become emotionally wrought up and closely involved, Chaucer the narrator brings us sharply back to his all-seeing eye and to a dis-tance. The same technique may also be seen elsewhere in the poem. This continual inversion of the telescope increases our sense of space and gives us a kind of literary equivalent to the perspective of depth in painting.

Chaucer, in his insistence on cultural relativity, not only empha-sizes chronological but also geographic variability. "Ek for to wyn-nen love in sondry ages,/In sondry londes, sondry been usages" (II.27–28). Above all we get this sense of spatial distance in the final ascent of Troilus to the ogdoad, the eighth sphere,[4] where in a sense he joins Chaucer in looking down on this "litel spot of erthe" and can even contemplate his own death with equanimity.

---

[4] Although irrelevant to the point I am making about the sense of distance in the journey to or through the spheres, there is some question as to the reading and mean-ing here (v.1809). I follow Robinson and Root who take the reading "eighth" rather than "seventh" as in most manuscripts. Boccaccio uses "eighth," and there is a long tradition extending back to classical antiquity which makes the ogdoad the resting place of souls (see Morton W. Bloomfield, *The Seven Deadly Sins* [East Lansing, 1952], pp. 16–17 ff.). Cf., however, Jackson I. Cope, "Chaucer, Venus and the 'Sev-enthe Spere,' " *MLN*, LXVII (1952), 245–246. (Cope is unaware of the ogdoad tra-dition and also assumes that Troilus is a Christian.) There is also the problem of the order in which the spheres are numbered. If the highest is the first then the eighth sphere is that of the moon, the one nearest the earth. Root believes Chaucer is follow-ing this arrangement. However, as Cope points out, Chaucer in the opening stanza of Bk. III names "Venus as the informing power of the third sphere" and therefore must be using the opposite numbering system. Troilus then goes to the highest sphere, that of the fixed stars.

E. J. Dobson ("Some Notes on Middle English Texts," *Eng. and Ger. Stud.*, Univ. of Birmingham, I [1947–48], 61–62) points out that Dante, *Paradiso* XXII, 100–154, which is Boccaccio's (and hence Chaucer's) source for this passage in the *Teseide*, makes clear that the emendation to "eighth" is justified.

The sense of aesthetic distance [5] is evoked by the continual distinction Chaucer makes between the story and the commentator, between the framework and the inner events. Although his basic "facts" are given, Chaucer never lets the reader doubt for long that he is the narrator and interpreter of the story. Once, at least, he adopts a humorous attitude toward his dilemma. He insists that he is giving his readers Troilus' song of love (1.400 ff.), "Naught only the sentence" as reported by Lollius but "save oure tonges difference" "every word right thus." This attitude is, however, rare. But it is not unusual for Chaucer to insist upon his bondage to the facts. Yet he strains against the snare of true events in which he is caught. Indeed Chaucer tries again and again, especially where the betrayal of Criseyde is involved, to fight against the truth of the events he is "recording." He never hides his partiality for that "hevennysh perfit creature" (1.104), and in this attitude as in others he notifies us of the narrow latitude which is allowed him. As he approaches the actual betrayal, he slows down; and with evident reluctance, as his reiterated "the storie telleth us" (v. 1037), "I fynde ek in the stories elleswhere" (v.1044), "men seyn—I not" (v.1050) show, he struggles against the predestined climax. The piling up of these phrases here emphasizes the struggle of the artist-narrator against the brutality of the facts to which he cannot give a good turn. As a faithful historian, he cannot evade the rigidity of decisive events—the given. Criseyde's reception of Diomede cannot be glossed over.[6] All this makes us more aware of Chaucer the narrator than ordinarily and

[5] Needless to say I am not using this phrase in the sense given it by Edward Bullough in his " 'Psychical Distance' as a Factor in Art and an Aesthetic Principle," *Brit. Jour. of Psychol.*, V (1913), reprinted in A *Modern Book of Esthetics: An Anthology*, ed. Melvin Rader, rev. ed. (New York, 1952), pp. 401–428. He refers to "distance" between the art object on the one hand and the artist or audience on the other. The distance here referred to is within the poem, between the character-narrator Chaucer and the events.

[6] Chaucer sets himself the problem of interpreting Criseyde's action here by his sympathetic portrayal of her character and by his unblinking acceptance of the "facts" of his history. Boccaccio evades it by his pre-eminent interest in Troilus. Henryson gives Troilus an "unhistorical" revenge. Shakespeare has blackened Cressida's character throughout. Christopher Hassall, in his libretto for William Walton's recent opera on the subject, makes Criseyde a victim of a mechanical circumstance and completely blameless. Only Chaucer, by a strict allegiance to the "historical" point of view, poses the almost unbearable dilemma of the betrayal of Troilus by a charming and essentially sympathetic Criseyde.

increases our sense of aesthetic distance between the reporter and what is reported, between the frame and what is framed.

Finally we may call certain aspects of Chaucerian distance religious. Troilus, Pandarus, and Criseyde are pagans who lived "while men loved the lawe of kinde" (*Book of the Duchess*, 1. 56)—under natural law. The great barrier of God's revelation at Sinai and in Christ separates Chaucer and us from them. Chaucer portrays them consciously as pagans, for he never puts Christian sentiments into their mouths.[7] He may violate our historic sense by making the lovers act according to the medieval courtly love code, but not by making them worship Christ. They are reasonable pagans who can attain to the truths of natural law—to the concept of a God, a creator, and to the rational moral law but never to the truths of revealed Christian religion. Chaucer is very clear on this point and in the great peroration to the poem he expressly says

> Lo here, of payens corsed olde rites,
> Lo here, what alle hire goddes may availe;
> Lo here, thise wrecched worldes appetites;
> Lo here, the fyn and guerdoun for travaille
> Of Jove, Appollo, of Mars, of swich rascaille! (v. 1849–53)

In general, until the end of the poem, Chaucer, as we shall see, plays down his own Christianity for good reason. He even, at times and in consonance with the epic tradition which came down to him, calls upon the pagan Muses and Furies, but he does not avoid the Christian point of view when he feels it necessary to be expressed. Although the religious barrier is not emphasized until the conclusion, we are left in no doubt throughout as to its separating

---

[7] The only exception is to be found in the Robinson text where at III.1165 we find the reading in a speech by Criseyde "by that God that bought us both two." I am convinced that the Root reading "wrought" for "bought" is correct. It would be perfectly possible for pagans to use "wrought" but not "bought." If we admit "bought" it would be the only Christian allusion put into the mouths of the Trojan characters and would conflict with the expressedly pagan attitude of these figures. I now take a stronger position on the matter than I allowed myself to express in "Chaucer's Sense of History," *JEGP*, LI (1952), 303, n. 17 (above p. 21). Various references to grace, the devil (I.805), a bishop (II.104), saints' lives (II.118) and celestial love (I.979) need not, from Chaucer's point of view of antiquity, be taken as Christian.

Chaucer from his characters. This sense of religious distance becomes at the end a vital part of the author's interpretation of his story.

A close study of Chaucer's proems written as prefaces to the first four books bears out the analysis offered here. In these Chaucer speaks out, and from his emphases and invocations we may gain some clues as to his intentions. At the beginning of the first proem, we are told of the subject of the work and of its unhappy fatal end. Chaucer does not allow us to remain in suspense at all. He exercises his role as historical commentator immediately at the outset. Tesiphone, one of the Furies, is invoked as an aid. She is a sorrowing Fury, as Dante had taught Chaucer to view her. She is responsible for the torment of humans, but she weeps for her actions. She is also in a sense the invoker himself who puts himself in his poem in a similar role. Chaucer is also a sorrowing tormenter who is retelling a true tale, the predestined end of which he cannot alter. Though ultimately he is to conquer it through religion, Chaucer the commentator is throughout most of the poem a victim of the historical determinism of his own poem. Although it is set down in the introduction to the poem, we may not understand the full meaning of Chaucer's entanglement and the escape provided by Christianity until we reach its end. There the Christian solution to the dilemma of the first proem is again presented but deepened by our knowledge of Troilus' fate and by a greater emphasis. Then, we shall have followed through the sad story under Chaucer the commentator's guidance and the answer is plain. In the proem, on the first reading, however, the problem and the solution cannot be clear in spite of Chaucer's open words. We too must discover the answer.

On the other hand, in the first prologue, he does tell us, so that we may understand, that he the conductor and recorder of his story is like Troilus after the betrayal, unhappy in love. In the *Book of the Duchess*, the dreamer's unhappiness in love is assuaged within the dream and inner story by the grief of the man in black, whose loss of his beloved foreshadows what would have happened to the dreamer's love in one form or another, for all earthly love is transitory. Death is worse than unhappiness in love. Chaucer the *Troilus* narrator who dares not pray to love "for myn unliklynesse" is also going to learn in his tale that the love of the Eternal is the only true love. Actually Chaucer, because he conceives of himself as historian, has already learned before he begins. Hence, it is not quite accurate to say as above that he is going to learn, for he already knows. The reader, however, unless he is extraordinarily acute, remains in ignorance until he finishes the whole work. He discovers in the course of the experience of the history what Chaucer already knows and has really told him in the beginning, for Chaucer concludes his first proem by calling on all lovers both successful and unsuccessful to join him in prayer for Troilus. It is, he says, only in heaven, in the *patria* of medieval theology, that we can find lasting happiness. Troilus will find a pagan equivalent for this in his pagan heaven at the end. One cannot, however, quite believe Chaucer here until one reads the poem and finds that he is deadly serious when he prays that God "graunte" unhappy lovers "soone owt of this world to pace" (1.41). It is the love of God which is the answer to the love of woman and of all earthly things.

In other words, Chaucer in his introduction to the poem indicates his bondage to historical fact, his own grief at his position, the problem of the unhappiness in this world which he, like Troilus and all unhappy lovers, must face, and the only true solution for all the lovers of this world.

The second proem appeals to Clio, the Muse of history, and alludes to the diversity of human custom and language. The sense of history and cultural relativity manifested here emphasizes the distance in time which temporal barriers impose. "For every wight which that to Rome went/Halt not o path, or alwey o manere" (11.36–37).

The opening of Book III calls upon Venus, goddess of love, and, although it makes other points as well, underlines again the pagan quality of the history. Venus in her symbolic, astrological, and divine role conquers the whole world and binds its dissonances and discords together. It is she who understands the mysteries of love and who explains the apparent irrationality of love. The proem closes with a brief reference to Calliope, Muse of epic poetry, as Chaucer wishes to be worthy, as an artist, of his great theme of love.

Finally, in the last proem, we have an appeal to Fortune the great presiding deity of the sublunar world. Here as always she suggests instability and transience. Chaucer then alludes to the binding power of his sources. He closes his prologue with an invocation to all the Furies and to Mars with overtones suggesting his unhappy role as commentator and the paganness of the story he is unfolding.

These proems cannot be completely explained in terms of my interpretation, for they are also, especially the third and fourth, appropriate artistically to the theme of the books they serve to introduce and the various stages of the narrative. In general they emphasize the tragic end of the tale, the unwilling Fury-like role Chaucer has to play, the historical bonds which shackle him, the pity of it all, the aloofness and distance between the Chaucer of the poem and the history itself he is telling, and the one possible solution to the unhappiness of the world. Nor are these sentiments confined to the prefaces. They occur again and again throughout the body of the poem.[8] Chaucer takes pains to create himself as a character in his poem and also to dissociate this character continually from his story.

The attitude of Chaucer the character throughout makes it possible for us to understand the crucial importance of the concept of predestination in the poem. In the past there has been much debate in Chaucerian criticism over the question of predestination in *Troilus*. We know that Chaucer was profoundly interested in this question and that it was a preoccupation of his age. It seems to me that, if we regard the framework of the poem—the role that Chaucer sets himself as commentator—as a meaningful part of the poem and if we consider the various references to fate and destiny in the text, we can only come to the conclusion that the Chaucerian sense of distance and aloofness is the artistic correlative to the concept of predestination. *Troilus and Criseyde* is a medieval tragedy of predestination because the reader is continually forced by the commentator to look upon the story from the point of view of its end and from a distance. The crux of the problem of predestination is knowledge. So long as the future is not known to the participants in action, they can act as if they were free. But once a position of distance from the action is taken, then all can be seen as inevitable. And it is just this position which Chaucer the commentator takes and forces upon us from the very beginning. As John of Salisbury writes, "however, when you have entered a place, it is impossible

[8] See note 2 above.

that you have not entered it; when a thing has been done it is impossible that it be classed with things not done; and there is no recalling to non-existence a thing of the past." [9] All this presupposes knowledge which is impossible *in media re*. It is just this knowledge that Chaucer the commentator-historian gives us as he reconstructs the past. Hence we are forced into an awareness of the inevitability of the tragedy and get our future and our present at the same time, as it were.

Bound by the distance of time and space, of art and religion, Chaucer sits above his creation and foresees, even as God foresees, the doom of his own creatures: God, the *Deus artifex* who is in medieval philosophy the supreme artist and whose masterpiece is the created world.[10] But Chaucer is like God only insofar as he can know the outcome, not as creator. Analogically, because he is dealing with history, and, we must remember, to the medieval Englishman his own history, he can parallel somewhat his Maker. He is not the creator of the events and personages he is presenting to us; hence he cannot change the results. On the other hand God is the creator of His creatures; but He is bound by His own rationality and His foreknowledge. The sense of distance that Chaucer enforces on us accentuates the parallel with God and His providential predestination. We cannot leap the barriers which life imposes on us, but in the companionship of an historian we can imitate God *in parvo*. As God with His complete knowledge of future contingents sees the world laid out before Him all in the twinkling of an eye, so, in the case of history, with a guide, we share in small measure a similar experience. The guide is with us all the way, pointing to the end and to the pity of it. We must take our history from his point of view.

It is, of course, as hazardous to attribute opinions to Chaucer as it is to Shakespeare. Yet I suspect both were predestinations—insofar as Christianity allows one to be. It is curious that all the great speeches on freedom of the will in Shakespeare's plays are put into

[9] *Policraticus*, II, 22, ed. C. C. I. Webb (Oxford, 1909), I, 126. The translation is by Joseph B. Pike, *Frivolities of Courtiers* (Minneapolis, 1938), pp. 111. Incidentally it should be noted that Calchas' foreknowledge through divination is on a basic level the cause of the tragedy.

[10] "We are looking on at a tragedy that we are powerless to check or avert. Chaucer himself conveys the impression of telling the tale under a kind of duress" (G. L. Kittredge, *Chaucer and His Poetry* [Cambridge, 1915], p. 113).

the mouths of his villains—Edmund in *Lear*, Iago in *Othello*, and Cassius in *Julius Caesar*. This is not the place to discuss the relation of Chaucer to fourteenth-century thinking or to predestination, but I think he stands with Bishop Bradwardine who, when Chaucer was still very young, thundered against the libertarians and voluntarists because they depreciated God at the expense of His creatures and elevated man almost to the level of his Creator. Even the title of his masterpiece *De causa Dei* reveals clearly his bias. God's ways are not our ways and His grace must not be denied. His power (that is, manifest in predestination) must be defended. Chaucer is probably with him and others on this issue and in the quarrel over future contingents which became the chief issue [11]—a reduction of the problem to logic and epistemology as befitted a century fascinated by logic and its problems. Regardless of Chaucer's personal opinion, however, I think I have shown that one of the main sources of the inner tensions of *Troilus* is this sense of necessity of an historian who knows the outcome in conflict with his sympathies as an artist and man, a conflict which gives rise to a futile struggle until the final leap which elevates the issue into a new and satisfactory context. This conflict causes the pity, the grief, the tears—and in a sense the ridiculousness and even the humor of it all.

Yet, throughout, the maturity of Chaucer's attitude is especially noteworthy. Predestination which envelops natural man implicates us all. Only from a Christian point of view can we be superior to Troilus and Criseyde and that is not due to any merit of our own, but to grace. As natural men and women we too are subject to our destiny whatever it may be. Chaucer links himself (and us) with his far-off characters, thereby strengthening the human bond over the centuries and increasing the objectivity and irony of his vision. We are made to feel that this is reality, that we are looking at it as it is and even from our distance participate in it.

There is no escape from the past if one chooses to reconstruct artistically, as Chaucer does, the past from the vantage ground of the present. Chaucer's creation of himself in *Troilus* as historian-narrator and his emphasis on the distance between him and his charac-

---

[11] On this dispute in the fourteenth century, see L. Baudry, *La Querelle des futurs contingents* (Paris, 1950), and Paul Vignaux, *Justification et prédestination au XIVe siècle* (Paris, 1934).

ters repeat, in the wider frame of the present and in the panorama of complete knowledge, the helplessness and turmoil of the lovers in the inner story. The fact that Chaucer regards his story as true history does not, of course, make his point of view predestinarian; in that case all historians would be committed to a philosophy of predestination. The point is that the author creates a character— himself—to guide us through his historical narrative, to emphasize the pitiful end throughout, to keep a deliberate distance suggested and stated in various ways between him and us and the characters of the inner story. He makes his chief character awake to the fact of predestination towards the end of the story and at the conclusion has this character join, as it were, us and Chaucer the character—in space instead of time—in seeing his own story through the perspective of distance. It is all this which gives us the clue. The outer frame is not merely a perspective of omniscience but also of impotence and is in fact another level of the story. It serves as the realm of Mount Ida in the *Iliad*—a wider cadre which enables us to put the humans involved into their proper place.

Every age has it polarities and dichotomies, some more basic than others. To believing medieval man, the fundamental division is between the created and the uncreated. God as the uncreated Creator is the unchanging norm against which all His creatures must be set and the norm which gives the created world its true objectivity. The true Christian was bound to keep the universe in perspective: it was only one of the poles of this fundamental polarity. The city of God gives meaning to the city of the world.

The impasse of the characters can only be solved on this other level and in this wider cadre. Actually for Troilus and Criseyde there is no final but merely a temporary solution—the consolation of philosophy—from which only the betrayed lover can benefit. Troilus begins to approach his narrator's viewpoint as he struggles against his fate beginning in the fourth book. The political events have taken a turn against him, and he tries to extricate himself and his beloved. But he is trapped and, what is even worse, long before Criseyde leaves he becomes aware of his mistake in consenting to let her go. In spite of her optimistic chatter, he predicts almost exactly what will happen when she joins her father. And he tells her so (iv.1450 ff.). Yet like one fascinated by his own doom he lets her

213

go. He struggles but, in spite of his premonitions, seems unable to do anything about it.

It has long been recognized that Troilus' speech in favor of predestination (IV.958 ff.) is an important element in the poem.[12] It certainly indicates that Troilus believes in predestination, and I think in the light of what we have been saying here represents a stage in Troilus' approach to Chaucer. When, in the pagan temple, he finally becomes aware of destiny,[13] he is making an attempt to look at his own fate as Chaucer the commentator all along has been looking at it. The outer and inner stories are beginning to join each other. This movement of narrator and character towards each other in the last two books culminates in the ascent through the spheres at the end where Troilus gets as close to Chaucer (and us) as is possible in observing events in their proper perspective—*sub specie ae-ternitatis.* As Boethius writes in the *Consolation of Philosophy*

> Huc [Nunc] omnes pariter uenite capti
> Quos fallax ligat improbis catenis
> Terrenas habitans libido mentes
> Haec erit uobis requies laborum,
> Hic portus placida manens quiete,
> Hoc patens unum miseris asylum. (III, metrum x)

Or as Chaucer himself translates these lines

> Cometh alle to gidre now, ye that ben
> ykaught and ybounde with wikkide cheynes

---

[12] I am aware, of course, that this famous speech was added only in the second or final version of the poem as Root has clearly shown. I do not think that this point is of much relevance to my argument one way or another. Inasmuch as we can probably never know why Chaucer added the passage, one explanation is as good as another. We must take the poem in its final form as our object for analysis. My case, which is admittedly subjective, does not rest on this passage. It may be that Chaucer felt that by adding this speech he was making clearer a point he already had in mind. Or it is possible that it was only on his second revision that he saw the full implications of his argument. Or finally it may have occurred to him that by bringing Troilus closer to his own position before the end, he would deepen the significance of what he wished to say. These explanations for the addition are at least as plausible and possible as any other.

[13] The location of this speech is not, I think, without significance. The end of pagan or purely natural religion is blind necessity, and in its "church" this truth can best be seen.

214

by the desceyvable delyt of erthly
thynges enhabitynge in your thought! Her
schal ben the reste of your labours, her is
the havene stable in pesible quiete; this
allone is the open refut to wreches.

From this vantage point all falls into its place and proper propor-
tion. Troilus now has Chaucer's sense of distance and joins with his
author in finding what peace can be found in a pagan heaven.

Just before this soul journey, Chaucer has even consigned his very
poem to time and put it in its place along with all terrestrial things
(v.1793 ff.) in the kingdom of mutability and change. As Chaucer
can slough off his earthly attachments and prides, even the very
poem in which he is aware of their transitory nature, Troilus his
hero can also do so.

Thus towards the end, in the last two books, we see the hero beginning to imitate his narrator and the narrator, his hero, and the
distance set up between the two begins to lessen and almost disappear. A dialectic of distance and closeness which has been from the
beginning more than implicit in the poem between God, Chaucer
the commentator-narrator, and the characters—notably Troilus—of
the inner story, becomes sharply poised, with the triangle shrinking
as the three approach each other.[14] A final shift of depth and distance, however, takes place at the end. The poem does not come to
a close with Troilus joining Chaucer. A further last leap is to establish again, even as at the beginning, a new distance. Beyond the
consolation of philosophy, the only consolation open to Troilus is
the consolation of Christianity. In the last stanzas, Chaucer the narrator escapes from Troilus to where the pagan cannot follow him;
he escapes into the contemplation of the mysteries of the Passion
and of the Trinity, the supreme paradox of all truth, which is the
only possible way for a believing Christian to face the facts of his

---

[14] Another triangle has its apex in Pandarus, who is, of course, the artist of the
inner story as Chaucer is of the outer one and as God is of the created world. Pandarus works on his material—Troilus and especially Criseyde—as his "opposite numbers" do with their materials. All are to some extent limited—Pandarus by the characters of his friend and niece and by political events; Chaucer by his knowledge and
by history; God by His rationality. All this is another story, however; my interest here
is primarily in the triangle with Troilus as apex.

story. The artist and the historian who have been struggling in the breast of Chaucer can finally be reconciled. Here free will and pre-destination, human dignity and human pettiness, joy and sorrow, in short all human and terrestrial contradictions, are reconciled in the pattern of all reconciliation: the God who becomes man and whose trinity is unity and whose unity is trinity. Here the author-historian can finally find his peace at another distance and leave behind for-ever the unhappy and importunate Troilus, the unbearable grief of Criseyde's betrayal, the perplexities of time and space, and the tyr-anny of history and predestination.

IV. Language and Linguistics

11. Canadian English and Its Relation to Eighteenth-Century American Speech

Although Canadian English is a branch of American English in more than a geographic sense, very little research has been devoted to it. One can echo today, without the least lessening of its force and truth, A. F. Chamberlain's statement of over fifty years ago, "Towards the investigation scientifically, of the spoken English of the Dominion little indeed has been done." [1]

With all the linguistic activity of the past half century in America, it is indeed surprising that the English spoken by some ten million people, a speech bound both historically, culturally, and socially with American English, should have been studied so little by scholars.[2] In the last thirty-five years, considerable attention, with corresponding results, has been given to the subject of American English, and we are now in possession of a large body of linguistic information and some general syntheses on the language spoken in the United States. Yet until Canadian English is studied and understood, the history of American English must be incomplete.

The probable explanation for this neglect lies in the fact that most American investigators, ignorant of Canadian history, are under the impression that Canadian English, as undoubtedly is the case with Australian, South African, and Newfoundland English, is a direct offshoot of British English and therefore does not belong to their field of inquiry. It is, however, necessary to know the history of a country before one can know the history of its language. As far

Reprinted with permission of the University of Illinois Press from *JEGP*, XLVII (1948), 59–67.

[1] "Dialect Research in Canada," *Dialect Notes*, I (1890), 45. This article, however, must be used with caution; see below note 11.

[2] G. P. Krapp, *The English Language in America*, 2 vols. (New York, 1925), the author of the only scholarly book on the whole subject, for instance, has nothing at all to say on Canadian English. H. L. Mencken, *The American Language*, 4th ed., Corrected etc. (New York, 1936) and *Supplement 1* to it (New York, 1945) include a number of references to minor and specific points of Canadian English usage. Mencken is under the common illusion that American English drove out the original British English in Canada; see *op. cit.* (1936). p. 609. A. Baugh, *A History of the English Language* (New York, 1935). pp. 397–398 has a paragraph on the subject which is inaccurate and incomplete. Baugh obviously also looks upon Canadian English as a direct outgrowth of British English, for he does not place the paragraph in his chapter on American English where it belongs, but rather in the chapter on nineteenth-century British English. Recently, however, there have been encouraging signs that scholars engaged in the study of American English are beginning to give attention to Canadian English. The *Linguistic Atlas* and discussions at the meetings of the Dialect Society testify to this awakening interest.

as Canada is concerned, scholars have usually ignored this principle.

It is not the purpose of this article to present a full study of Canadian English, which at present would in any case be impossible, but rather to give a brief outline of its history and affiliations, to suggest further lines of inquiry and to point out how a knowledge of Canadian English is of importance in the investigation of the history of American English. Although full studies of Canadian English are needed, not enough preliminary work has been done on the subject as yet to make that possible.[3] It is the hope of the author that this article will stimulate further studies upon which such fuller works can eventually be constructed.

Canada first became open to English speaking settlers when, by the Treaty of Utrecht in 1713, the Maritime Provinces (then called Acadia, later Nova Scotia, and later still Nova Scotia, New Brunswick, and Prince Edward Island) with the exception of Cape Breton Island, became a British possession. In the period between 1713 and 1763, English and American settlers (the latter mainly from New England and the largest in number) moved into Nova Scotia;[4] and in 1749, Halifax was founded.

[3] On Canadian English itself, besides Chamberlain's article, there are a few short word-lists in the early numbers of *Dialect Notes*; see I (1894), 377–381 and IV (1916), 332. E. L. Chicanot, "The Polyglot Vernacular of the Canadian Northwest," *MLR*, X (1915), 88–89, points out a few Indian, Gaelic, Mexican, and French words which are used in the Canadian West and Northwest. Most of them are not peculiar to Canada. M. B. Emeneau, "The Dialect of Lunenburg, Nova Scotia," *Language*, XI (1935), 140–147, and XVI (1940), 214–215, has studied a Canadian subdialect, but mainly from the point of view of possible German influence from the early settlers in Lunenburg. Evelyn R. Ahrend, in "Ontario Speech," AS, IX (1934), 136–139, has studied, rather uncritically, "the general speech of Canadians living between Toronto and Kingston." Ahrend recognizes a strong United Empire Loyalist influence from the United States but does not relate this important point to the Canadian English of today. She implies that it was only one element in the creation of Canadian English, although at the same time she recognizes the American character of Canadian speech without attempting to explain it. The "distinctive" Canadian sounds listed at the end of the article can all be paralleled south of the border. Morley Ayearst, "A Note on Canadian Speech," AS, XIV (1939), 231–233, is accurate in recording Canadian speech habits, but seems to imply that Canadian English owes its basic similarity to General American to borrowing or assimilation. He mentions, but minimizes, United Empire Loyalist influence.

[4] See J. B. Brebner, *The Neutral Yankees of Nova Scotia: A Marginal Colony during the Revolutionary Years* (New York, 1937).

Though in 1763, at the conclusion of the Seven Years' War, all of Canada including Cape Breton Island passed legally into British hands, for the following decade there was only a slight influx of Englishmen and Scotsmen into the new possession. Except for temporarily quartered soldiers, Canada did not grow in population to any great extent during this period.

After 1776, however, the situation changed and a large increase in population occurred, entirely owing to the movement north of many Tories or Loyalists who wished, or were forced, to leave the United States because of the American Revolutionary War. They carried with them, as a matter of course, the language spoken in the Thirteen Colonies at the time. They provided the bulk of Canada's original English-speaking population. Others also came. Gaelic-speaking Scotsmen, driven out of Scotland by economic necessity, settled in Cape Breton Island, in the eastern end of the Nova Scotian mainland and to some extent in Prince Edward Island, Quebec, and Ontario.[5] Except in Nova Scotia (Pictou county and Cape Breton Island), where they preserved their language and customs, they were soon assimilated by their English-speaking neighbors. Dutch and Germans, in small numbers, came to Nova Scotia and Ontario. Merchants and traders from Great Britain settled along the St. Lawrence, particularly in Montreal, the center of the fur trade. They were influential but few.

The important group, both in number and prestige, were the Loyalists, who, hardy and industrious, opened up Ontario, drove an English-speaking wedge into the Province of Quebec, settled in the Maritime Provinces where, since the 1740's, Yankees had been living, and sealed the devotion to their cause by checking the American invasions of Canada during the War of 1812.[6] They were conservatives who had suffered for their loyalty. Hence, to the normal conservatism of emigrating linguistic groups there was added, in

[5] On this movement and on Gaelic in Canada, see J. L. Campbell, "Scottish Gaelic in Canada" AS, XI (1936), 128–136. In this article, Campbell also deals with the influence of Canadian English on Gaelic in Canada, but not with the influence of the latter on the former in Nova Scotia. See below p. 226.

[6] See, for instance, A. G. Bradley, *Colonial Americans in Exile: Founders of British Canada* (New York, 1932), for the history of this northern movement from the British point of view. See, also, C. H. Van Tyne, *The Loyalists in the American Revolution* (New York, 1902), for an American view of the Loyalists.

221

this case, a strong political and psychological conservatism. This frame of mind was to have its effect upon Canadian English and Canadian life.

After this sudden spurt in population during the last quarter of the eighteenth century, Canada grew very slowly in the first half of the next century. The superior attractions of the United States gathered most of the immigrants from Europe. Although there was always some immigration from the States, the chief source of Canadian settlers after 1800 was no longer the south, but Great Britain and Europe. But English-speaking Canada had been created by the Loyalists.

One other group, not an ethnic one, should be mentioned, although its members were mostly transients in Canada—the military. Just what influence they had upon the language is difficult to estimate, but it should not be ignored.[7] Close investigation may reveal that certain lexical and phonological peculiarities of contemporary Canadian English are due to their presence.

In the early days of British Canada these soldiers provided the bulk of the British (that is, not American) population. After 1763, Canada was garrisoned by Great Britain, and Halifax and Quebec became important military bases. During and after the American Revolution, the military importance of Canada increased, and the garrisons and forts were all strengthened. After the bitterness of the War of 1812 had subsided—from 1818 onwards—the number of British troops were progressively reduced, until by the end of the century, inasmuch as relations with the United States had been peaceful for many decades, the remaining few British troops were withdrawn.

---

[7] In at least one case, the military left its mark on Canadian French. The use of *blood* among French Canadians, in the sense of *sporting, generous, frank*, no doubt goes back to this source. The word, in this sense, is only preserved in contemporary English in the phrase *young blood*. French Canadians say, "Sois blood" [swe blʌd], meaning "Be generous or sporting." The whole subject of English borrowings into Canadian French needs investigation, and the preliminary listing has been largely done in French Canadian dictionaries. Some words, e.g., *slide* for *sandwich*, seem inexplicable. The usual explanation of this term is that it is a corruption of the English *slice*, but that seems far-fetched and improbable phonetically. On the general subject, see A. M. Elliott, "Speech Mixture in French Canada, B.—English and French," *American Journal of Philology*, X (1889), 133–158.

Most of this military population was a floating one, but some soldiers settled permanently. During their stay, the officers led a dashing social life, and the men mingled with the masses. But neither they nor the small number of civilians from Great Britain affected the basically Loyalist nature of English-speaking Canada. This Loyalist frame had been firmly fixed by 1830 when immigrants from Great Britain, mostly poor, began to settle in increasingly large numbers. The Loyalists had molded Canada, created its ruling caste and set its social standards, among which was its language. It is they who gave Canada its tradition of intense loyalty to the Mother Country and, at the same time, its colonial complex.

From 1850 onwards their political and social position became less secure, and differences in social and ethnic background were less and less stressed. Participation in two World Wars has more recently produced a Canadian nationalism—always strong among French-Canadians—which no longer exclusively looks toward Great Britain. Linguistically, however, Loyalist influence is still very much alive, and Canadian English, which presents even fewer dialectical variations than its American mother, is one of these Tory Americans' most important legacies to contemporary Canada. There is, of course, speech mixture due to large-scale migration during the last century. Southern Standard, Northern, Scots, and Irish English, for instance, are spoken in Canada among first and second generation immigrants from Great Britain, as well as "foreign" English dialects, but gradually all varieties of English are being assimilated to the Canadian English of the Loyalists, which, in turn, has been modified to some extent by the process. The Canadian West was colonized, also, to some extent, by Americans from the Middle West, reinforcing the already American basis of Canadian English. Canadian English then is basically eighteenth-century American English modified by other influences, notable among which are Southern Standard English and the English taught by Scots school teachers. The continuing influence of the United States has also been a factor which cannot be ignored, although Canada's sense of inferiority and pride has generally kept it as slight as possible.

❧

Canadian English, as has been recognized by some observers, is to all intents and purposes General American with a few modified sounds, usually paralleled in American subdialects, and with some vocabulary variation.

The most striking Canadian phonetic divergence from General American—found also in Virginia—is the pronunciation of the General American diphthongs [ɑʊ] and [ɑɪ] as [ʌʊ] and [ʌɪ] before voiceless consonants, as in *about, out, house, nice, height*. There is also a strong tendency among Canadian speakers of English—stronger, I believe, than the same tendency among American speakers—to diphthongize final vocalic *l*, *m* and *n*, as in *mail* [meɪᵛl], *known* [nowən] *film* [fɪlam], elm [ɛləm]. Stress will occasionally follow the British rather than American pattern. *Corollary, capillary, laboratory* will, for instance, often be accented on the second syllable, especially in Eastern Canada among educated speakers. Yet words ending in *-ary* and *-ery* will usually have a secondary stress as in American English.

If the phonemes in good usage in the Chicago area as given by Leonard Bloomfield in *Language* (1933) are compared with those of educated second or third generation Canadian speakers, it will be found that, with the few exceptions listed in the previous paragraph, they coincide almost exactly. In the series of records prepared by Professors Ayres and Greet of Columbia University and put out by the Linguaphone Institute only one (#67) is devoted to Canadian speech (from Ontario). This record indicates clearly the General American nature of Canadian speech.[8] Most of the phonetic variations found within Canadian English (exclusive of British influence) are those also found in General American.

The differences between Canadian and General American vocabularies—in choice and oral style—are, of course, wider and more considerable, but still not numerous. The vocabulary of Canadian English is a subject which must be approached with some caution. It is sometimes difficult for observers [9] to determine correctly Ca-

[8] For phonetic transcriptions of Canadian English, see Appendix, pp. 230–231.

[9] Baugh, *op. cit.*, p. 398, for instance, incorrectly lists certain English terms as native Canadian.

224

nadian usage, as English people (that is, people born in England or their children) in Canada will often use, as is natural, British English terms, for example, *lift* for *elevator*, when native Canadians follow American usage. There is, also, among certain limited strata of educated native Canadians, a strong tendency to imitate or follow British usage, as in [jʊ] after *d*, and *s*, for example. In studying the vocabulary of a relatively new and sparsely populated country like Canada, a knowledge of the geographic origin and social status of the speaker is even more important than it usually is. Ultimately, of course, the question of native Canadian usage is bound up with the question of who is a native Canadian. In Canada, among English speakers, that question is not always easy to answer, although it is getting easier with the passage of the years. Native Canadians will use *chesterfield* as well as *sofa*, *zed* for *zee*, *copper* for *penny*, *porridge* for *oatmeal*, and distinguish in pronunciation *rout* and *route*; and say [ʃɔn] or [ʃan], not [ʃoᵛn] for the past tense of *shine*. In the case of many words, such as *schedule* and *tomato*, both the normal British and American pronunciations may be found in good usage. The past participles *got* and *proved* are generally used. Syntactically, Canadians will say "have you" rather than "do you have" as in American English, or, unlike American English, "will you *take* a drink" rather than "will you *have* a drink."

Canadians do not normally use *lift* for *elevator*, *pram* for *baby carriage*, *pavement* for *sidewalk*, *cinema* for *movies*, *sweet* for *dessert*, or *hoarding* for *billboard*. These terms, however, will be found among first generation British settlers in Canada or among imitators of British usage. In spelling on the other hand Canadians are generally taught British practice, yet *tire*, *curb*, and *jail* are spelled as in the United States.

In special or trade languages, such as those of mechanics, railwaymen, and printers, Canadians generally employ the same cant as their American fellow-trade-unionists, for they usually belong to International (that is, American) Labor Unions or Brotherhoods. In one important "trade," however, that of soldier and sailor, they follow British usage. The Canadian Navy, Army, and Airforce are patterned after, and were formerly trained by, their British counterparts. In Canada, unlike the United States, Royal Air Force slang of this past war, for instance, is well-known, and British military and naval terms are universally employed, although Canadians know, from movies and magazines, American military expressions and slang.

The cultural dependence of Canada on the United States and Great Britain, particularly on the former in recent years, has tended to introduce contemporary American and English locutions into its speech. In the past thirty-five years, it has been primarily the United States which, through motion pictures, magazines, books, and personal contact, has kept Canadian English "up-to-date."

English-speaking Canada from Nova Scotia to British Columbia is part of the General American speech area. There are, of course, subdialects and local usage, notably in the Maritime Provinces, and to a lesser extent in parts of Ontario, but it can be said that, allowing for recent immigrants from Great Britain, one type of English is spread over Canada's 3000-mile populated belt.

In the case of Nova Scotia, Prince Edward Island, and New Brunswick, the problem of dialect criteria comes to the fore. Chamberlain, writing in 1890,[10] argues that the language spoken in these provinces constitutes a separate dialect. It is doubtful whether this opinion can be maintained. The distinctive quality of Maritime speech phonetically comes down largely to its treatment [ɑ] before medial and final [r] and occasionally elsewhere, which is somewhat more fronted than in General American—somewhat similar to the New England treatment of this sound.

Otherwise, Maritime speech is similar to Canadian English (or General American) in pronunciation, intonation, and vocabulary (except for a few localisms which can probably be traced to New England). In the Scottish-derived areas of Cape Breton Island and Pictou County, however, a number of Gaelic words are to be found in ordinary English speech. Chamberlain, as his comments on the English spoken in Quebec and his concept of Canadianisms [11] show, is a highly unreliable observer. It is hard to maintain that the differentiating criteria are sufficiently significant to justify the title of a separate Canadian dialect. We are dealing with General American

[10] *Op. cit.*, pp. 45–46.

[11] *Ibid.*, p. 46. Chamberlain believes that Quebec English (English of the Eastern Townships) is similar to that of New England. See above. Many of the Canadianisms he lists could equally well be considered Americanisms.

slightly modified by the New England dialect—an admixture which possibly goes back to the eighteenth century and the original Yankee settlers and possibly reveals eighteenth-century New England speech as it was.

These distinctive Maritime sounds and words, if they are not traceable to the earliest settlers, can easily be explained by the proximity of the New England States and the close contacts with them over the past two centuries. There are more "Maritimers" in New England than in the Maritime Provinces, and every summer, in normal times, large numbers visit their relatives in both directions. There is also a close cultural connection which is as old as the eighteenth century. Geographically, the Baie de Chaleur and the boundary line between Maine and Canada make the Maritime Provinces an extension of New England rather than of Quebec. Their natural outlet, destroyed by the frontier, is to the south and west. Linguistically, however, the total New England influence, if it is influence, has been slight.

It should be noted, however, that, although geographical proximity is obvious, English speakers in Quebec Province have *not* been influenced at all by the English of Vermont or the upper New York subdialect. The English speakers of Quebec have not had the cultural and social contacts with the natives of New York, Vermont, and New Hampshire that the inhabitants of the Maritime Provinces have had with New Englanders over the past two hundred years.

Mencken's words, "In Canada, despite the social influence of English usage, the "flat *a*" has conquered, and along the Canadian-New England border it is actually regarded as a Canadianism, especially in such words as *calm* and *aunt*," [12] bear out the fact that New England has affected Canadian speech very little and reveal, at the same time, Mencken's ignorance of the source of Canadian English, for the "flat *a*" in most cases never had any rival *a* to conquer. In the Maritimes, the linguistic influence of New England is confined to the [ɑ] before [r] and to a few terms, both possibly borrowed dur-

[12] *The American Language*, 4th ed., Corrected etc. (New York, 1935), p. 338. Further, as Hans Kurath, in "Mourning and Morning," *Studies for William A. Read*, ed. N. M. Coffee and T. A. Kirby (Baton Rouge, 1940), pp. 166–173, shows, the vowels in *mourning: morning; hoarse: horse* are distinguished in New England. This is not the case in Canada where, as in Maryland, no distinction is made.

ing the eighteenth century or even more likely, reflecting New England speech of the eighteenth century, and in Quebec, it has been absolutely nil.

❧

A study of the geographic origins of the Loyalists might contribute to an understanding of eighteenth-century American English. The troublesome problem of the origin of the three main American dialects may be solved—or partially solved—by an examination of contemporary and early Canadian English. It may be possible perhaps to show the necessity of modifying some of the current explanations of the origin of American dialects.[13]

Most of the distinguishing characteristics of New England and Southern American English may not have developed until the late eighteenth and early nineteenth centuries—that is, *after* the exodus of the Loyalists to Canada. The ubiquity of General American in Canada testifies to its ubiquity in the country of its origin around 1775–1785 and even earlier, since there is no evidence that the Loyalists came only from the central Atlantic states.[14] It is possible, however, that, as the speech of the Maritimes as noted above testi-

[13] See Krapp, *op. cit.*, I, 52–57; Hans Kurath, "The Origin of the Dialectical Differences in Spoken American English," MP, XXV (1928), 385–395; Baugh, *op. cit.*, pp. 450 ff.; and Anders Orbeck, *Early New England Pronunciation as Reflected in Some Seventeenth Century Town Records of Eastern Massachusetts* (Ann Arbor 1927) (which contains an excellent bibliography on early American pronunciation).

Professor John S. Kenyon, however, in a private letter to me (Nov. 1946) writes: ". . . G A was probably more widespread in America in the 18th c. than now. 'Speech Islands' like Martha's Vineyard in Mass. where G A is spoken, indicate this, as does also the fact that Eastern New England cities show the "Boston" type more than the immediately adjacent country and villages. My grandparents, who came from R. I. from a spot where the Eastern type is now prevalent, spoke G A. But they may have lost their early speech in the Western environment. But many things convince me that the "Boston" type was a class dialect, imitated from London and fostered by the elite. I believe the same to be true in New York City and in Richmond, Va."

[14] Chamberlain, *op. cit.*, p. 46, states that the early Loyalist settlers of Ontario came from New York and Pennsylvania. Assuming that he is correct, there is nothing surprising in the fact that Ontario today speaks General American. Where, however, did the Loyalists of Quebec and Nova Scotia come from? Most likely from New England. Loyalists from the Southern States, particularly Virginia, also settled in Canada, but probably in smaller numbers. A study of their settlements in Canada would be of great interest.

fies, the changes in [ɑ] in New England were taking place around 1770. A study of the geographic origins of the Loyalists would be a valuable contribution to the solution of the problem.

It has always been recognized, of course, that the northern and southern sea-board states were influenced by certain eighteenth-century changes in Southern Standard English,[15] for example, the substitution of [ɑ] for [æ] in certain words, and the dropping of the medial and final [r] before consonants.

Those who hold that the origin of the three major American dialects is to be found in English dialectal divergence believe that at least the seeds of this triple distinction had emerged by the late seventeenth and early eighteenth centuries. This theory, however, cannot account for the clear General American characteristics of Canadian English. Some modification of this hypothesis seems to be called for.[16]

More specifically, a study of local dialects in old Loyalist settlements will reveal information on eighteenth century speech in the United States. *The Linguistic Atlas of the United States and Canada* will contribute to the solution of problems in American English on which Canadian English can shed light. But more investigation than that required for the *Atlas* will be necessary. A study of Loyalist settlements in Canada will reveal much even today. Both the oldest town records and old native inhabitants can provide much linguistic information. And above all, when the time for it is ripe, a synthesizing study of early Canadian speech will either substantiate old, or create new, theories of eighteenth-century American English.

Canadian English is, of course, a subject of intrinsic interest, but it should also be considered as a part of the history of the English language in America to which it primarily belongs. The enlargement of the boundaries of American English will benefit all students of the subject and make possible a more exact understanding of the history of the English Language in America.

[15] Unless we assume that these changes antedate the eighteenth century, for which assumption there is some evidence.

[16] I am *not* saying that English dialects are of no value in studying variations in American English. I am questioning the attribution of the origin of American major dialects to English dialectical variety.

APPENDIX

For most of the following phonetic transcriptions of Canadian English, I am indebted to the kindness of Professor John S. Kenyon of Hiram College. The sources are not in every case free from cross influences, nor are the phonetic symbols always used consistently as the transcriptions were taken by different recorders. In other words, only a rough approximation is here offered. I question the accuracy of certain transcriptions; I have, however, followed my sources. When two pronunciations are given, both are attested. In most examples, only the main stress is indicated. The General American character of the phonology is quite obvious.

	Maritime (Halifax)	Quebec (Montreal)	Ontario*	Western (Saskatchewan)
aseptic	[æ'sɛptɪk]	[ə'sɛptɪk]	[ə'sɛptɪk]	[ə'sɛptɪk]
aunt	[ænt]	[ænt] or [ant]	[ænt] or [ant]	[ænt]
beauty	[bjuti]	[bjuti]	[bjutɪ]	[bjuti]
boss	[bɔs]	[bɒs]	[bɔs]	[bɒs]
brewed	[brud] [brjud]	[brud]	[brɪud]	[brud]
camphor	['kæmfɚ]	['kæmfɚ]	['kæmfɚ]	['kæmfɚ]
caterpillar	['kætɚpɪlᵘr]	['kætɚpɪlᵘr]	['kætɚpɪlᵘr]	['kætɚpɪlᵘr]
chocolate	['tʃɔklət]	['tʃaklət]	['tʃɔklət]	['tʃaklət]
choose	[tʃuz]	[tʃuz]	[tʃɪus]	[tʃuz]
coffin	['kɔfən]	['kɔfən]	['kɔfn̩]	[kɑfn̩]
cushion	['kʊʃən] [kʊʃʌn]	['kʊʃən]	['kʊʃn̩]	['kʊʃn̩]
doll	[dɔl]	[dɒl]	[dɔl]	[dɔl]
fatality	[fə'tælɪti] [fe'tælɪti]	[fə'tælɪti]	[fə'tælətɪ]	[fe'tælɪti] [fə'tælɪti]
food	[fud]	[fud]	[fud]	[fud]
feud	[fjud]	[fjud]	[frud]	[fjud]
gooseberry	['guzbɛri]	['gusbɛri]	['gusbrɪ]	['gusbɛri]
gourd	[gɔrd]	[gʊrd] [gɔrd]	[gʊrd]	[gʊrd]
grease (*verb*)	[gris] [griz]	[gris]	[gris]	[gris]
greasy	['grisi]]'grizi]	['grizi]	['grizɪ]	['grisi]
hew	[ju] [hju]	[hju] almost [çu]	[hɪu]	[hju]
hiccup	['hɪkəp]	['hɪkəp] ['hɪkʌp]	['hɪkʌp]	['hɪkəp]
hoof	[hʊf]	[huf]	[huf]	[hʊf]
horror	[harrər]	[hɔrɚ]	[hɔrɚ]	[hɔrɚ]
house	[hʌʊs] [haʊs]	[haʊs]	[haʊs]	[hʌʊs]

	Maritime (Halifax)	Quebec (Montreal)	Ontario*	Western (Saskatchewan)
Latin	[lætn̩]	[lætn̩]	[lætn̩]	[lætn̩]
march	[martʃ]	[martʃ]	[martʃ]	[martʃ]
miracle	['mɛrəkl] ['mirəkl]	['mɪrəkl]	['mɪrəkl]	['mɪrəkl]
mock	[mɑk]	[mɒk] [mɔk]	[mɔk]	[mɑk]
moth	[mɑθ]	[mɔθ]	[mɔθ]	[mɑθ]
nausea	['nɑʊziə]	['nɔsiə] [n'ɑsɪə]	˙'nɔsiə]	['nɑsɪə]
nominative	['nɑmnətɪv]	['nɑmnətɪv]	['nɔmnətɪf]	[nɑmnətɪv]
of	[ɔv] [əv]	[əv]	[əv]	[əv]
persist	['pɝˑsɪst]	[pɚ'sɪst]	[ɔɝˑsɪst]	[pɚ'sɪst]
poor	——	[pʊᴧ]	[pur]	[pʊᴧ]
romance	[ro'mæns]	['romæns]	[rʌ'mans]	[rʌ'mæns]
sirup	['sɪrəp]	['sɪrəp]	['sɝˑʌəp]	['sɪrəp]
swath	[swɑθ] [swæθ]	[swɑθ]	[ɛwɔθ]	[swɑθ]
tune	[tun]	[tjun]	[trʊn]	[tjun] [tun]
waft	[wɑft] [wæft]	[wɑft]	[wɔft]	[wɑft]
wasp	[wasp]	[wasp]	[wɔsp]	[wasp]
what	[wat]	[wʌt]	[hʍɔt]	[hwɔt]
wife	[wʌɪf]	[wʌɪf]	[waɪf]	[wʌɪf]
wives	[waɪvz]	[waivz]	[waɪvz]	[waɪvz]
yoke	[jok]	[ɪok]	[jok]	[jok]

* The Ontario source has been particularly subjected to various non-Canadian phonetic influences, especially that of Southern Received standard.

12. Final Root-forming Morphemes

Although the study of morphemes can never perhaps be put upon a strictly scientific basis,[1] there still remains much to be done in identifying, analyzing, and understanding this characteristic of language structure. The purpose of this paper is to present an extensive list of one type—the final root-forming [2] or terminal [3] morpheme—and to make certain tentative suggestions concerning the phenomenon in English.

A final root-forming morpheme is a phonemic block which terminates in the same language at least two different words (or is preceded by differentiating sounds or morphemes) and which functions as a unit conveying the same or a similar meaning. The *-ash* morpheme in English, for example, conveys a sense of violent striking action, as in *bash, clash, crash, dash, gash, gnash, hash, lash, mash, pash, quash, slash, smash,* and *thrash.* This particular morpheme is very widely distributed; most occur no more frequently than twice.

In the list of words at the end of this article, upon which my comments are based, I have taken a strict definition of morpheme, excluding words like *fresh* and *brash* which show phonetic divergence in the final morpheme in most English dialects but which undoubtedly have mutually influenced each other and could under a broad definition be considered the same final morpheme. English and American provincial dialects could provide, I am sure, many more examples than those given here; but in general I have stayed close to standard English. I have also avoided what Bolinger has called neutral morphemes,[4] such as affixes which indicate syntactic functions which would have swollen the lists without adding much to our knowledge. I have not allowed metathetic units as seen in *dirt* and *grit.* But I have ignored differences in parts of speech and have permitted functional shift.

The examples fall into two major groups—onomatopoeic and

Reprinted with permission of Columbia University Press from *American Speech,* XXVIII (1953), 158–164.

[1] See Dwight L. Bolinger's important article, "Rime, Assonance and Morpheme Analysis," *Word,* VI (1950), 117–136. Cf. also his earlier "Word Affinities," *American Speech,* XV (1940), 62–73.

[2] So called by Leonard Bloomfield, *Language* (New York, 1933), pp. 245–246.

[3] Bolinger's term in "Rime," p. 120.

[4] *Ibid.,* p. 117.

what, for lack of a better name, I call "abstract." In the first, we find some kind of basic imitative sound pattern which suggests various types of noise, size, movement, light, periodicity, etc. These may be illustrated by the following pairs: *bash, clash; bleat, tweet; bounce, jounce; burble, gurgle; buzzy, fuzzy; flimmer, glimmer; thwack, wack;* and so forth. The second embraces a wide variety of types the subclassification of which is difficult. Here we find pairs like the following: *basket, casket; bitch, witch; breast, chest; callow, shallow; solid, stolid; rub, scrub;* and so forth. These similarities are not based on an attempt to imitate sound or sense patterns.

Before we proceed further, however, we must distinguish these rhyming words from other lexical and morphic phenomena with which they may often be and have often been confused. This group must be sharply differentiated from playful repetitive compounds like *namby-pamby; hurly-burly;* [5] *hoity-toity; lazy daisy; harum-scarum; hocus-pocus;* and so forth, [6] although there are some points of contact between them. However, in their basic pattern and function, final root-forming morphemes are different from these compounds in that they do not occur in one composed word and in that most do not have a humorous connotation nor rise from playful motives. The repetitive principle is also dominant in the latter. The compounds are examples of what Sturtevant calls "contamination," [7] whereas final root-forming morphemes are not fundamentally so. [8] The only significant similarity between the two groups is that both make use of rhymes. In the case of *hurly-burly* (and possibly some others), there is evidence of an amalgamation of two words which were originally separate with the final root morpheme *-url* (related to noise and activity), together with the addition of the fanciful *y* ending. Here *hurl* and *burl,* the latter losing its separate identity permanently, amalgamated to become a playful com-

[5] On this word see Gösta Langenfelt, "Hurly-Burly, Hallaloo, Hullabaloo," *Neuphilologische Mitteilungen*, LI (1950), 2–18.

[6] See the list of these playful compounds gathered by Alice MacFarland in the Webster-Merriam *Word Study*, XXVI (1950).

[7] See Edgar Howard Sturtevant, *An Introduction to Linguistic Science* (New Haven, 1947), pp. 110 ff.

[8] In some cases there may have been in the history of the various groups of words some cross influence or contamination; however, most words seem to be of relatively the same date when such can be determined or guessed.

234

pound *hurly-burly.* But *hurl,* along with *whirl,* still remains as a sep-arate word, illustrative of the morpheme.

Then, too, we must distinguish rhyming slang [9] from the material presented here. Rhyming slang, like rhyming compounds, owes its origin to a playful fancy [10] and probably also to a desire to be secre-tive, but it is by no means so widespread as the compound group. It is the device found in English chiefly since the nineteenth century, although the motives behind it may be seen in English as far back as the Old English riddles and kennings, of half hiding a meaning in a rhyming phrase. Koziol gives as examples *birdlime-time; brown hat-cat; captain cook-book.*

Finally, we must maintain the distinction which Leonard Bloom-field makes between initial and final root-forming morphemes. In the first, the unifying principle is alliteration; in the second, it is rhyme. Certain initial root-forming morphemes have certain rela-tively fixed semantic suggestions, usually of an onomatopoeic sort. Some of the examples Bloomfield gives are ‛fl], "moving light," as in *flash, flare, flame, flicker,* and *flimmer* and ‛skr], "grating impact or sound," as in *scratch, scrape,* and *scream.* The confusion between initial and final root-forming morphemes is less likely to occur than with rhyming compounds and rhyming song.

When we examine closely the list below, we can clearly see the importance of semantic-sound parallelism in our language. As part of the wider subject of word affinities, a subject often neglected by linguists, these final root-forming morphemes occupy an important position. Yet mutually contradictory forces may be at work. The need to differentiate, for instance, may outweigh and submerge the morphemic function.[11] The morpheme will only become effective when it does not clash with other morphemes or established words. The sound group *-oon,* for example, suggests unpleasantness and awkwardness in *goon* and *loon,* but not in *moon* or *boon.* There are also complicated and tenuous cross patterns and influences which

---

[9] See D. W. Maurer, " 'Australian' Rhyming Argot in the American Underworld," *American Speech,* XIX (1944), 183–195; H. Koziol, "Rhyming Slang," *Die Sprache, Zeitschrift für Sprachwissenschaft,* II (1950), 77–84.

[10] On humor in language and word formation, see Robert M. Estrich and Hans Sperber, *Three Keys to Language* (New York, 1952), pp. 276–309.

[11] Bolinger, "Rime," p. 124.

make scientific accuracy impossible. Yet characterizing generalizations about morphemes are possible.

In English, it may be argued on the basis of both initial and terminal morphemes as well as of other evidence, we sense many of our words as consisting of an initial sound or sound cluster (or even a zero sound) and an ending, either of which may theoretically be replaced. Generally, we divide our words psychologically into a beginning and an end without a middle. There are exceptions to this principle, as may possibly be seen in certain long polysyllabic words (which, however, belong chiefly to the written vocabulary) like *satisfaction, dictionary,*[12] *revolution*, etc., and certainly in our ablaut survivals which we sense in terms of a variable middle such as *dr-nk* as in *drink, drank, drunk*. In general, however, in our spoken vocabulary the widespread use of initial and final morphemes argues that it is as beginning plus ending that we conceive our words.

Even in the many cases where there is no possibility of meaningful variants being established by changing the beginning or the end of our words, we allow for the possibility within our phonemic framework. This is revealed in the type of nonsense or root formation creations we find. A most profitable study of the principles of word formation used, say, by Lewis Carroll could be made as a contribution to ascertaining our structural sense of our vocabulary. It is also revealed in the fact that we would accept a product named "duzz," for instance, as both *d-* and *-uzz* are initial and final morpheme possibilities in English; but we would reject "sfuzz" because *sf-* is not. All this, of course, probably moves on a subconscious level.

In fact, by comparing our structural sense toward the English vocabulary with that of speakers of other languages toward their own, we may be able to penetrate more deeply into the morphemic nature of various languages: in fact, lay the basis for comparative structural morphemics. It would be especially interesting to compare the English sense of its own vocabulary structure with that of the speakers of those Indo-European languages which retain in large measure the inflections we have lost. Moreover, I am sure that speakers of Semitic languages sense their words differently—as consisting of a trilateral (usually) root center which can be modified

---

[12] Although here, as in some other polysyllabic words, I suspect we really think of it as a beginning plus two endings, as *dict+ion+ary*.

by affixes of an initial, medial, or final type and by the insertion of vowels. In some word pairs in English wherein we distinguish meaning by means of prefixes, for example, *please* and *displease*, *legal* and *illegal*, or in some of our remaining ablaut (strong) verbs, we may have a weak sense of this kind of structural organization, but in general we do not. This type of structural organization is not so widely sensed as in, say, Arabic.

In general, morphemic analysis is not historical.[13] The etymologies are irrelevant to our structural sense, although in some cases a study of the etymology of the pairs or triplets gives us the reason—or at least the antiquity—for the formation of the final root-forming morpheme. In some instances it is demonstrable that the form of one word has influenced the other.[14] In others, folk etymology has probably been at work. In yet others, the root is due to borrowing from foreign languages, as in *bathos* and *pathos*. It is, however, the semantic not the historical union which is decisive.

Yet there can be no doubt, I think, of mutual influences and attractions at work in the past. This is usually impossible to prove, yet it frequently seems a reasonable assumption. If one word came into the language later than the other, it is possible that the existence of the first aids in the acceptance of the second. In the more literary words this cross-influence may not be very active. It is amazing, however, to note how many of these words are colloquial and how many go back to Old English and Primitive Germanic, even though this antiquity must sometimes be assumed without proof.

The members of some pairs or triplets are mere natural phonetic variants of each other, as, for instance, *bottle* and *pottle*. In some cases one form is at present obsolete or obsolescent. Often, however, both are still very active in our present-day vocabulary. Sometimes the variants had the same meaning, but with the widespread English habit of near but not exact synonyms slightly different meanings have developed. Sometimes the opposite has occurred

---

[13] See Bolinger, "Rime," *passim*.

[14] Not always to bring forms closer together. I have always suspected that OE *scyttan*> NE *shut* rather NE *shit* in order to avoid the taboo morpheme. It would be natural to assume that the more common pattern as in OE *pytt* > NE *pit* and OE *brycg* > NE *bridge* would be followed. There are examples, of course, of OE [y] > NE [ʌ], as *rysc* > *rush*; but the question of why one alternative rather than the other was taken in this case still remains.

when the words have come closer in meaning from an original wider semantic separation because of phonetic similarity.

Most of the word groups here listed consist of words rhyming but having a related but distinctly different meaning. The ending suggests the relationship, whereas the beginning suggests the difference. The difference and similarity are often on a high level of abstraction. The semantic similarity of words like *solid* and *stolid,* for instance, is not immediately obvious. Yet it is clear, I think, that the mere existence of the one bears upon the meaning of the other.

That these words are often openly sensed to be related may be observed in the widespread euphemistic habit of using words like *dastard, muck,* and *witch* to avoid taboo rhyming words. It is all beautifully summed up in a scene in Congress as reported in the *New Yorker* of September 15, 1951:

> We've been told that one snag at Kaesong, like so many international snags of late, has resulted from the inability of the rival negotiators to agree on definitions of certain basic words—the Communist definition of "peace," to cite one notorious example, failing by the thickness of an unabridged dictionary to match our own. Here at home, where until recently nobody bothered much about precise shades of meaning except lexicographers and lawyers, we've been noticing signs of a complementary trend in terminology. During a debate on the Senate floor several weeks ago, after Senator Lehman had referred to Senator McCarthy's conduct as dastardly and a colleague had risen to take exception to the term, Lehman obligingly shifted to cowardly, and everybody seemed to feel better, though, as nearly as we can figure out, the two adjectives are synonymous.

LIST OF WORDS [15]

affect, confect, effect, perfect	bastard, dastard
amble, gambol, ramble, scramble	bathos, pathos
babble, gabble	batten, fatten
bash, clash, crash, dash, gash, gnash, hash, lash, mash, pash, quash, slash, smash, thrash	betray, bewray
	bitch, witch
	blab, gab
basket, casket	blackguard, braggart

[15] For some of these morphemes I am indebted to the articles by Bolinger alluded to in the text of this paper and to Mr. and Mrs. David Hite.

238

blare, flare, glare
bleat, tweet
blowsy, frowsy
blunt, stunt
blush, flush, gush, lush, mush, slush
boil, broil
bore, gore
bother, pother
bottle, pottle
bounce, flounce, jounce, trounce
brash, rash
breast, chest
brew, stew
bub, cub
bump, clump, dump, hump, lump, thump
burble, gurgle
burrow, furrow
buzzy, fuzzy (of tones in music)
callow, shallow
can, pan
cask, flask
champ, clamp, stamp, tramp
chip, snip
chubby, tubby
clap, rap, slap, snap, tap, trap
clasp, hasp
claw, paw
clunk, plunk
coil, toil (snare)
condemn, contemn
crimp, scrimp
crinkle, wrinkle
crook, hook
crude, lewd, nude, prude, rude
crumple, rumple
cry, sigh
cuddle, huddle
cuff, muff, scuff
curl, furl, hurl, purl, swirl, twirl, whirl
dank, rank
dart, start
daze, faze, haze, maze
diddle, fiddle, piddle
dimple, pimple
doodle, noodle (music)
doom, gloom
dotage, nonage
draggle, straggle
dram, gram

drone, groan, intone, moan
drop, flop, slop
drub, dub
drum, strum
dumb, numb
dunk, sunk
dusty, fusty, musty, rusty
elide, glide, ride, slide, stride
exacerbate, exasperate
fettle, mettle
flail, rail
flavor, savor
fleck, speck
fleer, jeer, leer, sneer
flimmer, glimmer, shimmer, simmer
flip, tip, trip
flop, plop
floss, gloss
flummery, mummery
flurry, hurry, scurry
flute, lute
foil, spoil
foist, hoist
frail, pale
frill, trill (music mainly)
frock, smock
fuck, muck, suck
fuddle, muddle
fuss, muss
gig, rig
glower, lower
goggle, ogle
goon, loon
grope, hope
group, troop
grouse, louse, mouse, souse
growl, howl
gruff, huff, sough
guile, wile
ham, sham
hassle, rassle
haunch, paunch
heel over, keel over
hoot, toot
hush, shush
impale, nail
jab, stab
jagged, ragged
jealous, zealous

jitter, titter, twitter
lacerate, macerate
land, sand
lime, slime
ludicrous, ridiculous
mar, scar
maunder, wander
mere, sheer
moil, toil
mutter, splutter, sputter, stutter, utter
pack, sack
pack, stack
pick, prick, stick (in certain senses)
pine, whine
potato, tomato
prattle, tattle
prod, rod
quake, shake
refrain, rein, restrain
roast, toast

rub, scrub
scatter, shatter, spatter
scoot, shoot
screwer, skewer
scuffle, shuffle
skip, slip, trip
slim, trim
smooth, soothe
solid, stolid
sooth, truth
spraddle, straddle
spur, stir
spurt, squirt
squiggle, wiggle, wriggle
sweat, wet
sweet, treat
swell, well
thwack, wack
withe, writhe

13. A Grammatical Approach to Personification Allegory

Although personification allegory is considered the most unimportant part of the general subject of allegory and symbolism and has earned the epithets of "reality-drained" and "paper-thin," [1] it has nevertheless been the subject of a good deal of speculation in modern literary theory and has not been entirely avoided by modern writers. If, indeed, we view the whole range of Western literature from Homer down to today, we may say that it has been one of the most popular of all literary modes. Even in an age which, following Coleridge and Schelling and Hegel, damns personification and elevates symbolism that is set in absolute opposition to it, there has been some reluctance to follow various critics in completely cutting off personification from symbolism. In England and America, Coleridge, who disapproved of certain kinds of symbolistic-figurative writing by calling them allegory and who instigated "numerous pedantic distinctions between symbolism and allegory," [2] has not entirely had his own way.

The whole subject of personification, allegory, and symbolism is obscured by conflicting theories and a wavering, and even contradictory, terminology. Although I shall not be able to avoid entirely some of the general questions and problems involved, I wish as far as possible to avoid the pitfalls of this subject and to concentrate on personification allegory itself in the hope of clarifying what it is and how it is used, by employing a more objective approach which might be called grammatical and logical. I am well aware of the fact that the subject has many ramifications with which I shall not

Reprinted from *Modern Philology*, LX (1963), 161–171.

[1] The first phrase comes from Edwin Honig's *Dark Conceit: The Making of Allegory, Allegory and Its Use by Melville, Hawthorne, James, Lawrence, Joyce, and Kafka* (reprint; Cambridge, Mass., 1960), p. 181. The second was used, I believe, by Don Cameron Allen at a meeting of the Medieval and Renaissance Symbolism Conference Group of the Modern Language Association in December 1960. This present paper was presented in shortened form at the Triennial Conference of the International Association of University Professors of English, August 17, 1962.

[2] Honig, *op. cit.*, pp. 44. Honig's book is not basically concerned with personification allegory. It is concerned with the more general subject of allegory, to which he brings a keen sense of literary and historical complexity. However, he does not make clear just exactly what he is writing about. He deplores at times the common distinction between allegory and symbolism and yet makes it himself, without clarifying exactly what he means by allegory. In a way he is turning Coleridge upside down by using the word "allegory" to designate those symbolic works he favors. The book is, however, full of good things.

be concerned and that much more may be said of it from other points of view than mine. I am trying merely to see whether grammatical analysis of some sort may not help us as scholars and critics in our task of understanding certain literary phenomena. More than the grammatical approach is needed, but we should not neglect this aspect of the subject.

There have been some grammatical analyses of personification in English literature, many of them dissertations at Kiel University,[3] but they have been mostly concerned with the problem of gender. In the hope, perhaps, of getting to the root of the use of grammatical genders, their authors have been concerned with the sex of personifications. The subject is particularly interesting in English, because a writer of English after about 1300, unlike his German or French counterparts, had more or less freedom in choosing masculine or feminine gender for his personified figures. The Germans seem to have been particularly fascinated with this freedom of choice denied them. The gender of their personifications, and even the very possibility of personification, was determined by forces outside their control. One might say that languages with grammatical

---

[3] Some of them make general remarks of interest, but they are all basically given over to classifying the genders; e.g., Gustav Tietje, "Die poetische Personifikation unpersönlicher Substantiva bei Cowper und Coleridge" (Inaugural-Dissertation . . . der Königlichen Christian-Albrechts-Universität zu Kiel, 1914); Werner Brandenburg, "Das poetische Genus personifizierter Substantiva bei James Thomson und Edward Young" (Inaugural-Dissertation . . . des Königlichen Christian-Albrechts-Universität zu Kiel; Hamburg, 1914); Julius Plaut, "Das poetische Genus personifizierter Substantiva bei Alfred Lord Tennyson" (Inaugural-Dissertation . . . der Königlichen Christian-Albrechts-Universität zu Kiel; Heidelberg, 1913); W. Franz, *Shakespeare-Grammatik* (3d ed.; Heidelberg: Germanische Bibliothek, 1924), I, 1, 12; Martin Liening, "Die Personifikation unpersönlicher Hauptwörter bei den Vorläufern Shakespeares (Lyly, Kyd, Marlowe, Peele und Greene)" (Inaugural-Dissertation . . . der Universität Münster i. W.; Borna-Leipzig, 1904); Herbert Cramer, "Das persönliche Geschlecht unpersönlicher Substantiva . . . bei William Wordsworth" (Inaugural-Dissertation . . . der Christian-Albrechts-Universität zu Kiel; Halle / Saale, 1919); Johann Trede, "Das persönliche Geschlecht unpersönlicher Substantiva . . . bei Lord Byron" (Inaugural-Dissertation . . . der Königlichen Christian-Albrechts-Universität zu Kiel, 1914); Erich Ausbüttel, *Das Persönliche Geschlecht unpersönlicher Substantiva . . . seit dem Aussterben des grammatischen Geschlechts* ("Studien zur englischen Philologie," XIX (Halle / Saale, 1904); Victor Schultz, "Das persönliche Geschlecht unpersönlicher Substantiva . . . bei Spenser" (Inaugural-Dissertation . . . der Königlichen Christian-Albrechts-Universität zu Kiel; Heidelberg, 1913). On gender in English see Lorenz Morsbach, *Grammatisches und psychologisches Geschlecht im Englischen* (2d ed.; Berlin, 1926).

244

gender, unlike English, have automatically built-in personification of some sort. These German studies may be taken as contributions to the history of gender rather than to the understanding of allegory. Grammatical analysis in this paper is to be employed for the sake of clarifying personification allegory and not for a linguistic or grammatical goal.

The application of grammatical (and rhetorical) analysis to literature can be, I am convinced, most fruitful. Many grammatical, phonological, and phonetic studies have, of course, been made, though sometimes of a rather barren sort, and Leo Spitzer and some of the stylistic analysts have brought philological acuity to the analysis of the aesthetics of literature. We are all appreciative of the work of Professor Roman Jakobson who is using modern syntactic analysis in the study of poetry, as well as that of Josephine Miles, Käte Hamburger, Francis Berry, Christine Brooke-Rose, and others. But on the whole, a great deal remains to be done by linguists and philologists with some literary sensitivity. I see here a new and important field for literary critics and scholars. Robert Browne has urged that we should approach aesthetic and poetic meaning through grammatical (and rhetorical) structure.[4] Although one can exaggerate the effectiveness of this method and although some literary works are less adapted to it than others, nevertheless the close relations between language and literature need to be studied in detail in literary texts so that the claims of linguistics to clarify literature may be fully justified.

The origins of personification lie deep in the past and are related to primitive animism. The nineteenth century saw much probing on the subject of the relation between gods and early personifications which shall not detain us here.[5] It has been argued that the origin of literary personification is to be found in ritual drama, for Canaanite and Egyptian rituals use abstract qualities as divine and semidivine names.[6] In any case the earliest Western writings, in the

[4] "Grammar and Rhetoric in Criticism," *Texas Studies in Literature and Language,* III (1961), 144–151.

[5] See the brief discussion of the probing in Karl Reinhardt, "Personifikation und Allegorie," *Vermächtnis der Antike, Gesammelte Essays zur Philosophie and Geschichtsschreibung,* ed. Carl Becker (Göttingen, 1960), pp. 7 ff.

[6] See Theodore H. Gaster's Foreword to the recent paperback edition (original ed., Cambridge, England, 1914) of Francis Macdonald Cornford's *The Origin of Attic Comedy* (New York, 1961), pp. xxi–xxiii.

Bible and Homer, use personifications, and they are found throughout all Greek and Roman literature. In late antiquity Prudentius' *Psychomachia* gave this mode a great boost, for it represented a breakthrough in which Judeo-Christian notions were given an epic quality built entirely around personifications.[7] Boethius' *De Consolatione Philosophiae* and Martianus Capella's *Marriage of Mercury and Philology* use personifications for their chief characters. I have argued elsewhere that personification allegory is to be found in *Beowulf*,[8] and it certainly appears in early medieval Latin literature. However, as far as the West is concerned, the great efflorescence of personification began in the late twelfth century with the extensive use of animated concepts and notions, many of them psychological, in romance, lyric, and debate.[9]

The period from 1200 to 1700 was the great era of personification allegory in European literature. Indeed it has had periods of resurgence since then as in the late eighteenth-century ode and to some extent in modern poetry beginning with Baudelaire. At all times, of course, it has been used for incidental effects. Even Wordsworth, who attacked the trope in his critical writings, used it in his poetry. There is no question, then, of its importance in literary history.

Before any clarity can obtain in this subject, it is necessary to make certain distinctions. Not all personifications are of the same nature or used for the same literary purpose. Certain verbal usages look like personifications and are frequently confused with them, but are not actually personified allegory. As a very general definition, it may be said that personification allegory is the process of animating inanimate objects or abstract notions, and that a personification is the animate figure thereby created. We can discover whether a figure is a true personification by certain grammatical tests. The use of nouns as names of living beings or gods is one test.

---

[7] See Hans Robert Jauss, "Form und Auffassung der Allegorie in der Tradition der *Psychomachia* (von Prudentius zum ersten *Romanz de la Rose*)," *Medium Aevum Vivum, Festschrift für Walther Bulst*, ed. H. R. Jauss and D. Schaller (Heidelberg, 1960), pp. 187 ff.

[8] See "*Beowulf* and Christian Allegory: An Interpretation of Unferth," *Traditio*, VII (1949–1951), 410–415.

[9] For the background of this efflorescence and its significance see Jauss, *op. cit.*, and Charles Muscatine, "The Emergence of Psychological Allegory in Old French Romance," *PMLA*, LXVII (1953), 1165–1179.

246

In languages with natural gender, pronouns, provided that they maintain gender distinctions, are helpful. Verbs which are normally only used of living beings also provide tests of value. The use of the vocative case or vocative form and any other forms that are normally only used of living creatures (such as the relative *who* in English) are often decisive in the matter. Occasionally the absence of a linguistic form is useful. We do not, for example, use "the" in English with an animate proper noun. But even with grammatical markers, as we can see, caution is necessary. If we take the first two lines of the Prologue to the *Canterbury Tales*, we get some idea of the difficulty of simple identification:

> Whan that Aprill with his shoures soote
> The droghte of March hath perced to the roote.

Here *his* is of no use whatsoever in determining whether "Aprill" is personified, for in Chaucer's time (and even as late as the eighteenth century) *his* could refer to both masculine and neuter nouns. "Perced" is ambiguous. It is normally a verb of animation used of living things, but the metaphoric habit is so widespread that it may be simple metaphor. When we say "the storm is howling outside," it is highly dubious that we are personifying the noun in spite of the animate nature of the verb. Language, created in a primitive past and spoken still by humans who have a good deal of the primitive with its tendency to animism in them, is full of these simple metaphors. The problem arises chiefly in connection with an odd decorative personification, for if personification allegory is extended over any considerable length, the grammatical evidence becomes overwhelming. However, in short passages the matter is not always clear. In the case of the Chaucerian lines just quoted it is highly dubious that we have true personification, as we most certainly do have three lines further on when Chaucer writes:

> When Zephirus eek with his sweete breeth
> Inspired hath in every holt and heeth
> The tendre croppes.

Here the name "Zephirus" as well as a verb of animation is the revealing sign of this pathetic fallacy.

247

This discussion has given us knowledge of one pseudo-personification: simple animate metaphors. Another type of pseudo-personification may be seen when in modern English we use feminine pronouns for inanimate objects. When we call a ship a "she," we are usually not really personifying it. The verbs used with these pronouns tell us whether we are truly personifying the ship or not. We may say of a ship, "she has broken down," but the verb here tells us that we are really not animating the machine. A further type of pseudo-personification may be found in certain phrases of common use. When Kant speaks in *The Critique of Pure Reason* of reason putting certain questions to nature, we are not dealing with a genuine personification. These types of partial grammatical animation may be called, following Schultz,[10] formal personification.

Another type of pseudo-personification may be called emblematic and frequently accompanies genuine personification. We find this type when trees, rivers, and buildings are given abstract names. The City of Covetousness, the Slough of Despond, the Tower of Truth provide examples. In extended personification narrative inanimate objects are frequently given emblematic names of this sort and help to carry out the impression of generality, combined with naturalistic detail, which is, as we shall see, most characteristic of this literary mode.

Finally, we find another type of pseudo-personification in certain naming habits of novelists and dramatists. Fondlove, Wringhim, Quiverful, and Thwackum, in spite of the fact that their names reveal their outstanding personal characteristics, are not true personifications. They are a kind of shorthand, often humorous, which writers, especially in the past, like to use. They are usually appended to minor characters who move in a world of concrete beings with ordinary accidental names and possess none of the other characteristics of true personification. Their names are often phrasal rather than simple nouns, or if nouns, as with Lord Steyne, are frequently metaphoric rather than direct. Lord Steyne is degeneracy which is a *stain* on the nobility.

Before we discuss some of the different literary uses of personification, let us look at it a little more closely from a grammatical

[10] *Op. cit.*, pp. 2 ff.

point of view. When we make inanimate nouns animate, we are making deictic (or pointer) nouns out of nondeictic nouns. In other words, unless the animation is individualized, it is not a true animation. The inanimate notion or object must take on the general characteristics of an individual human being, not just any animate characteristics. It is characteristic of all nouns, except deictic nouns, to be polysemous. Deictic words, on the other hand, are unisemous. Or to put it another way, we are making proper nouns out of our source nouns, that is making them one member class nouns, and giving them an existential quality. Truth consists of a class of many truths, but the class "Lady Truth" contains only one member, the being who is the subject (or object) of the sentences in the literary work. We indicate in English this deictification by dropping the definite article, if it is normally used with the noun, by employing verbs of animation when making predications about the personified noun, and animate personal pronouns and "who" and "whom" instead of "which" when referring to it. If along with the generative grammarians we regard animateness and inanimateness as a grammatical rule of English we may say that in personification we violate English grammar in this respect. Poets and writers frequently violate English grammar for artistic effect, but in personification allegory the grammatical rule which is violated is that of animateness.

Historically, in English, we find a curious phenomenon. As personification came into the literature on a vast scale, the language was at the same time undergoing a process of neutralization by which many masculine and feminine nouns were becoming neuter.[11] Personification in English had to contend with neutralization in the common and public language. Whether this struggle made personification more or less attractive to English writers, given the general poetic tendency to violate grammar. I cannot say, but it seems to me that a comparative investigation into this matter in other literatures where this process was not going on may be of con-

---

[11] See Ausbüttel, *op. cit.*, p. 127. The phenomenon of neutralization is found sporadically in other Indo-European languages, even where grammatical gender did not disappear (see Edgar H. Sturtevant, "Neuter Pronouns Referring to Words of Different Gender or Number," *Studies in Honor of Hermann Collitz . . . Presented by a Group of His Pupils and Friends . . . February 4, 1930* [Baltimore, 1930], pp. 16–24).

siderable interest to an understanding of Middle English and Renaissance literature.

Of all the grammatical signs of personification it seems to me that the use of animate verbs and predicates is the most characteristic and important, except perhaps in dialogue or debate. The stress in most personification allegory is on the action. The personifier throws his creativeness into what he has his figures do. The really characteristic part of personification allegory in terms of aesthetic effect lies not in what nouns the writer chooses but in what predicates he attaches to his subjects. It is this misunderstanding I think which gives rise to the impression that personification allegory is mechanical and dull.

If we regard personification purely as a matter of nouns, we may say that they are open and clear and even on occasion dull. But if we consider personification in its sentence context, as it should be, we find a curious phenomenon. If a poet writes "Truth always treads down error," that is, if he uses personification, instead of writing, say, "Jerusalem always defeats Babylon," that is, if he uses symbolism, the verb in the first sentence, "treads down," is although presumably factual, symbolic and metaphorical and carries the tension of the sentence, whereas the verb in the second sentence, "defeats," is literal in its reference. The "higher" meaning in the first sentence is hidden in the verb; whereas in the second it is hidden in the nouns or in the sentence as a whole, but not particularly in the verb.

Indeed we cannot even tell that "Truth" in the first sentence is a personification at all until we come to the verb. We could very well have a sentence like "Truth is a virtue," where the subject is clearly not a personification; or we could have an ambiguous (in our sense) predicate as in the sentence "Truth is nobler than error," wherein Truth may or may not be a personification. Even though we cannot always decide from one sentence whether the noun is personified or not, we must at least have the whole sentence before us before any decision is possible.

Sometimes qualifying words or phrases may carry the metaphoric load, so to speak. Or complements ("Nature is the kindest mother still," Byron, *Childe Harold*, II, 37) or pronouns may weakly do the task. But we may say that, although it appears in the first instance

250

in the subject, personification is in some basic sense linked to predicates.

The verb (or occasionally some other part of speech) drives us back to the subject so that we may reinterpret it as a personification, and the verb must be metaphoric in every statement using personifications that is descriptive or narrative.[12]

The personifier, like the cartoonist, throws his creativeness into what he has his figures do. He does not wish to expend his artistic energies on the subjects of his discourse but on their actions. A cartoonist wishes to say something about the United States and almost automatically draws the figure of Uncle Sam, but the point is in the whole context, in what Uncle Sam is doing or having done to him.

Pope speaks of the throne of Dulness as follows:

> Beneath her foot-stool, Science groans in chains
> And Wit dreads Exile, Penalties, and Pains.
> There foam'd rebellious Logic, gagged and bound,
> There, stript, fair Rhet'ric languished on the ground.
> His blunted arms by Sophistry are born,
> And Shameless Billingsgate her robes adorn.
> Morality, by her false Guardians drawn,
> Chicane in furs, and Casuistry in lawn,
> Gasps, as they straiten at each end the cord,
> And dies, when Dulness gives her Page the·word
> <div align="right">The <i>Dunciad, IV,</i> ll. 21–30.</div>

Is this not artistic creativity of the highest order? But the creativity does not merely lie in thinking up the figures of Science, Wit, Logic, Rhetoric, Sophistry, Billingsgate, Morality, Chicane, Casuistry, and Dulness, but in what Pope has them do or causes to be done to them and in the mastery of his language. I do not, however, wish to deny the force of the cohesion of the nouns in this

---

[12] As stated above, speeches by personifications and in some cases apostrophes present a somewhat different problem. Of course, once we determine from an early sentence in a piece of writing that the abstraction or object is being personified, we need not redetermine it in every subsequent sentence, although our interest will continue to be in the action. Donald Davie, *Purity of Diction in English Verse* (New York, 1953), pp. 38–39 saw, as no doubt others have, the importance of the verb in personification.

251

passage. They also create a feeling of the presumed but actually false literalness of the action.

My colleague W. J. Bate makes the same general point (although he does not relate it to personification in general) about Dr. Johnson's prose style, which is full of abstract nouns. He writes, "but what is surprising is to find these abstract nouns . . . sometimes jostled and always invigorated by the most frequent use of verbs in English prose: 'employed in *collecting importance* into our faces'; '*diseased* with vain longings'; '*dissolved* in listlessness'; the belief that weather and change of seasons affect invention is 'imagination *operating* on luxury.' " [13]

Personification was defended and praised in the eighteenth century for the very qualities—imaginative creativity, boldness, concentration, passion—that it has since been considered most deficient in. It was the "fairy" quality of personification, its being created out of nothing, so to speak, that endeared it to Addison and many other figures of his century. Of course, it was recognized that there were good and bad, successful and unsuccessful, personifications; but if prosopopoeia was successfully used it was frequently thought of as of the essence of poetic creativity. [14] Yet the eighteenth century did

[13] *The Achievement of Samuel Johnson* (New York, 1955) (reprinted as a Galaxy Book, 1961), p. 173.

[14] Of all the eighteenth-century comments on personification allegory (many conveniently summarized in Earl R. Wasserman, "The Inherent Values of Eighteenth-Century Personification," *PMLA*, LXV [1950], 435–463, which also has some valuable general remarks about its use in that period), perhaps only George Campbell's (*The Philosophy of Rhetoric*, edition of 1834, New York, pp. 296–299) openly puts the matter somewhat as I have. The other commentators more or less take it for granted. Campbell writes: "when the concrete is used for the abstract, there is, in the first place, a real personification, the subject being in fact a *mere* quality both inanimate and insensible: nor do we lose the particularity implied in the abstract, because, where this trope is judiciously used, *there must be something in the sentence which fixes the attention especially on that quality*" (p. 299; my italics). For some recent treatments of personification allegory in the Renaissance and eighteenth century besides those already mentioned and to be mentioned later, see Chester F. Chapin, *Personification in Eighteenth-Century English Poetry* (New York, 1955); Bertrand H. Bronson, "Personification Reconsidered," *New Light on Dr. Johnson, Essays on the Occasion of his 250th Birthday*, ed. Frederick W. Hilles (New Haven, Conn., 1959), pp. 189–231 (a reworking of his earlier article with the same title in *ELH*, XIV [1947], 63–77; Joshua McClennan, *On the Meaning and Function of Allegory in the English Renaissance*, "University of Michigan Contributions in Modern Philology," No. 6, April, 1947; Harry Berger, Jr., *The Allegorical Temper; Vision and Reality in Book II of Spenser's Faerie Queene*, "Yale Studies in

not, on the whole, prolong the action of personifications as the Middle Ages loved to do. It favored a more static, pictorial type of personification allegory. Dr. Johnson in his *Life of Milton* reveals this preference by writing "to give them [personifications of Fame and Victory] any real employment or ascribe to them any material agency is to make them allegorical no longer, but to shock the mind by ascribing effects to non-entity." [15]

Perhaps a partial explanation for this eighteenth-century love of relatively static and descriptive allegory is due to the impact of painting and sculpture. Of all the sister arts, eighteenth-century poetry preferred painting. Because of technical limitations and its iconological nature, personification is one of the few technical devices common in more than a metaphorical sense to both the fine arts and to literature. In poetry, painting, or sculpture today, we rarely find victory, reason, or fame appearing as a noble lady or an upright man. If we do have occasional sculpture entitled "Truth" or "The Spirit of 1776," they are either hopelessly old-fashioned or something else altogether. Perhaps, as we have suggested, only in political cartoons do we still find significant uses of static personification, and even here it is usually limited to "Uncle Sam" or "John Bull" or a frightened lady, "Peace," and the like. However, personifications were common in Renaissance and post-Renaissance art.

This type of static personification allegory was by no means unknown to the Middle Ages, but it was less common than dynamic or narrative allegory. Describing wall paintings or buildings such as temples, the late classical trope of *ekphrasis*, was widespread and was a favorite mode down to the eighteenth century. Even with this type of personification, the emphasis is on, and the metaphoric con-

English," No. 137 (New Haven, Conn., 1957); Ellen Douglas Leyburn, *Satiric Allegory, Mirror of Man*, "Yale Studies in English," No. 130 (New Haven, Conn., 1956); Jean H. Hagstrum, *The Sister Arts: The Tradition of Literary Pictorialism and English Poetry from Dryden to Gray* (Chicago, 1958); Norman MacLean, "Personification but Not Poetry," *ELH*, XXIII (1956), 163–170, and his "From Action to Image: Theories of the Lyric in the Eighteenth Century," *Critics and Criticism, Ancient and Modern*, ed. R. S. Crane (Chicago, 1952), pp. 408–460; and Edward A. Bloom, "The Allegorical Principle," *ELH*, XVIII (1951), 163–190.

[15] Quoted in Bloom, p. 184. Johann George Sulzer, *Allgemeine Theorie der schönen Künste* . . . (Leipzig, 1771–1774) in his article on Allegory (pp. 27 ff.) also speaks of the dangers of letting personification go on for too long (p. 33).

tent is in, the predicate. Although it may involve any syntactic relationship of which the noun in English is capable, personification allegory, in most of its manifestations, is in a basic sense extended or simple predicative metaphor.[16]

Personification allegory, whether static (descriptive) or dynamic (narrative), has slightly different functions in different literary genres. Although there is a common ground to all its manifestations, it fills different roles in different literary contexts. We shall omit short personification passages and refer briefly to its functions in dialogue or debate and in apostrophes. Narrative we have already dealt with. Some personification may, of course, be imbedded in other literary forms and in nonpersonification contexts.

In dialogue and in apostrophe or, as we may call them, confrontation literature, personification allegory does not have this predicative function in quite the same way. Here I think directness and openness are chiefly in the writer's mind. However, in dialogue the use of personifications throws emphasis on the speeches. They may be considered extended complement-predicates to a kind of statement like "X says." In the debates of love and reason, or of the heart and the head, or of the artist's persona (a kind of self-personification) with Lady Philosophy or Lady Holy Church, the poet is not interested in the effects of the agitation or conflict on a character but in the substance of the dispute. We are enabled to see the general import of the issue and at the same time to be both distanced from and implicated in it as human beings.

A work totally arranged around an allegorical debate is primarily organized around the substance of the quarrel. What happens when an owl and a nightingale debate is that we are left in obscurity as to what these birds stand for, but when Philosophy and the Boethius persona talk we have no doubt as to the frame of reference in which the issues are set. Personification debates are not as metaphorical as allegorical descriptions or narratives, but they serve to throw light on what is being debated. The speeches are the predicates, so to speak.

[16] Robert Frank in his very interesting article, "The Art of Reading Medieval Personification-Allegory," *ELH*, XX (1953), 237–250, following L. L. Camp, makes this point too in less linguistic fashion by referring to the action as carrying the secondary meaning.

In apostrophes, or lyric personification, the existential reality, the deictic nature of the abstraction, is being stressed. It is a way of bringing alive an abstract quality for temporary variation, and at the same time it uses the strengths of predicative metaphor.

The theories of C. S. Lewis are perhaps the best-known attempt to present a theory of personification allegory.[17] Following John Ruskin and others, Lewis makes a more or less absolute distinction between allegory (personification) and symbolism. They are essentially opposite ways of expressing meaning. The allegorist starts from the immaterial, usually passions or thoughts, and materializes them. The symbolist starts from the material and puts an immaterial meaning into it. Or "the allegorist leaves the given—his own passions—to talk of that which is confessedly less real, which is a fiction. The symbolist leaves the given to find that which is more real." [18] Lewis goes on to say that "symbolism is a mode of thought, but allegory is a mode of expression." [19]

Bronson has criticized the Lewis position.[20] After pointing out that one cannot contrast a mode of thought with a mode of expression, he denies the centrality of the opposition between symbolism and allegory. The true opposite of allegory, he argues, is naturalism, and symbolism may employ either allegory (personification) or naturalism.[21] The more detailed a naturalistic character is the less use is he to symbolism. Before a naturalistic character can become symbolic, he must in some sense be allegorical (that is, typical). Bronson is also not happy with Lewis' idea of immateriality. To regard passions as immaterial seems dubious to him.

Without necessarily agreeing with Bronson entirely, I suggest he has put his finger on a fundamental difficulty in Lewis' exposition—the clear-cut opposition of symbolism and allegory.[22] However, a more fundamental objection to Lewis' definitions is that they are

[17] *The Allegory of Love: A Study in Medieval Tradition* (London, 1936), esp. pp. 44 ff.

[18] *Ibid.*, p. 45.

[19] *Ibid.*, p. 48.

[20] *Op. cit.*

[21] This is more or less the position Graham Hough takes in "The Allegorical Circle," *Critical Quarterly*, III (1961), 199–209, except that he uses the term "realism" rather than "naturalism."

[22] Frank also seems, at least by implication, to favor this absolute opposition—as I myself did some years ago.

psychological rather than linguistic.[23] They find the basic difference between symbolism and allegory (personification) in the intention and internal procedures of the poet. They place the core of the difference in whether the poet starts from the "immaterial" passions or from the material facts of experience. This is extremely difficult to determine exactly, and his mental procedures could be the same in both personification allegory and symbolism. His linguistic means do, however, differ and differ objectively in terms of their transformation of sentences.

If we take the two examples used above, we may actually say that when a poet writes "Truth always treads down Error" or when he writes "Jerusalem always defeats Babylon," he may actually have started from the same intention. He has chosen a different way to express himself, but the "meaning" in the sense of empirical or testable meaning is the same.[24] In other words, there is a difference in aesthetic effect, but not in empirical meaning. If we can get away from psychological definitions in this matter, we shall be on firmer ground.

Personification allegory combines the nonmetaphoric subject with metaphoric predicate and yokes together the concrete and the metaphoric in the presentation of generality. It attempts to gain the advantages of both the general and the concrete at the same time without sacrificing one to the other. It effects a concordance of discordance—the opposition between literalness and metaphor—within the work itself by uniting what is often separate without sacrificing aesthetic effect. It increases the area of applicability of generalizations and by the artistic force of metaphor makes them more memorable.

[23] Jauss, *op. cit.*, has a strong criticism of Lewis' psychological interpretation of personification allegory. He sees figures in the *Psychomachia* and the *Romance of the Rose* as more than individual qualities in the heart of a man or woman, they are also superpersonal and mythological. Medieval man depersonalized the personal. The battle in the *Psychomachia* is not in the soul, but for the soul.

[24] "Empirical meaning is what remains when, given discourse together with all its stimulatory conditions, we peel away the verbiage. It is what the sentences of one language and their firm translations in a completely alien language have in common." Willard V. Quine, "Meaning and Translation," in *On Translation*, ed. Reuben A. Brower (Cambridge, Mass., 1959), p. 148. In our examples here, "a completely alien language" would have to be one outside the Judeo-Christian tradition in which Jerusalem and Babylon are merely neutral place names.

When Prudentius presents artistically the moral struggle by means of personified abstractions, he is creating a work which makes clear the norm and the ideal without losing the vividness of the concrete. Philosophy is directly yoked to narrative and imagery, two of the most powerful aesthetic modes. Unlike his source,[25] he does not wish to tack an obvious moral on the story of the battle of Abraham with the four kings to which he refers in his preface or let the story tell itself, for it can be interpreted in a variety of ways. Tropologically in Philonic and patristic Biblical exegesis this episode in Abraham's life had been interpreted as the battle of reason against the vices. Yet instead of detailing this story at length, Prudentius turns to the use of personifications. I suspect it was that he wished to avoid any ambiguity about the subject and at the same time employ the vividness of detail and of metaphor which would make it appealing. He wished to teach his audience both what the vices can do to the soul and also, as his conclusion makes clear, what aid Christ can give us. At the conclusion of the poem, in his thanks to Christ, he indeed tells us that Christ wishes us to know what perils hide in our corporeal envelopes and the hazards of the battles of the soul.[26]

There is much detail in personification allegory, as in, for example, *Piers Plowman* and *Pilgrim's Progress*, but it is transmuted into metaphor. We are given a concrete world of action or of humanness which is immediately transcended metaphorically. Personification enables the artist to use experience without being too localized or pinned down in time and yet give us a sense of "this-ness." The *haeccitas* of the world points to another world of values and enables the artist to escape the danger of misplaced concreteness. The frame of true personification in narrative is not usually a naturalistic world but rather some kind of moral, mythic, or cosmic universe. This is why a naturalistic narrative cannot be automatically made into a personification allegory by changing the names of the characters into personification names. The frame of most naturalistic tales would not carry a true personification allegory. Hence per-

[25] See Morton W. Bloomfield, "A Source of Prudentius' *Psychomachia*," *Speculum*, XVIII (1943), 87–90.

[26] "Tu nos corporei latebrosa pericula aperti/Luctantisque animae voluisti agnoscere casus" (ll. 891–892). See n. 23 above.

257

sonification allegory is not purely a linguistic device, although we must start from the linguistic. In our literary world today, we are mostly realistically and naturalistically oriented and find idealized and generalized literature, of which personification allegory is a notable type, hard to take, although there are signs of change in the air. I suspect that we shall not wholeheartedly accept personification allegory until we have some firm basis onto which we may anchor a new rationalism.

Personification allegory and symbolism are in general modes of understanding expressed through different grammatical means. They are characteristic in different ways of the generalizing and unifying powers of the human mind. Personification allegory is not then simply the opposite of symbolism in any fundamental sense, but it is opposite to it in its clarity of subject. In personification, usually to serve a didactic purpose, the subject—that is, what is talked about, what is the subject of the predication to come—is unveiled and clear. As a recent writer in the *Times Literary Supplement* puts it, "it is the nature of allegory not to be ambiguous," [27] but this is only part of the story. The predicate is the most veiled part of personification allegory, although it may not be heavily veiled. Symbolism is more than veiled predicates; it is veiled nouns and/or sentences, although not necessarily every noun or every part of the sentence. The writer gives up the openness, we might say, of subject and predicate in order to suggest rather than present another universe of myth or idea. The personifier only gives up the openness of the predicate.

The immateriality of which Lewis speaks is better thought of as generality. Personification allegory is a method of presenting generalized and idealized notions in literature by literary means. These general notions may, however, be presented in the predicate with great concreteness and detail, but they are so presented as to drive the mind immediately to the universal. To the Middle Ages, or to any age which is committed to a set of organized beliefs, the more general is not necessarily the more immaterial. As Owen Barfield writes, "For us, the characters in an allegory are 'personified abstractions,' but for the man of the Middle Ages, Grammar or Rhet-

[27] Review of Edward Wagenknecht's *Hawthorne* . . . and Daniel G. Hoffman, *Form and Fable* . . . in *TLS*, September 29, 1961, p. 638.

oric, Mercy or Daunger were real to begin with, simply *because* they were 'names.' And names could be representations in much the same solid-feeling way as things were." [28]

The opposition which Bronson sets between personification allegory and naturalism, or between the general and the particular, creates difficulties. For although allegory is more generalized than naturalism, in the predicate it is only generalized through symbolism in the same way as naturalism itself may be symbolic. We have also seen that in much personification allegory we actually get a great mass of naturalistic detail. We cannot say the more allegory the less naturalism, a statement that would certainly be possible if they were true opposites. The concrete (which is the stuff of naturalism) and the general (which is the stuff of meaning and of the subjects, though not the predicates, of personification allegory) exist in different proportions in literary works. Only if we regard personification as the figure itself and not as part of a whole sentence context may we say that it is the opposite of naturalism. However, full personification entails a complete proposition, and in this sense personification makes use of naturalism, even to the extent, as we have seen, of defining itself as personification.

In view of the great popularity of personification and personification allegory, it is surprising that in classical and medieval rhetorics personification is a relatively minor item in the classification of tropes. Is is almost always a subdivision of a broader classification, but it is obvious that the rhetorical tradition recognized its vigor and clarity. Quintilian classifies prosopopoeia as a type of ἐνάργεια, vivid illumination, and sees it as one type out of many which give animation to a speech.[29] In the Renaissance Richard Sherry in *A Treatise of Schemes and Tropes* [30] described prosopopoeia as a type of *energia* (possibly a mistake for *enargia?*), and he defines it as

[28] *Saving the Appearances: A Study in Idolatry* (London, 1957), p. 86. See also Reto R. Bezzola, *Le Sens de l'aventure et de l'amour* (*Chrétien de Troyes*) (Paris, 1947), pp. 47–61.

[29] The main sections on prosopopoeia in Quintilian occur in *Institutio oratoria* IX, iii, 29 ff. and VI, ii, 32 ff. Cf. also *Ad C. Herennium De ratione dicendi* IV, liii, 66 ("conformatio est, cum aliqua, quae non adest, persona confingitur quasi adsit, aut cum res muta aut informis fit eloquens, et forma ei et oratio attribuitur ad dignitatem accommodata").

[30] Facsimile reproduction with Introduction and Index by Herbert W. Hildebrandt, Scholars Facsimiles and Reprints (Gainesville, Fla., 1961), p. 60.

259

"when a thynge is so described that it semeth to the reader or hearer that *he beholdeth it as it were in doing*" (my italics). George Campbell, in the eighteenth century, makes more or less the same point.[31] To Quintilian and Sherry and Campbell, as well as to other rhetoricians, it is a sense of activity which gives personification its peculiar potency and hold. And it need not be emphasized that it is the verb and the whole predication which is the action part of the sentence.[32] If we look at personification in this light, we can understand its hold on ages in which order, clarity, and imagination were regarded highly enough to be sought in literary activity as the highest goals, for personification yokes together rationality, directness, and metaphoric boldness.

[31] See n. 14 above.

[32] Robert L. Montgomery, *Symmetry and Sense: The Poetry of Sir Philip Sidney* (Austin, Texas, 1961) sees personification as one of the main methods whereby Sidney attains to an energetic style, in the analysis of which he applies my general point, without relating it, except incidentally, to grammatical structure. He writes, "No other element of Sidney's style [than personification] is so surely responsible for the energy of *Astrophel and Stella*" (p. 94) and elsewhere, "for although personification may be a living vessel for speech, it tends to remove attention from the main subject of the verse" (p. 40). See also Friedrich Brie, "Umfang und Ursprung poetischen Beseelung in der englischen Renaissance bis zu Philip Sidney," *ES*, L (1916–1917), 383–425. It should be pointed out that the term "prosopopoeia" is being used in this paper not in its stricter sense as found in the old rhetorical tradition but as a general synonym for "personification."

I wish to thank Professor Robert W. Frank, Jr., for his criticisms and suggestions in the writing of this paper.

14. The Syncategorematic in Poetry: From Semantics to Syntactics

"Poets must seek, not as Wordsworth thought, words in common usage, but a powerful and passionate syntax."—W. B. Yeats

Professor Jakobson, who has made us aware of so much in language and its functioning, was the first linguist who distinguished between the metaphoric and metonymic or the symbolic and contiguous dichotomy in the linguistic process.[1] I propose to carry a little further this distinction in language, employing it in a slightly different way, in order to show its usefulness in studying literary work. My emphasis will be upon metonymy—the role of contiguity and linguistic context—which as Professor Jakobson has said has been neglected in comparison with metaphor.

It has long been recognized [2] that words have two major roles in language—to refer and to indicate internal relations. In the one, words point outward to concepts, macro- or micro-cosmic; in the other they point inward to their sentence or constituent context. The first convey meaning: they name; the second convey grammatical function: they connect or relate. One function is vertical; the other horizontal. Words or morphemes in their referential role need the world of meaning to disambiguate them; words or morphemes in their syncategorematic role need only the linguistic or grammatical world.

The difference between these two functions is often seen as a difference between two types of words, although I think there is really not such a sharp distinction between these functions as such a verbal division implies. Charles Morris in discussing semiotic, the theory of signs, designates these functions by the terms, semantic and syntactic.[3] Other terms have been employed, usually indicating a distinction in words rather than in function: autosemantic and synsemantic, lexical and grammatical, full and empty. Bertrand

Reprinted by permission of Mouton and Company n.v. from *To Honor Roman Jakobson* (The Hague, 1967), I, 309–317.

[1] *Fundamentals of Language*, Part II (= *Janua Linguarum*, 1) (The Hague, 1956), pp. 76–82.

[2] See, e.g., Aristotle, *Poetics*, XIX 7 ff. (= 1456bff.) and *Rhetoric* III, 5, 2 (= 1407a). See also R. H. Robins, *Ancient and Medieval Grammatical Theory in Europe with Particular Reference to Modern Linguistic Doctrine* (London, 1951), p. 43 *et passim*.

"Besides the words which are used to *name* ideas, we need those which signify the *connection* of ideas or propositions." Leibnitz, *New Essays Concerning Human Understanding*, III, 791, trans. Alfred G. Langley, 3rd ed. (La Salle, Illinois, 1949), p. 364).

[3] *Signs, Language, and Behaviour* (New York, 1946), p. 219.

Russell calls syntactic words incomplete symbols. They have also been called form or functional words. The medieval logicians used the "syncategorematic" (as opposed to "categorematic") for these grammatical words, a term which has the advantage to us today of being relatively uncluttered by various irrelevant associations. Syncategorematic words provide the structure of the sentence or proposition, whereas the semantic or referential words are the variables. To put it in more modern terms, syncategorematic words are the words used as such in the pre-morphophonemic rules (although there are other syncategorematic words which come in on the morphophonemic or lower levels). Logic is a study of the possible manipulations of the syncategorematic element in propositions, even if the Aristotelian symbolization is replaced, as it is in modern symbolic logic, by less palpable and more mathematical symbols. Syncategorematic words are more predictable than categorematic words. The possibility of filling the gaps in an open sentence like the following are practically endless: The ____ ____ in the ____. On the other hand any speaker of English would probably be able to fill the following gaps without much trouble: ____ dog lives ____ ____ kennel. He may be wrong, but his possible fillers are very few.

Syncategorematic words function, it will be noted, metonymically, that is, in relation to their verbal or morphemic environment. Categorematic words function metaphorically inasmuch as they symbolize concepts. The metonymic-metaphoric distinction can then be applied to words in their language use. "Metaphor" must be employed somewhat loosely in this context and not strictly as Professor Jakobson employs the terms in his writings. "Metaphor" is here not being used as Aristotle defined it—the finding of similarity in dissimilarity—but rather in a looser but more etymological sense of "carrying over" or "transferring." "Metonym" is also being used more broadly, somewhat in the sense of "contextual."

In ordinary language usage, it is extremely doubtful whether any hard or fast division between these categories of words or morphemes can be made. This is why referring to the function of words rather than to the words themselves has advantages. At the most we can say that some words are more syntactic (or semantic) than others. Syntactic words have some meaning even if on a different level, often only in metalanguage, from that of semantic words. The fact that one cannot ordinarily be substituted for another even though a perfectly well-shaped sentence will result, shows that they have a different meaning. "The man" does not mean the same as "a man" in English in spite of the fact that "the" and "a" share a formal class—that of article—together. I think everyone more or less recognizes the semantic aspect of syncategorematic words. It is, however, less commonly recognized that lexical words have some syntactic or relational role, even when undistinguished by a syntactic bound morpheme as in inflectional languages. The parts of speech into which these words may be put, for instance, provides an elementary syntactic category. The part of speech to which a word belongs determines its possible sentential roles, which are made more precise by word order or syntactic markers.

Take the word *home* in English. This word, which would ordinarily be considered a semantic word, can function in certain roles and only in certain roles in a sentence. *Home* is relatively open syntactically and can act as a verb, noun, adjective, or adverb, depending on context. The context immediately establishes its syntactic function.

> He came [   ]. *adverb*
> [   ] is where the heart is. *noun*
> He hit a [   ] run. *adjective*
> The pigeon will [   ] on its release. *verb*

Anyone having a knowledge of English rules can immediately classify the syntactic role of the word by virtue of the context. Owing to the prevalence of functional shift, the relative ease with which words can be shifted in English from one part of speech to another, most English semantic words are relatively open syntactically. However, some words are more restricted than others, with a syntactic role limited to two or even one possibility. In the latter case, the part of speech to which it belongs may ordinarily, if the word is known to the speaker, be determined at once. Pronouns and adverbs ending in *-ly* [4] are usually syntactically closed in English, for they are generally incapable of functional shift (except in metalanguage).

[4] I am aware of the fact that there are *-ly* adjectives in English too.

265

In the case of adverbs with *-ly* the presence of a bound morphemic ending, which is the syntactic part of the word, forces its syntactic function to a single role. In inflected languages where functional shift is relatively limited, the syntactic morphemes, if unambiguous, perform a similar role. When they are ambiguous, experience solves the possible ambiguity. *Mensā* in Latin could be the ablative of a noun *mensa* or the second person singular imperative of a verb *mensare*. However, the speaker knows of no verb *mensare*, whereas he knows of a noun, *mensa*. *-s* in oral English is more ambiguous, but the context determines whether it is a genitive or a plural or belongs to a noun or a verb category. Most endings in inflected languages, however, make the problem a rational not an empiric one.

In any case, lexical words carry, so to speak, some kind of grammatical load which can easily or with a little difficulty be interpreted by means of sentence context. Semantic categories in one system of grammar may become syntactic in another. Until recently the animate-inanimate distinction in English was regarded as a purely semantic distinction, but it is now realized that such a distinction has grammatical implications and indeed determines the compatibility of certain nouns and verbs. It becomes a grammatical rule rather than a semantic feature in generative-transformational grammar. In other words, words and morphemes squint in two directions at once—toward the world of concepts and toward the world of words, although in almost every case the squint in one direction is stronger than in the other.

Syncategorematic words then are words which function MAINLY in terms of context—intrasententially: "words with inherent reference to the context." [5] Categorematic words are words which function MAINLY in terms of the world of meaning, extrasententially.

In terms of the listener or reader, words and immediate constituents function transitively and intransitively. They are both means to other words or concepts as well as ends in themselves. In general the artistic use of words works to increase the intransitivity of

[5] Roman Jakobson, "The Cardinal Dichotomy in Language," in *Language: An Enquiry into its Meaning and Function*, ed. Ruth Nanda Anshen, Science of Culture Series, VIII (New York, 1957), p. 161.

words. This feature of literary language is similar to the notion of "foregrounding," to use the happy translation of P. L. Garvin, which Jan Mukařovský of the Prague School suggested was its main characteristic. Poetic language calls attention to itself.

The "object" of words which are mainly lexical is the world of meaning; the "object" of words which are mainly functional is its own verbal or syntactic context. Because of the heavy metonymic rather than metaphoric function of syncategorematic words, paradoxically we become more aware of such words as words. When words lead to other words we are more conscious of their own wordhood than when they lead to concepts. When words lead to concepts, we tend to forget the word in the concept. In other words the transitivity of syncategorematic words increases their own intransitivity. The transitivity of categorematic words on the other hand decreases their own intransitivity. Inasmuch as one of the main purposes of literary art is to increase meaningfully intransitivity, the problem of the artist is much greater when working with semantic words than with syntactic words. Syntactic words carry much intransitivity by their very presence; whereas to increase the intransitivity of semantic words poses a great problem. Poetry not only says something about the world, it also says something about the language, about its own form of expression.[6] Poetic language not only communicates concepts; it also communicates itself to the reader and listener. Poetic devices enable the artist to do so. Poetic devices are the artist's weapons in his fight against the transitivity of lexical words.

Again Professor Jakobson makes a similar point although not quite in our terms when he writes, "The function of poetry is to point out that the sign is not identical with its referent. Why do we need this reminder? Because along with the awareness of the identity of the sign and the referent (A is A:), we need the consciousness of the inadequacy of this identity (A is not A:); this antinomy is essential, since without it the connection between the

---

[6] "If there is one meaning which the metrical pattern enforces on all language submitted to its influence, it is this: *Whatever else I may be talking about*, I am talking also about language itself." John Thompson, *The Founding of English Metre* (New York-London, 1961), p. 13.

sign and the object becomes automatized and the perception of reality withers away." [7]

Almost all theorists on the nature of poetry are aware of the fact that poetic devices function at least partially for the purpose of getting attention and of emphasizing certain words. To list the many critics who have discussed these aspects in various ways and in various terms would be otiose and unnecessary.

Sigurd Burckhardt puts the matter in his article "The Poet as Fool and Priest" [8] in a most arresting way and in a manner close to my approach.

I propose that the nature and primary function of the most important poetic devices—especially rhyme, meter, and metaphor—is to release words in some measure from their bondage to meaning, their purely referential role, and to give or restore to them the corporeality which a true medium needs. . . . He [the poet] can . . . drive a wedge between words and their meanings, lessen as much as possible their designatory force and thereby inhibit our all too ready flight from them to the things they point to.

Burckhardt is interested in the phenomenon from a psychological point of view. He emphasizes the fight of the poet with his material, and his necessity of stripping it of its ordinary force as used in everyday life. The media of the painter and sculptor and composer do not need this stripping: words do. My interest is more linguistic than psychological. The stripping does not interest me as a manifestation of the poet's will but as a grammaticization of language. [9]

---

[7] Victor Erlich's translation of a sentence from "Co je poesie," *Volné směry,* XXX (1933–34) in his *Russian Formalism: History—Doctrine,* Slavistic Printings and Reprintings, IV (The Hague, 1955), p. 154.

[8] *ELH,* XXIII (1956), 279 ff. The quotation is from pp. 280–281.

[9] Murray Krieger makes a similar point, but I think explains it in the opposite (and I think, wrong) way when he writes: "It [Poetic language] is language in rebellion against the ways in which we normally use it as a counter for things; it is language that subverts its normal auxiliary function of denying its own terminal existence in order, instrumentally, to lead us to the world; language that proclaims itself as substance and its own world of multiplying meanings as sovereign." "The Poet and His Work—and the Role of Criticism," *CE,* XXV (1964), 408.

The important, though not the only feature of poetic language, is its terminal quality, its intransitivity, not its instrumentality. Cf. Roger Caillois, *Babel, orgueil, confusion et ruine de la littérature* (Paris, 1948), pp. 238 ff.

What I am arguing here is that language affords in its normal functioning a means of self-attention. The syntactic functon of morphemes, words, and phrases leads to an intransitivity which makes us aware of their own forms and leads us back to the sentence. Poetic effort, among other things, is directed to increasing the syncategorematic and decreasing the semantic element of language. The poet heightens the normal syntactic function of his words and phrases as much as he can by means of poetic devices.

Now, literature has other goals than foregrounding. It presents a point of view, it organizes experience, it attempts to catch attention, not to speak of social and other indirect aims. But great literature, especially poetry, has a linguistic message as well, and in the last analysis this is what gives it much of its greatness. This is why paraphrase even when necessary, destroys a poem or a finished work of art. It has always been recognized that a poem gives fresh meanings to words. "La poésie est ainsi re-sémantisation du discours." [10] That it also re-grammatizes discourse has not I think been widely recognized. Poetry is a kind of syntactization of referential words. They become more metonymic and less metaphorical. Poetry has a syntactic as well as a semantic density.

It should also be noted that certain genres like the novel are less concerned with foregrounding than others. What I have to say applies more forcefully to poetry than to prose. Yet poetic devices are by no means rare in novels or short stories, but they are not so persistent or frequent.

Let us look at some of the better known poetic devices with this function in mind. It is of course clear, I hope, that the confines of an article make any kind of complete analysis impossible. Nothing less than a handbook would fulfil the task of showing how poetic devices work in enforcing foregrounding and intransitivity. However, a few words may not be inappropriate and will perhaps make my point clearer.

(1) Under the broad head of repetition, we may group a number of well-known poetic devices: rime, sound-repetition, alliteration, assonance, meter and rhythm, parallelism, verbal or grammatical repetition, and so forth. All of these gain their primary force from

---

[10] Paul Zumthor, "Stylistique et poétique," in *Style et Littérature* (The Hague, 1962), p. 34.

their linguistic context and first of all operate intrasententially or intersententially. The semantic power must of course combine successfully with the linguistic repetition to be accounted aesthetically satisfying. None of these poetic devices can be mechanically applied. When yoked with semantic significance, they produce great literature.

Rime, sound-repetition, alliteration, and assonance are different types of segmental phonetic repetition that effects an immediate sound linkage and captures a kind of primitive attention. The linked sounds provide a "macro-context" [11] in which intra- and intersential patterns become perceptible. They force us to dissociate partially words from their normal meanings and perceive them as words.

Meter and rhythm are also phonetic types of repetition relying on segmented time and suprasegmental phonetic representation. They are more strongly intersentential, since in order to gain their effect they must persist over a minimum period of time.[12] They link together sentences and clauses and set up a foregrounding pattern for the whole poem—a kind of contextual adhesive. Rhythm and meter also operate powerfully on the physiological apparatus and have a deep biological effect. This effect is not my concern here, but it certainly links together the reader or listener and the poem. The rules of meter and rhythm must also be distinguished from the actual performance of the verse. They pertain to the deep rather than the surface grammar.

Parallelism affects more directly the verbal and syntactic level of communication. It operates both intra- and intersententially and is a more obvious type of repetition than the phonetic types.

Robert Frost's "Acquainted with the Night" could be analyzed at great length, but I shall examine it only for the purpose of looking at some different types of repetition.

[11] See Michael Riffaterre, "Stylistic Context," *Word*, XVI (1960), 213.

[12] There are some very short poems—of two or three lines—in which the rhythmical or metric effect, when it is relied on to any extent, is based on close juxtaposition. Occasionally we get a strong effect from the rhythm of a phrase or sentence; these cases are rather rare and the foregrounding is often subordinated, though not of course eliminated, to the referential power and wit of the words—or sometimes to repetitive devices other than rhythm and meter. Poems generally, however, are at least four and usually more lines long.

I have been one acquainted with the night.	1
I have walked out in rain—and back in rain.	2
I have outwalked the furthest city light.	3
I have looked down the saddest city lane.	4
I have passed by the watchman on his beat	5
And dropped my eyes, unwilling to explain.	6
I have stood still and stopped the sound of feet	7
When far away an interrupted cry	8
Came over houses from another street,	9
But not to call me back or say good-bye;	10
And further still at an unearthly height,	11
One luminary clock against the sky	12
Proclaimed the time was neither wrong nor right.	13
I have been one acquainted with the night.	14

"Light" rimes with "night" and "lane" with "explain." The second word in each of these pairs is linked to the first. The odd last word in the second line of each triplet becomes the major rime of the next triplet, for "rain" (line 2) rimes with "lane" and "explain." Besides the referential value of "night," we have a syncategorematic value which forces us to link it with "light" making us aware of both words as words and setting up an opposition (which is picked up again in reconciliation in the second to last line "Proclaimed the time was neither wrong nor right," reinforced by the rime "right" which drives us back to "light" and "night"). Rimes as always exhibit assonance, and the [ai] diphthong sounds through the poem. There is another riming word "height" in line 11 and [ai] occurs in "eyes" (line 6), "cry" (line 8), "good-bye" (line 10), "time" (line 13). Other sounds like [ei] also reverberate through the poem.

Throughout the poem the five beat rhythm both in deep structure and performance runs steadily except for line 11 where only 4 beats can appear in performance—"And further still at an unearthly height." The stress there on "still" emphasizes its ambiguity—a semantic feature which causes us to waver syntactically.[13]

Except for the final couplet, the poem is written in *terza rima*

---

[13] A type of syntactic ambiguity. See below, p. 273. (The poem itself is from *Complete Poems of Robert Frost*, copyright 1928 by Holt, Rinehart and Winston, Inc., © copyright 1956 by Robert Frost; reprinted by permission of Holt, Rinehart and Winston, Inc.)

with the unrimed final word of the middle line of each triplet picked up as the rime of the next. The odd rime of the fourth trip-let becomes the rime of the final couplet which is also the rime of the first couplet.

Alliteration also effects linkage within lines as in "I have stood still and stopped the sound of feet" (line 7). Less noticeable we have two "l's" in line 4, which also echoes the *l* of "light" in the preceding line. Alliteration links "cry," "came," "call" running over lines 8, 9, and 10. Line 10 offers us *but*, *back*, and *bye*. These are the main alliterative linkages.

This sonnet also offers a number of significant parallelisms on the verbal and grammatical level. Words like 'I," "night," "rain," "still," "acquainted" occur more than once, and we also have a fas-cinating inversion "walked out" (line 2) and "outwalked" (line 3), all emphasizing the profound despair of the repetition of nature and life—the lack of interest which a perpetual cycle creates. This is all heightened by the repetition of the first line in the last line, giving the effect of a circle which never gets anywhere. The first four lines are each complete sentences.

Note the repetition of the perfect tense "I have been, walked, outwalked, looked down, passed by, dropped (with a variation by which 'have' is only understood), stood, stopped ('have' under-stood), and finally 'been' again." The perfect with its sense of com-pleted action comes again and again. There are only two other finite verbs, both in the preterite, emphasizing the pastness of the past as seen in the coming of the "cry" (line 9) and the proclaiming of the "clock" (line 12).

(2) Under the broad head of deviation, we find ungrammatical-ity of various types—violations of the syntactic or lexical rules of English.[14] Lexical deviation belongs properly to semantic behavior and is a normal process of the use of words. Grammatical deviation of various sorts shocks us into intransitivity and is hence of our im-mediate concern. That poets deliberately violate the rules of gram-mar is a commonplace. These violations force us into an awareness of syntactic context and of the word or words themselves and are part of the general metonymic process. This aspect has not I think

---

[14] See Samuel R. Levin, "Deviation—Statistical and Determinate—in Poetic Lan-guage," *Lingua*, XII (1963), 276–290.

been noted before. When Dylan Thomas writes "a grief ago," "all the sun long" or "robed in the long friends," "His golden yesterday asleep upon the iris" or E. E. Cummings, "Blow soon to never and never to twice / (blow life to isn't: blow death to was)," the syntactic deviations are arresting. More common in the poetic tradition is variation from normal word order and original conversions of words into new parts of speech. All syntactic deviations are attention-getting and serve the function of making us more aware of the metonymy of words and phrases. They all help to dissociate words from their meanings and make us aware of words as words.

Deviations of style, tone, metrical pattern, even genre are also common. Sudden shifts in person, point of view, direct and indirect narration: all these are types of deviation which effect foregrounding.[15] One can at present do little more than point them out.

(3) The third heading is ambiguity, especially syntactic ambiguity. It is not a common occurrence, but it occurs frequently enough to be thought of as a poetic device. Here a close reading of the context is necessary to resolve the ambiguity if indeed it is resolvable. Even if it is resolvable, it also always suggests its other possibility. We have already referred to one of these ambiguities above in the word "still" in Frost's poem where the ambiguity of adjective and conjunction/adverb remains unresolved, in suspension, until "proclaimed" in line 13 favors the second alternative. With a similar suspended ambiguity Archibald Macleish writes "To feel the always coming on / The always rising of the night" where "always" suggests a noun until "of" converts it into an adjective.

We find another type of syntactic ambiguity in English when an inverted or possible inverted word order creates suspension as to what immediate constituent a word belongs. In "And brass eternal slave to mortal rage" (Shakespeare, Sonnet 64), "eternal" hovers between "brass" and "slave." Or in "and beauty making beautiful old rhyme" (Sonnet 106) where "beautiful" may be an attributive adjective (with "old rhyme") or a predicative adjective (after "making").

All these syntactic ambiguities serve to push us to scrutinize the

---

[15] Even the shift from count to mass noun effects such a shock. See for example Shakespeare's "the twilight of such day / as after sunset fadeth in the west" (Sonnet 73) where "day" becomes a mass noun for the nonce.

context, hesitate over it, and become aware of the syntactic possibilities. They partially separate their lines or sentences from their meaning and create an intransitivity which bars the easy leap to referential meaning.

The richness of poetry is syntactic and metonymic as well as semantic and metaphoric; and one ignores the former at the cost of the understanding which can open new vistas upon language and life. Poetry and verbal art must rest upon the manipulation of the powers of language. We not only perceive new meanings in the extralinguistic world in great poetry, but we see new possibilities in the world of language itself.

V. Essay-Reviews

15. *Kenneth Sisam*, The Structure of Beowulf *(New York and Oxford, 1965)*

The Structure of Beowulf is a short and direct answer to the newer schools of *Beowulf* scholarship and criticism. It starts from the premise that "*Beowulf* is an heroic narrative poem, composed to entertain an audience of Anglo-Saxons" (p. 1), "a tale of marvels set in the Heroic Age" (p. 58), and that "great difficulties stand in the way of all explanations that make the poet a deep thinker, attempting themes and ways of conveying them that might be tried on a select body of readers in a more advanced age" (p. 77). It is fundamentally a brief and often acute defence of the older traditional approach—with the assumption of an essentially semi-Christianized "upper-class" audience ("the listeners would be the kind of people who appear in Heorot" [p. 9]), which was primarily interested in a good story well told and not likely to be bothered by the symbolic, mythical, theological, or even artistic subtleties which modern critics have found in *Beowulf*.

Having made this assumption and others on the genesis of the poem, its nature, and the quality of old Germanic life and indeed on the proper method of literary study, the author tries to refute some of the recent arguments of *Beowulf* scholars and critics, occasionally putting some of them in historical perspective. Sisam does

Reprinted by permission of the Medieval Academy of America from *Speculum*, XLI (1966), 368–371.

sometimes venture into aesthetic matters, almost always happily, as in his suggestion that the poet is trying to present simultaneous actions in the return from the mere (lines 837–927) section (pp. 29 ff.). His criticisms of the Klaeber theory that Beowulf is a king who dies for his people (pp. 11–12), of reading into the text more than is there (as in the supposed villainy of Hrothulf and in the supposed destruction of the Geats by the Swedes) and of traditional assumptions (as that Heoroward was slighted when Heorogar left his battle gear to Hrothgar) are most welcome. Although one feels that ingenuity is at times pushed too far (for example, when Unferth is whitewashed), Professor Sisam's criticisms are almost always worth reading. At the very least, *Structure* will serve as a corrective, especially when Sisam analyzes the text, to some of the wilder flights of critical and scholarly fancy.

Yet the author makes a number of historical and critical assumptions which are at least open to doubt. These former should occupy our chief attention so that Professor Sisam can be met on his own ground. Besides, I am with him in his attack on the position that we should be concerned only with what the poem means to us today and not be bothered with history, a position which would completely by-pass Sisam's criticisms and indeed much modern scholarship. This is the classic dilemma posed in our time by "New Criticism"—what has the genesis of a poem got to do with its significance to us? This assumption lies behind some of the modern comments on *Beowulf* which Sisam and others oppose. It involves problems of too great a magnitude to discuss here, but briefly it might be said that history is part of the meaning of a literary work as it is part of the reader's own meaning to himself and to others. The question should not be posed as history (traditional scholarship) *or* meaning (modern criticism), but rather history *and* meaning. Like Professor Sisam, I wish to save history; we cannot approach literature innocent and naked. We must know what a poem meant before we can fully know what it means.

I do meet Sisam, however, on the ground of history and do oppose his view of the historical circumstances of the poem. He assumes, for instance, an assumption shared by almost all commentators on the poem and indeed students of the early Middle Ages, that early Christianity was exclusively a religion of love. By using certain selective comments of Jesus and by ignoring others not to our modern taste, we are led to an individualistic and sentimental view of Christianity. This view makes one believe that the desire for vengeance is unchristian (pp. 78 and 79).[1] One has only to read carefully Ambrose, Augustine, Gregory, and Jerome, not to speak of others in the West less distinguished, to be disabused of this notion. It is true that to love one's enemies was the highest of virtues, but this was a counsel of perfection and did not preclude at any time punishment for crimes or sins, or righteous anger. These Fathers recognize that without justice and its concomitant of punishment, no society would be possible. In a Germanic society, justice was in general carried out by personal efforts. This did not of course mean approval of endless blood feuds.

Further, Sisam favors an oral theory of composition but seems a little confused as to what it implies. He thinks of the scop as memorizing his poem (for example, p. 3, note 4) and does not refer to the formulaic method of composition. He also clearly separates the fictional from the historical element in the poem (pp. 51 ff.) but confuses the objective truth with what the poet himself thought was true. Although Beowulf himself and his exploits are clearly fictional, it is by no means clear that the poet thought so.

Moreover, the purpose of the poem is not merely entertainment but also heroic celebration. The general rhetorical stance of *Beowulf* is not due to the personal desire of its author to tell an interesting and entertaining story—at least not only that—but rather to the social desire to recall and memorialize a hero. And in this he was carrying out one of the traditional roles of the court poet (or if a monk, of a monkish chronicler). Entertainment yes, but not as the main end or goal. It was not that the *Beowulf*-poet had a personal view to give to the world by means of objective correlatives as a romantic poet might have, but rather he wished to present the *res gestas* of a hero so that he may be remembered, to give his audience new strength and a model. His artistry was primarily used to attain that goal. The hero and his companions could be schemers (although Beowulf personally was not) and still be worthy of imita-

---

[1] See Dorothy Whitelock, *The Beginnings of English Society*, Pelican History of England 2, A245 (Harmondsworth, 1952), pp. 37, 42–45, and *The Audience of Beowulf* (Oxford, 1951), pp. 13 ff.

tion ("How did this set of schemers [Hrothulf, Unferth, Wealh-
theow, etc.] get the reputation of heroes?" [p. 43]). Besides the
trickster hero of folklore, we may recall Jacob and Odysseus as well,
who were no less heroes for all their wiliness.[2]

In other words, I do not agree with some of Sisam's views about
the historical setting of the poem and the attitudes of the poet and
original audience. But even assuming his theories to be correct, is it
not reasonable to look for some general principles and attitudes behind the poem in their light? True, such speculation is dangerous,
but surely good sense will reassert itself and no permanent harm is
done if some explanations are improbable or far-fetched. In the last
analysis, *Beowulf* must have some general meaning and significance
to us if it is to be continued to be read as literature. I am no lover
of ingenious and subtle symbolic and mythic readings of poetry, but
I would not deny their right to be expressed because they may be
wide of the mark or purely subjective. Historical research also may
be and has on occasion been wide of the mark. Professor Sisam himself admits the right of conjecture (pp. 60 and 71), but in practice
he will in effect allow little of it or of critical structural analysis. At
one point (p. 36) he denies the presence of any dramatic irony at
all in Anglo-Saxon heroic poetry. The literal admittedly has a kind
of built-in priority in literary criticism, but one does not have to be
confined exclusively to it.

Let us see how literary criticism can help one of Professor Sisam's
own arguments. If he were not so sensitive himself to literary values
one would perhaps not wish to make this suggestion. In spite of his
bluff no-nonsense approach to *Beowulf*, Sisam is not only a great
scholar but also a most perceptive and intelligent man. In discussing
the section devoted to Beowulf's return (lines 1888–2199), he is
concerned with the fact that "this part of the poem has had few
admirers" (p. 44). Along with the other parts of this section, the
author defends Beowulf's famous and frequently criticized recapitulation (lines 2000–2162). His defense centers on its verisimilitude
to Germanic life and on what is expected of a Germanic hero. He
also tries to account for the variations from the earlier narrative—
by the use of the verisimilitude principle, the poet's tendency to ex-

---

[2] One further disputable point. Going to hell is not incompatible with facing the
Last Judgment (p. 75).

aggerate in order to make a strong impression, and the normal expectation in a long poem of some inconsistenecy. Yet if we use the critical principle of the "point of view," Beowulf's recapitulation makes sense and has a satisfying aesthetic force.

Up to this point in the epic, we have never heard Beowulf speak from his own heart, nor have we really had his point of view on the first two adventures. In this long speech, for the first time, we see how the Danish expedition looked to the chief participant in it. We get Beowulf's opinion of and report on the fights and his own reactions to them. This was the only way to present the psychology of the chief character in an age not used to psychological probing. We are given a fitting close to these adventures by at last seeing them from the protagonist's point of view.

Just as literary criticism, although in a somewhat different fashion, enables us to understand Friar Lawrence's long recapitulation in *Romeo and Juliet* (V, iii, 229–277), so it helps us to see the rationale of Beowulf's long apparently repetitive speech. It is, of course, true that not every element in a literary work was necessarily consciously put there by its creator; no doubt a poor memory or unthoughtful composition can lead to consciously unmotivated parts or episodes. Yet it is a dangerous principle to adopt in literary investigation that nothing we do not readily understand can be rationally explained. We must as a working principle assume that everything in a work of art is capable of explanation even at the cost of oversubtlety and even error. Besides, today we know that not only conscious but also unconscious motives shape our conduct. We must not assume, unless we are finally forced to it, that the writer or composer did not know what he was doing.

Whatever Professor Sisam writes is worth paying heed to, and it is no less true of this little book as of his other work. Yet one could wish that his impatience with the exaggerated use of certain methods had not led him to be so sternly exclusive.

16. Nevill Coghill, The Pardon of Piers Plowman (Proceedings of the British Academy, 1945)

The *Pardon of Piers Plowman* is the latest contribution to the small but significant number of articles and books which have appeared in the wake of Professor Henry W. Wells's articles of the twenties [1] and which attempt to interpret the meaning of *Piers Plowman*. At present the authorship dispute, which was the main concern of scholarship—American, British, and Continental—for some twenty-five years after Manly's shattering work in the early part of the century, is no longer considered a burning question. Most, if not all, scholars concerned with the poem (or poems) have tacitly agreed to let the matter rest and to assume, even without proof positive, that it is the work of one man, until further evidence turns up. The unity of authorship has not been proved (if the burden of proof lies there), but it is the most reasonable assumption and offers the least stubble for the blade of Ockham's razor. Even the last heretic to this view, Father Dunning, has recently recanted.[2]

In increasing volume, attention is being bestowed on the poem as

Reprinted by permission of the Mediaeval Academy of America from *Speculum*, XXII (1947), 461–465.
[1] "The Organizing Ideas in Piers the Plowman," *PMLA*. XXXVII (1922), and "The Construction of *Piers Plowman*," PMLA, XLIV (1929), 123 ff.
[2] "Langland and the Salvation of the Heathen," *Med. AE*., XII (1943), 45–54.

a poem and as a product of medieval civilization. The contemporary mood in scholarship is more attuned to this approach; and the modern world-view makes possible, I think, a fuller appreciation of Langland's aims and methods than was possible a generation ago. Just as one cannot help being impressed by the analogy between certain pieces of modern music and medieval music, so one cannot help seeing similarities between certain modern literary works and the kind of medievalism represented by *Piers Plowman*.[3]

Mr. Coghill, in the Sir Israel Gollancz Memorial Lecture for 1945, brings to this work of interpretation a concern with the problems of the poem extending over at least fifteen years. In this recent work, he takes as his starting and unifying point one of the most disputed scenes in the poem, the tearing of the pardon which Piers receives in Passus VIII of the A-text, a passage upon which much exegesis and effort have already been expended. He sees in this incident the key to the interpretation of the poem.

His general argument may be summed up as follows. Langland, stimulated by such contemporary social satires on the state of England as *Wynnere and Wastoure*, attempted, in the thirteen sixties, a similar, though richer ("enriched by a moral meaning") work in the A-text of *Piers Plowman*, an "anatomy of England," with "a longish moral *significacio*" (Passus IX–XI) at the end. As a result of the Pardon Scene, Langland becomes aware of more elaborate and complex problems involved in his subject than he had previously imagined; and, after a somewhat stumbling attempt to solve them and at the same time to keep to his main theme, he gives up the attempt somewhere in Passus XII. John But who "medleth of makyng" later adds some lines to this unfinished poem.

Some ten or fifteen years later, Langland returns to his task, revises and lengthens the A-text as far as it goes, and completes his earlier work by the addition of a number of passus to bring the poem to its present end. While engaged on the new part of the poem, he finally arrives at the solution of his problem by using the figure of Piers, whose earlier treatment had already foreshadowed this development, as a mystical unifying symbol to answer the ques-

---

[3] On this point, see H. W. Wells, *New Poets from Old: A Study in Literary Genetics* (1940), pp. 13, 19, 44, 48–49, 66–68, 117, 196, 201, 253, 323 *et passim*.

tions raised by the Pardon Scene. Mr. Coghill emphasizes the fact that B is a different *kind* of poem from A, different because of its intention and treatment. This difference, he urges, is due to the full employment in B of the four senses of allegorical meaning—the literal, allegorical, tropological (or moral), and anagogical (or mystical). He suggests that *Wynnere and Wastoure* is written on two levels, the A-text on three, and the B-text on all four. It was only thus, Mr. Coghill believes, that B could satisfactorily complete A.

Although his lecture is full of splendid insights which make a genuine contribution to our understanding of the poem, Mr. Coghill's central thesis, as outlined above, cannot, I think, bear close inspection.

My objections to his hypothesis may be summed up as follows:

1. Mr. Coghill in his argument assumes that allegory and symbolism, really quite different processes, are the same. In spite of various warnings,[4] this is a confusion which is serious and yet very common in medieval studies. The method (allegory or, better, personification) used in the *Romance of the Rose* is not the method (symbolism) used in the *Divine Comedy*. In some ways, they are the exact opposite of each other. Symbolism starts from a literal story, historical or created, and interprets it in various senses (often, in medieval times, four). It is a movement from the concrete to the abstract. Allegory, on the other hand, is really personification. It is a movement from the abstract to the concrete. Certain abstract concepts are made concrete by being personified. Langland employs both methods, but he follows that of the *Romance of the Rose* much more frequently than that of Dante. It is irrelevant to quote, as Mr. Coghill does, Dante's comments on the fourfold method in the *Convivio*. Langland is using, for the most part, allegory, not symbolism. We can find a fourfold meaning (often called, in order to add to the confusion on the subject, the *allegorical* interpretation) in parts of *Piers*, and this contributes to our understanding of the poem. But most of the poem is an allegory, and it is highly doubtful whether quadruplicate meanings can be applied to person-

---

[4] See, e.g., John Ruskin, *Stones of Venice*, II, 55 (*The Chesterfield Society Edition*, VIII, 322–323); W. P. Ker, *English Literature Medieval* (1912), pp. 184 ff.; C. R. Post, *Mediaeval Spanish Allegory* (1915), pp. 3–4; C. S. Lewis, *The Allegory of Love* (1936), pp. 44 ff.; and Edwin B. Place, "The Exaggerated Reputation of Francisco Imperial," *Speculum*, XXI (1946), 462–463.

ification. What are, for instance, the four meanings of Dame Study, Imaginatif, or the Sin of Sloth?

2. Even if Langland were using the fourfold interpretation throughout the B-text (and this is highly doubtful), it is unlikely that he would not also use it in the A-text. A mystical meaning can be found in parts of the latter. In the later Middle Ages (even in St. Thomas), this method of interpretation, it should be noted, was rapidly losing favor, as compared say, to its popularity with the Victorines.

3. In Mr. Coghill's theory, a large part of the A-text (Passus IX–XI) is a mere fumbling around with problems which arise out of the Pardon Scene. One cannot deny that Langland is greatly concerned with intellectual questions in this part of the poem (the *Vita*), but it seems reasonable to assume, with Professor Chambers, that this section was part of Langland's plan, not something extraneous or a mere *Significatio*, and that the problems here arise from his not having thought through such questions as the salvation of the righteous heathen. Mr. Coghill, on the basis of his theory, cannot account for the obvious break and new beginning of Passus VIII. Why start a *Vita* at all? Or if Langland couldn't solve the Pardon problem, why not eliminate the scene which includes it? It seems to me we must assume that the tearing of the Pardon and at least the general outline of the poem must have been in Langland's mind as he wrote. He was not a slipshod artist who had no sense of form.

4. It might be argued *contra* that B is more topical than A. It certainly includes more political and social allusions.

5. Mr. Coghill's thesis is weakened by two assumptions: (a) that Langland was not a learned man and (b) that esthetic considerations were not in Langland's mind when he wrote his poem. (a) has been widely assumed in Langland scholarship. I believe, on the contrary, that in Langland we have one of the most learned of English poets. As far as (b) is concerned, Mr. Coghill pays tribute to Langland's great poetic gifts and, at the same time, refuses to bring in artistic considerations when interpreting the order and meaning of the poem. "Foretastes" such as Mr. Coghill finds in the poem are characteristic of all great art—foreshadowings of later themes.

On a number of minor points, I raise certain questions. Mr. Coghill assumes that Langland never heard of the *Romance of the Rose*

(p. 7). It is difficult to believe that an educated man reared in England in the last half of the fourteenth century would not have known this famous allegory, which is preserved in so many manuscripts in England and was translated by several hands. To explain the leaps in Langland's thought and poetry, Mr. Coghill suggests the influence of the *Psalter* (p. 21). Need we make a similar assumption to explain the jerkiness of the poetry of Mr. T. S. Eliot or John Donne? There is no doubt, of course, that Langland knew his *Psalter*, but if we need to assume that one of the essential traits of his style and point of view was due to his reading of that book, it seems to me that we become involved in a series of rather strange hypotheses about poetic creation and miss one of the basic elements of Langland's genius.

Again, in discussing the three types of life—active, contemplative, and mixed—Mr. Coghill quotes St. Thomas (p. 22) and following Mr. Wells, suggests him as the source. It is unnecessary to assume a Thomistic origin for a widespread medieval belief. There are no particular verbal or unique conceptual echoes to lead us to posit borrowing from the Angelic Doctor. Our author seems surprised (p. 27) that David was considered saved by Langland whereas Solomon was not. Mr. Coghill seems to forget the purpose of the Harrowing of Hell, which saved most Old Testament figures. Solomon was one figure in dispute, but as for David, Adam, Moses, Isaiah, etc., there was no problem. Solomon was perhaps not saved, not because he lived before the New Covenant, but because of his evil deeds.

Mr. Coghill also assumes that Langland brought the A-text to an end (Passus xii) "by the simple literary device of killing off the author" (p. 29). He excludes the possibility that these lines are by John But and refer to Langland's actual death. Another surprising assumption is Mr. Coghill's apparent belief that the habit of thinking in trinities (threes) is quite unusual in medieval thought (pp. 55–56).

On the other hand, I am much impressed with his analysis of the character of the changes in the B-text over the A-text; with his interpretation of the Pardon Scene itself (especially with the point that Piers rejected the pardon because it was based only on justice and not on mercy, for I think Langland's main message was mercy

287

and love); with his emphasizing certain eschatological elements in the poem (for I believe the apocalyptic nature of *Piers Plowman* has been largely ignored); and above all with his fine esthetic perceptions (although he disclaims any such intention on the part of Langland), especially in pointing out how Langland takes themes up briefly only to develop them more fully later—"foretastes" as Mr. Coghill calls them—and in comparing the fourfold method to a fugue. All students of the poem will want to read this work and will be grateful to the author for help in elucidating a great poem, which, like all great literature, is difficult.

It seems to me, however, that we must continue to assume that A and B are the same kind of poem, however much they may vary in emphasis and treatment. We must still continue to believe that the *Visio* is essentially a treatment of this world (especially England) in terms of ordinary Christian living and that the *Vita* is essentially a treatment of this world in terms of the Christian mystery. When the dreamer asks in Passus I how he may be saved, he is first given a picture of life in the ordinary work-a-day world (the *Visio*) and then he is led into a timeless world of Christian truth, as Langland interprets that truth (the *Vita*). Langland ran into difficulties in his first try at the second part and couldn't complete his scheme, but he came back to it later in B and successfully (as far as these mysteries can be successfully interpreted in the terms of human speech) carried it out.

17. D. W. Robertson and Bernard F. Huppé, Piers Plowman and Scriptural Tradition (Princeton, 1951)

In this handsomely printed book Professors Robertson and Huppé have attempted to fill a serious gap in *Piers Plowman* scholarship— a study of the numerous Biblical quotations and allusions of the poem in terms of the medieval scriptural tradition. In spite of its many virtues, however, the present work is not an entirely satisfactory contribution to this aim, notwithstanding the authors' modest statement, "Our study is not exhaustive. It is merely a beginning which indicates a direction for fruitful study of the poem" (p. 16).

Except for the introductory and concluding chapters, the authors take us through *Piers Plowman seriatim*, elucidating its *sentence* presumably insofar as medieval Biblical exegesis, and to some extent, medieval theology and philosophy, enable us to do so. My criticisms of their effort may be subsumed under two headings: fact and approach.

As to fact: The writers misunderstand certain basic medieval philosophical concepts. They continually confuse epistemological and metaphysical categories with psychological and ethical categories. They also seem to misapprehend the difference between a cat-

Reprinted with permission of the Mediaeval Academy of America from *Speculum*, XXVII (1952), 245–249.

egory per se and a category in terms of its end. In the following quotations, for example, they do not understand the nature of the active intellect, the function of which is to abstract from the ordered sense impressions (phantasms) the universals which the possible intellect alone can apprehend. Here, too, they also assume that the practical intellect can or cannot be heeded at will, when it is surely a matter of to what end the practical intellect is directed.

p. 108 n. 13, "The *intellectus agens* has as its purpose the guidance of the Will."

p. 109, ". . . the evil of those who disregard the practical intellect . . . Those who are ruled by the practical intellect . . . ."

p. 111, ". . . those who are not ruled by practical intellect . . ."

p. 119, "To do well is to act in accordance with the true nature of man, formed in the image of the Trinity, to be governed, that is, by the active intellect, not by the whims of the will."

p. 132, "Since the *intellectus agens* is the faculty which makes judgments of this kind so that the will may act reasonably, it is clear that the stage of the poem has been reached in which this intellect is operative."

p. 147, ". . . the *intellectus agens,* which enables him to feel shame and to distinguish between evil and good."

p. 120, ". . . before he [Will] has learned through the practical intellect the discipline of faith . . ."

The authors equate *Kinde Witte* with both *scientia* and the speculative intellect (p. 152), which are by no means synonymous. They properly say that the speculative intelligence is concerned with things in themselves, not with the object of action (p. 152) and then say that *Kinde Witte* showed Piers the way (p. 76) and that Will "cannot properly act upon the possibilities of both good and evil presented by Wit, the speculative intellect" (p. 243). Here is evidence of a most serious confusion between the concepts of the practical and speculative intelligences.

Again, no medieval theologian would ever fall into the error of the following: "Since to know Dowel 'kyndely' the whole man is required, Will meets Anima, a combination of mind, memory, reason, the senses, love, and the spirit, all various aspects of the soul" (p. 177). There can be no "whole" man without the body (or matter). Besides, every man cannot but have these qualities, for, to the medieval philosopher they are constitutive parts of the soul and are not psychical attributes which may be attained or developed by moral and intellectual effort, as a modern might say of at least some of them. The same error of attributing modern thought patterns to medieval man is to be found in a note on page 147 where the authors imply that the *virtus phantastica* in a quotation from Godefroid de Fontaines is the equivalent of the modern imagination.

Although *ratio* and *intellectus* are occasionally used in medieval philosophy interchangeably as the authors do (for example, on pp. 110 and 119), usually and for good reason medieval philosophers made a clear distinction between the two. On the one occasion Robertson and Huppé equate reason with the practical intellect and on the other with the active intellect.

In all these cases, we find some very serious misunderstandings of medieval philosophical terms. As we know, medieval philosophy embraces a wide variety of attitudes and theories, but common to almost all of them after the development of scholasticism in the twelfth and thirteenth centuries is a generally understood philosophical vocabulary. If Robertson and Huppé believe that Langland is using his terms peculiarly or is following some not well-known medieval thinker who employs the common terms of medieval philosophy such as the active intellect, the possible intellect, the phantastic power, reason, *scientia*, and so forth in a special sense, they should at least explain these divergences from ordinary philosophical usage.

On a theological level, we also find statements like the following which are very strange:

p. 13, "Obversely, cupidity is the end of human failing, descending from the love of the world and a love of the flesh to a union with the Devil in his struggle against charity, that is the sin against the Holy Spirit." (An unusual definition of the Sin against the Holy Ghost.)

p. 101, "At the close of Passus vii, in spite of the dramatic clarity of what he has seen, Will has not achieved a state of grace; far from it, he does not understand the basic doctrine of grace . . ." (Do we know when we have attained a state of grace? Do we have to understand the doctrine of grace in order to obtain grace?)

291

p. 120, "Only through grace, through the true marriage of the soul with the Church, can man achieve salvation and avoid eternal punishment." (This violates the concept of the Mystical Body. All Christians, even sinners, are members of the Church. This doctrine is close to the Cathar and gnostic heresy of the *perfecti*. The image of the marriage of the soul to the Church is a most unusual one [cf. p. 121, "the well-wed intellect is necessary to his (Will's) recovery of grace"]).

On pages 191 ff. the authors confuse the concept of the trees of virtues and vices (which, incidentally, are the only reproductions in the book and are taken from the pseudo-Hugh of St. Victor's *De Fructibus Carnis et Spiritus*) with the *Lignum Vitae* and the tree of charity, the genera to which the tree in Passus XVI certainly belongs.

On Page 241, the authors assume that Holy Church of Passus I is the church militant. In view of all that Langland has said about the church militant, as the authors themselves have pointed out, it is highly unlikely that Will would be instructed toward truth by the church militant. It is obviously the true and triumphant church which is there personified.

Some of these quotations have been taken out of context, but I don't believe I have done so unfairly. It is impossible to quote in a review the complete passages involved. In every one I have cited is revealed a basic confusion of a most serious nature—either a misunderstanding of medieval philosophical terms, a reading into medieval philosophy of modern psychologism and Kantianism, or a misapprehension, or unusual interpretation, of a theological doctrine.

Now as to approach: Assuming that part of *Piers* can be explained by the scriptural tradition of the Middle Ages, is it permissible to ignore almost all the commentaries of the twelfth, thirteenth, and fourteenth centuries and to rely almost exclusively on the commentaries of St. Augustine, Bede, the *Glossa Ordinaria*, St. Bruno Astensis, and Peter Lombard? Some most important changes in exegetical approach occurred during the twelfth century, as Miss Smalley has pointed out, and yet the authors rely for the most part on Biblical commentaries which do not adequately reflect the variety of Biblical interpretations available to a writer such as Langland.

The reason for this preference is due to another serious misunderstanding—an attempt to read the so-called four symbolic levels into *Piers Plowman. Piers* is essentially an allegorical, not a symbolic, work. It is closer in method to the *Romance of the Rose* than to the *Divine Comedy.* In actual practice, the authors do not succeed very often in finding a fourfold meaning although in the introductory chapter they imply that it is present everywhere. I do not think that we can deny at times a four- (or three- or two-) level meaning in *Piers,* but it does not occur very frequently. After the Victorines, the multileveled symbolic interpretation became much less popular than in the earlier Middle Ages, and in general by the fourteenth century its influence was weak. Yet, in order to find four-leveled Biblical commentaries the authors must go back 800 to 400 years before Langland's time. Of course, it must be admitted that later commentaries are not easily available, although Nicholas of Lyra's work does not fall into that category. Yet, as far as I know, there is not one allusion in this book to this influential commentator who would a priori be more likely to have influenced Langland in his Bible interpretation than St. Bruno or Bede.

As far as theologians are concerned, the authors limit themselves primarily to St. Augustine, Peter Lombard, and most curiously to Godefroid de Fontaines, a relatively minor scholastic. Here, too, the authors have been misled by another misunderstanding. They point out, quite rightly, that one of the chief targets of the poem is the friars. But, acting on this, they immediately assume (1) that all criticism of the mendicants came from the seculars and (2) that such an attitude made Langland hesitant to use the philosophy and theology of the great friars of the thirteenth and fourteenth centuries. As far as (1) is concerned, the most violent criticism of the friars came from the friars themselves, especially in the Franciscan Order from those called the Spirituals and the Fraticelli. As for (2), it is highly doubtful if Langland's criticism of the friars would extend to such figures as Aquinas, Bonaventure, and Scotus, all of whom by his time were recognized as great thinkers. In fact, I think that much in *Piers* can be explained by the Franciscan tradition. In mentioning those who have been omitted, the authors refer to Occam (p. 10). But he himself in his later years became a bitter enemy of the friars and joined actively with Michael of Cesena in a struggle against the pope and the corruption of mendicant ideals.

293

Although the whole antimendicant tradition goes back to, and draws on the works of, William of St. Amour, the authors rely far too much on his texts [1] to explain the attacks on the friars in the poem. More to the point would be the assaults on the friars found in fourteenth-century England, especially in the works and sermons of Fitzralph, Uhtred de Boldon, and others.

The authors also do not always make clear their interpretations of several crucial and difficult parts of the poem, such as the tearing of the Pardon, the meaning of the figure of Piers, and the clothes of Hawkin (where the commentaries on *Joshua*, ix, 5, should have been looked at).

Yet the virtues of the book are by no means minor. As a commentary on the poem, the work is often enlightening, especially for the final passus beginning with the Dobet section (of the B-text, which the authors use throughout). Fortunately the authors do often give us an *explication de texte* and a structural analysis which enable us to see the meaning of some dark passages and sections. As an excellent example of their elucidation, we may cite the extensive parallelisms made between the last two passus of the poem (xix–xx) and the first part (the *Visio* and in particular the Prologue). They emphasize points such as the significance of the symbols of clothing and food throughout the poem, contributing thereby to our sense of the author's purpose. They see the character Will as an allegory of the will, a welcome revival of an old theory. Although they overestimate its structural unity (the poem "is no less perfect structurally than" the *Divine Comedy*, p. 247), the authors have certainly made us more aware of the guiding artistic plan of *Piers*.

Most of these achievements are not, however, dependent on a knowledge of what the Biblical commentators have said about the Biblical quotations and the imagery in the poem. But the medieval exegetes used by the authors do occasionally help us to apprehend directly the point of an allusion and, even more important, give us a

---

[1] In quoting William of St. Amour, the authors mainly use the summary of his work printed in Perrod and others. No library in America has, I believe, a copy of the hard-to-find seventeenth-century edition of his works, but it would be possible to get a copy on microfilm. *De Periculis* and some other of his writings are also available in Edward Brown's edition of Gratius, *Fasciculus Rerum Expetendarum* (London, 1690).

sense of the religious and theological milieu in which these allusions and quotations become comprehensible.

This book, then, must be used with caution, for while it reveals on the one hand a real sensitivity toward the poetic values of *Piers*, it also reveals on the other an incomplete knowledge of certain facets of medieval thought and feeling. As the authors themselves have so well put it (p. 234) "to understand *Piers Plowman* we must be prepared not only to see it in terms of the bitter controversy between the friars and the seculars or in the light of the tradition of Biblical commentary; we must understand its full human import, the permanent symbolic value of the search for Piers Plowman."

This is a sensitive and wise comment, but the ostensible purpose of the book rests upon certain misunderstandings of the nature of the poem the authors are studying and upon certain errors of fact and approach.

18. *Sanford B. Meech*, Design in Chaucer's "Troilus" *(Syracuse, 1959)*

This book is a learned, well-organized and extremely detailed comparison of *Troilus and Criseyde* with its source. It is divided into four long chapters, the first of which is devoted to a close comparison of the sequence of the narrative in *Troilus* and the *Filostrato*; the second to the modifications of the source in matters such as age, person, dress, love, time, place, and other such general categories; the third to the modifications of the imagery of the original; and the fourth to changes in the characters including that of the narrator.

Although there are some welcome generalizing passages (as on pages 99 ff., 181 ff., 319, 397 and 404 and in the introduction and conclusion), Professor Meech employs for the most part a method of extremely close comparison of hundreds of details and many categories. However his scholastic sense of systematic argument always keeps us informed of the structure of his book.

The study is, in spite of its clear organization, hard to read because of the piling up of detail, a difficulty compounded by a style which is often awkward or turgid and a predilection for unusual phraseology and vocabulary (for example, minify, toll [in the sense of deceive], gestalt, conceiting, thereof, congeed, Trojaninity, ideality, videlicet, aporia, sans, and so forth). The book is also not writ-

Reprinted with permission from *MLN*, LXXV (1959–60), 431–434.

ten for a reader ignorant of Italian, for only a few of the numerous quotations from that language are translated.

At times the author makes some extremely cogent remarks of an esthetic or historical nature as on the internal parallels in *Troilus*, on the character of Diomede, on the sense of destiny in the poem, on the probability that the *Filocolo* was used as a direct source for Chaucer, and others. Yet in spite of its title, we get very little sense of the design of Chaucer's great poem, and we are continually being bogged down in masses of detail the relevance of which is not very clear. We arise from the book with the mental equivalent of eyestrain, for through five hundred pages we have been forced to look at Troilus from a very special angle without ever being able to refocus our eyes on a more distant view. To put the dissatisfaction in scholastic terms: all is explained in terms of the material cause of *Troilus*; nothing in terms of its final cause.

A close and extensive analysis of any sort, whether of the poem itself or of the source of the poem, is of dubious value in works of the length of *Troilus*. The brilliant achievements attained in our time by close analysis of lyric poetry cannot be paralleled when studying very long poems or dramas. A change in length of such magnitude as that between say Keats' *Ode on a Grecian Urn* and *Troilus* creates, without even taking genre or aims into consideration, a qualitative change in the work which makes the same method of analysis of dubious value for both. In minute analysis, we lose our sense of the unity and structure of the long poem. The whole context of the literary effect and feel is too different to benefit by close extended textual analysis, although it may do for portions of the poem.

However, the fundamental weakness of the book lies in Professor Meech's conception of the methods and value of source study. It is a commonplace of modern literary historical scholarship that a knowledge of the source (or reconstructed source) of a work of art is valuable inasmuch as it enables a reader to understand the intentions of the author. By seeing what he did with his material, what he stressed, minimized, and eliminated, the reader can better comprehend his artistic purpose. This line has been strongly urged in the past twenty-five years against some of the excesses of the "New Criticism." Historical scholars, it is admitted, must give up *Quellen-*

forschung as practiced in the hey-day of positivism when every scrap of source or possible source material was treasured for its own sake, in order that they may intelligently probe, by source analysis, into the esthetic properties of a work of art.

But, unless we start from some theory as to what a work of art is all about, that is, what is the esthetic aim of the artist, all source investigation is a hit-or-miss affair. A review is no place to discuss this principle thoroughly, but we may say that if we are ever to get out of the philological circle of using the source to determine the aim of the work and using the aim to determine the analysis of the source, we must break out at the latter point. We cannot determine the purpose of the artist purely by an examination of his source because (1) the same element in a source can be used by different writers or even the same writer for different kinds of effects: the artist's goal determines the meaning of the borrowing; and (2) all changes made in a source are not necessarily made for esthetic purposes. We can strengthen our case for a particular interpretation of a work of art by reference to a source, but we cannot thus primarily establish it.

Without the guiding force of an interpretation of the work to be studied, there is no satisfactory method of setting up the proper categories for investigating the source and of distinguishing esthetic from other changes between the two works to be compared. Changes per se have no meaning. Professor Meech stresses the greater realistic detail, the greater emphasis on destiny, the sharpening of characters in *Troilus* over its sources, all of which differences he thinks prove Chaucer's greater artistry. But by themselves, that is, without any comprehension of Chaucer's and Boccaccio's aims in their respective romances, these differences prove nothing and may even be insignificant.

As an instance of a change which may have no direct esthetic effect we may take the point Meech stresses that in *Troilus* there is much more feudal imagery than there is in the *Filostrato*. This may merely be due to the respective audiences of the poems or to the fact that feudalism meant little in fourteenth-century Italy and a great deal in fourteenth-century England. In other words, this point may be irrelevant to the fundamental esthetic aims of Chaucer. The stress on this kind of imagery may help of course to give an

esthetic density to *Troilus,* but its absence or slightness in the original does not enable us to determine Chaucer's aims in making the
change. He might have had much feudal imagery regardless of the
source.

It must be admitted that Professor Meech has analyzed his two
poems from many aspects and that some of his categories are certain to be of value in any interpretation of the poem. A study of the
change in characterization, for instance, is pretty certain to be so.
On the other hand numerous comparisons seem to lead nowhere,
because we do not have any place to get to. Whether Boccaccio refers to the gods 95 times as compared to 145 times in Chaucer, to
take a typical but not exact example of much of Meech's work, can
mean nothing whatsoever by itself, unless we have some theory as to
why Chaucer uses so many more of these allusions than the Italian
writer. If we can account for the change, then we can welcome the
statistics in giving factual support for our case. Otherwise we feel
we are listing meaningless facts. Source study cannot be done mechanically.

Meech does attempt to give a statement of his interpretation of
the poem, but it is of such a general nature that it is not of much
help. In any case, he does not use it as his main methodological
control as he should. The interpretation is the goal, not the starting
point of his investigations. If he desired to write lists of changes, it
would have been much better to have cut the length of the text in
half or more and given tables at the end for the benefit of those who
needed references.

A few minor points may be raised. Professor Meech uses the
phrase "in propria persona" to refer to the narrator (not the author
Chaucer) throughout, a misleading usage. There is much subjective interpretation of Chaucer's motives in the book as to why certain changes were made (for example, pages 125 and 196). Meech
assumes that realism is per se a good thing; he does not regard realism as another literary mode but as life itself. On pages 245–246 he
sets up distinctions between various types of metaphoric language
but in his discussion of imagery makes very little use of these classi-
fications. He gives every little detail a natural explanation. Every
change really cannot be significant per se.

On the other hand, Meech's summaries of scholarship on the

poem (up to 1956) are excellent; the author has missed little if anything written on *Troilus*. At times Professor Meech sheds vivid illumination on parts of the poem in happy and satisfying passages which only make one wish that he had organized his whole book differently. To do source work on the poem or to find support for certain interpretations of the poem this book will be of some use, although one must still check the original for serious study, but unfortunately certain weaknesses of methodology will keep it from ranking as an original or exciting contribution to the elucidation of the design of *Troilus and Criseyde*.

Index

Index

Index

Index

Index

310

Index

Index

319

Index

Tacitus, 63, 116
Tales, secular heroic, 66
Tam (Hebrew), 39
Tatlock, J. S. P., 19
Taxonomy of episodes, 102
Teaching, 76
Teleological universe, 34
Teleology, 51
Telonia, *see* τελώνια
Temperance, 80, 161
Temple, pagan, 214
Templum Domini, 9n
Temptation theme, 142, 143, 148, 156
Tempting God, 107
Ten Brink, B., 139
Tenses, 155
Tension in sentence, 250
Terza rima, 271–272
Tesiphone, 208
Testament of the Twelve Patriarchs, 4–5
Text, 92, 132
Thackeray, W. M., 201
Thales, 32
Thebes, 21, 204
Theodicy (Babylonia), 76
Theodore of Mopuestia, 83n
Theology, 83, 91; science against, 41;
   and science, 50; Biblical, 54; Patristic,
   66, 94 (*See also* Fathers); Medieval,
   289
Theophany, 169
Theories of history, 15n
Theseus, 18
Thomas, Dylan, 272–273
Thompson, Stith, 101
Time, 25, 35; Chaucerian sense of, 20 ff;
   sacred, 72; proper, 79; cyclic, 154; of
   nature, 154; in *Gawain*, 154–155, 156;
   of troubles, 161; spatialization of, 186;
   in *Troilus*, 204; perplexities of, 216
Timelessness, 185, 288
Title, 179, 186, 193, 195
Tobias, 122
Topoi, 65
Torah, 43, 72. *See also* Law
Tories, *see* Loyalists
Totting of Oyta, Henry, 94n
Tournaments, 157
Tradition, scriptural, 289, 292
Tragedies, 18, 141
Tragic objectivity, 24
Transcendentals, 44n
Transformation of sentences, 256
Transience, 204, 209; human, 21
Transitivity, of categorematic words, 267

Translatio Regni, 204
Tree, 67; analysis, 128; God, 142
Trickster, divine, 108; hero, 280
Trinity, 27–38, 215, 216
Troilus and Criseyde, 17, 20, 21, 186–
   187, 193; proems of, 208 ff; source of,
   297 ff; design of, 298, 301; character-
   ization of, 300
Tropes, 259
Tropological level, 285
Troy, 186–187
Truth, 249; air of, 177, 181–182, 184;
   claims, 182n; Christian, 288
Twelve torments, 6
Typology, 89

Uhtred de Boldon, 294
Ulrich of Strasbourg, 45
Ulster cycle, 144n
Uncle Sam, 253
Unferth, 64, 378
Uniqueness, 51, 52, 53, 85
Unitas, 165
Unitive, grade, 50; way, 163
Universal, 86, 87, 258, 290
Universe, 257; providential and ordered,
   86
Unknown, the, 113, 198
Unlimited, 36
Unreality of narrative, 196
Untruth, 196
Usus, 38
Utilitas, 91
Utopia, 49
Utopia, 24
Utopianism, 53, 73
Utrecht, Treaty of, 220

Vanities of world, 195
Variability, geographic, 205
Variables, semantic words as, 264
Varro, 62
Vegetation, God, 142; myth, 144–145
Venus, 209
"Ver," 146
Verbs, 247, 250, 260; strong, 237; ani-
   mate, 247, 350; metaphoric force of,
   251; finite, 272
Verisimilitude, 194, 280
Vernacular literature, 88
Vices, *see* Sins
Victorines, 46, 286, 293
Victory songs, 65
Vikings, 67
Virgil, 90

320